Hands-On Sencha Touch 2

Lee Boonstra

Beijing · Cambridge · Farnham · Köln · Sebastopol · Tokyo

Hands-On Sencha Touch 2

by Lee Boonstra

Printed in the United States of America.

Published by O'Reilly Media, Inc., 1005 Gravenstein Highway North, Sebastopol, CA 95472.

O'Reilly books may be purchased for educational, business, or sales promotional use. Online editions are also available for most titles (*http://my.safaribooksonline.com*). For more information, contact our corporate/institutional sales department: 800-998-9938 or *corporate@oreilly.com*.

Editors: Meghan Blanchette and Brian Anderson
Production Editor: Nicole Shelby
Copyeditor: Rachel Monaghan
Technical Editors: Kevin Jackson, Max Rahder, and Paul Carstens

Proofreader: Jasmine Kwityn
Indexer: Ellen Troutman
Cover Designer: Ellie Volckhausen
Interior Designer: David Futato
Illustrator: Rebecca Demarest

July 2014:   First Edition

Revision History for the First Edition:

2014-07-11:   First release

See *http://oreilly.com/catalog/errata.csp?isbn=9781449366520* for release details.

ISBN: 978-1-449-36652-0

[LSI]

To Michele, the person who always stands by me and believes in me. (Even the few times when I was wrong. Just a few times, though…)

Table of Contents

Part II.   Building the FindACab App

Preface

This book helps you gain hands-on experience with Sencha Touch 2.3. You can use the code techniques explored here as a starting point for your own projects.

Over the course of this book, you will build a single application: the FindACab app. With this mobile app, a user can search for and call nearby taxis. The book will cover all of the fundamentals of Sencha Touch, including:

- Scaffolding a mobile app with Sencha Cmd
- Learning the Sencha essentials, the class system, and events
- Mastering the Sencha layout system
- Working with the Sencha Model-View-Controller (MVC)
- Sending/retrieving external content
- Loading/saving data offline
- Implementing Sencha view components
- Using and handling forms
- Styling a Sencha Touch application with Sass and Compass
- Building a package for testing or production
- Creating a native package with Sencha Cmd and PhoneGap

Why Sencha Touch?

Sencha Touch is based on Ext JS and has roots in JQTouch and Raphael (a JavaScript/SVG framework for cross-browser vector graphics on the Web). Unlike jQTouch or jQuery Mobile, however, it's not dependent on jQuery. By abstracting the differences in underlying hardware and mobile operating systems, Sencha Touch can push apps from a single code base to different platforms such as iOS, Android, Black-Berry, Windows 8, and more.

Sencha Touch *is* serious app development, and is great for building large and complex (enterprise) apps that look and behave like native touch applications. I think Sencha Touch is the best mobile framework around. You might think that my opinion is somewhat biased because I work for Sencha, but that's not the case and I don't get paid to say this! Before I joined Sencha I worked with lots of other frameworks, and they all have their good and bad points. The Sencha frameworks, however, are just so complete: they include lots of widgets, animations, effects, and styles, as well as great documentation and online resources. The Sencha MVC approach makes it easier to extend and maintain apps (because multiple developers are working on the product). Sencha Touch ships as open source (totally free) or commercial, and is backed by a company with many years of experience. Now for the downloads: I have to admit, because Sencha Touch takes a fully JavaScript coding approach, the learning curve can be steep. But that's why I wrote this book—to get you up to speed with developing real-world Sencha Touch applications.

Now, what about the other frameworks?

Sencha Touch Versus jQuery Mobile

jQuery Mobile is open source and runs on top of jQuery. It's easy to learn, it uses DOM-based syntax, you write "tags" on multiple HTML pages, and everybody knows jQuery. jQuery Mobile works like the jQuery UI. It doesn't ship with many mobile widgets, but because it's open source there are lots of widgets to be found in the community. And that can be a good or a bad thing. It's great for creating mobile sites. Personally, I would not recommend using it for serious app development for performance reasons, and you would need an additional framework to implement a design pattern. Without one, the app would be hard to maintain.

Sencha Touch Versus Appcelerator Titanium

Titanium is a mobile app development framework compiler that it compiles; XML and JavaScript into native iOS and Android code. It's developed by Appcelerator. It's open source and it's great for building hybrid applications with the webview component. However, it can be hard to debug and the compilation times can add up.

Sencha Touch Versus Kendo UI Mobile

Kendo UI, developed by Telerik, is a relative newcomer in the app development world. Like Sencha Touch, the Kendo UI has a lot of view widgets, effects, and stylesheets. It is a mix of HTML syntax with JavaScript code on top of jQuery. It uses the Model-View-

ViewModel (MVVM) design pattern, which helps developers separate the Model from the View. However, Kendo UI Mobile is not free (open source).

About Sencha Inc.

Most people know Sencha Inc. from its JavaScript framework, Ext JS, which was originally built as an add-on library extension of YUI (the Yahoo! Interface Library) more then five years ago. With Ext JS, you can build rich Internet applications (RIAs) for desktops. It's primarily used for web and software development, and works with jQuery and Prototype. Since version 1.1, it has no dependencies on other external libraries or scripts, but you have the option of using them. Sencha Touch is Sencha's mobile product; it is actually one of the first mobile HTML5 frameworks. Clients of Sencha Inc. include CNN, Cisco, Adobe, Samsung, and many more.

While Ext JS and Sencha Touch are Sencha Inc.'s main products, the company offers other products, tools, and services on its website. See Table P-1 for an overview of all Sencha products.

Table P-1. Sencha products

Name	Definition
Ext JS	Cross browser JavaScript component framework for developing rich mobile web applications.
Sencha Touch	HTML5 framework for building mobile touch (web) apps for phones and tablets.
Ext JS GWT	Java framework for building rich web apps with Google Web Toolkit.
Sencha Architect	A desktop application for prototyping Sencha Touch and Ext JS apps.
Sencha Animator	A desktop application that helps you to create CSS3 animations.
Sencha.io Src	A cloud service that provides tools for image resizing.
Sencha Cmd	Command-line tool to develop and deploy desktop and touch applications based on design standards.
Sencha Space	A secure and managed environment for deploying HTML5 business applications that run on multiple devices. See Figure P-1.

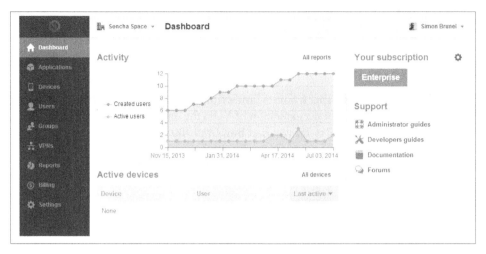

Figure P-1. Sencha Space, a secure managed environment for deploying enterprise apps that run on multiple devices

This book will focus on Sencha Touch (the open source version including Touch Charts) with the use of the Sencha Cmd tool.

Audience and Approach

This book is written for developers who want to learn Sencha Touch 2.3, or try out new techniques that address common programming tasks for building mobile web apps with Sencha Touch.

You should have some programming experience and familiarity with the following technologies:

- JavaScript
- JSON
- CSS3
- HTML5

Some examples in this book require server-side scripting. Throughout this book, I will make use of PHP. However, you don't need to be a server-side expert, and the use of any other server-side language would be fine too.

Before you start reading this book, understand that the learning curve for mastering Sencha technologies can be steep. I know that from experience; I have been there as well. My advice is to continue learning Sencha, read this book, and try to build a real-world MVC application. Once you understand the core Sencha concepts, your developer life will be so much easier. I can't remember coding in JavaScript without any of the Sencha frameworks. No, I'm not saying this because I work for Sencha—I really believe the framework is powerful and complete. I guess that makes me a fangirl!

In the process of writing this book, I used the FindACab app as an example for building a real-world MVC Sencha Touch app. Every chapter in this book starts with a general introduction before I dive into specific techniques. Every technique includes a broad explanation and then a real-world example of how you can implement it in a real Sencha Touch MVC architecture app. All the code examples and the full code listings for the FindACab app can be found on my GitHub repository (*http://bit.ly/host2-ex*). A preview of the FindACab app is available on my website (*http://www.ladysign-apps.com/finda cab*). Sencha has very powerful API documentation and guides, and I will show you the crème de la crème.

This is not a book with advanced, in-depth information about Sencha Touch or Sencha technologies. It's a hands-on book for tips and tricks, and I try to focus on the beginner to intermediate Sencha Touch developer. However, every now and then I will share some more advanced techniques.

This book also won't cover every Sencha Touch view component in high detail. Instead, this book will prepare you to start developing real-world MVC architecture applications. I will explain to you how the technology works; I will give you the tools, tips, and reference sources; and I will hold your hand while we build the FindACab app.

If this does not describe what you are looking for, there are some other great books that might be helpful to you:

- *Sencha Touch 2 Up and Running* by Adrian Kosmaczewski (O'Reilly)
- *JavaScript Patterns* by Stoyan Stefanov (O'Reilly)
- *Sencha Touch in Action* by Jesus Garcia, Anthony De Moss, and Mitchell Simoens (Manning)

Sencha Touch Releases

The first release of Sencha Touch was version 0.90 beta on July 17, 2010 (this version supported only Android and iOS devices). The first stable 1.0 version was released in November 2010. At the time of writing, the latest stable version is 2.3. This version includes support for Android, iOS, BlackBerry 10, Kindle, Windows Phone, MS Surface Pro and RT, Chrome Pixel, and Tizen devices.

Between version 1.* and 2.*, lots of API changes were made; thus, parts of the code have been deprecated, which means that you cannot use it anymore because it is outdated. For this book, you will start using version 2.3.

If you have some experience with Sencha Touch version 1, my advice is to upgrade as soon as possible to the latest version. Version 2.x is much faster and is based on MVC patterns to create best practices for clean code creation. Always try to use the latest version for the best performance.

The FindACab App

The FindACab app (see Figure P-2) is the demo application I have built for this book, and will be used as the common thread between chapters. Short code snippets are nice, but when it comes to building real-world touch applications, they can result in a lot more questions than answers. The FindACab app is a touch application for tablets that can be used to browse through nearby taxi services (provided by Yelp). This MVC app uses almost all the techniques covered in this book: implementing layouts and components (interface), requesting live data through the Yelp API web service, storing data offline, handling forms, theming your app, and creating production/native device builds.

In theory it should be possible, when you follow the chapters in order, to build the FindACab app from scratch. However, we developers never have enough time. Therefore, it's also totally fine to pick up this book and read only the chapters you'd like, in random order. In that case, it might be helpful for you to just quickly review the code, so you will have an idea of how to code real MVC architecture apps. The demo code can be forked from my GitHub account (*http://bit.ly/host2-ex*). For a preview of the FindACab app, just browse with a modern web browser or tablet browser to the app's web page (*http://www.ladysign-apps.com/findacab/*).

FindACab is a mobile app made for tablets. Unfortunately, this app is not optimized for mobile phones just yet, although you could do this by integrating device profiles (*http://bit.ly/device-profiles*).

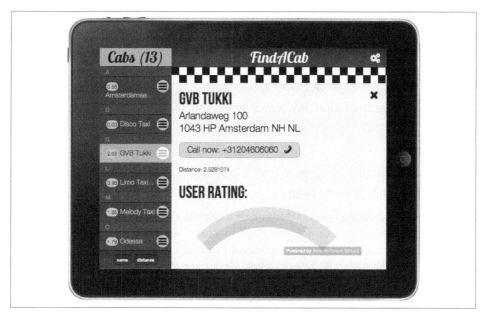

Figure P-2. After you've completed the tutorials in this book, the FindACab app will look like this

Using Code Examples

Supplemental material (code examples, exercises, etc.) is available for download at *https://github.com/savelee/cookbook-examples/*.

Use a modern mobile or desktop browser—such as Google Chrome, Safari, WebKit, Microsoft Internet Explorer 10, Mozilla Firefox 21+, and the mobile browsers for iOS, Android, BB10, Windows Phone 8, and Tizen—to access these apps and files.

This book is here to help you get your job done. In general, if example code is offered with this book, you may use it in your programs and documentation. You do not need to contact us for permission unless you're reproducing a significant portion of the code. For example, writing a program that uses several chunks of code from this book does not require permission. Selling or distributing a CD-ROM of examples from O'Reilly books does require permission. Answering a question by citing this book and quoting example code does not require permission. Incorporating a significant amount of example code from this book into your product's documentation does require permission.

We appreciate, but do not require, attribution. An attribution usually includes the title, author, publisher, and ISBN. For example: "*Hands-On Sencha Touch 2* by Lee Boonstra (O'Reilly). Copyright 2014 Lee Boonstra, 978-1-449-36652-0."

If you feel your use of code examples falls outside fair use or the permission given above, feel free to contact us at *permissions@oreilly.com.*

How This Book Is Organized

This book is organized into two main parts and includes 14 chapters and two appendixes.

Part I

Chapter 1, *Introduction to Sencha Touch*

The first chapter does not cover techniques but is more about Sencha Touch in general. It describes the important things you need to know before developing with Sencha Touch. I will talk about Sencha as a company, its products, Sencha Touch releases and licenses, the Sencha Network, where to find help, the API documentation, and the environment setup.

Chapter 2, *Installation*

The details of setting up your environment for Sencha Touch are covered in this chapter. I will discuss the tools and dependencies that can help you get up to speed with writing Sencha Touch code.

Chapter 3, *The Fundamentals*

This chapter describes all the basics, including how to create and configure components in Sencha Touch, work with templates, create references (selectors) to components, traverse components, and fire and remove events.

Chapter 4, *The Class System*

This chapter explores how to work with the Sencha Touch class system. It covers getters and setters, how to define singleton and static members, and how multiple inheritance works in Sencha Touch.

Chapter 5, *The Layout System*

In this chapter, we take a look at the Sencha Touch layout system. Topics include how to implement a horizontal or vertical layout, fit (full-screen) layouts, card layouts (layouts on top of each other), and docking components.

Part II

Chapter 6, *Structured Code*

This chapter describes how to structure your code. I will talk about design patterns as well as MVC architecture in general and how it translates to the Sencha Touch (client-side) MVC. This chapter also includes an introduction and implementation of data models, stores, controllers, and views. This chapter will be the starting point for building a real-world application, the FindACab app.

Chapter 7, *Data Models*

Models are part of the Sencha data package. This chapter describes how to validate models, how to save a record to the server, and how to implement model associations (relationships between models). You will build the models for the FindACab app.

Chapter 8, *Remote Connections (Server Proxies)*

Server proxies are part of the Sencha data package. This chapter describes how to retrieve external data for your app with AJAX and JSONP proxies. Beyond proxies, this chapter will also discuss retrieving and posting data in general: AJAX, JSONP requests, and AJAX with CORS. You will implement a server proxy for the FindACab app to retrieve real-time data from the Yelp web services.

Chapter 9, *Data Stores*

Stores are part of the Sencha data package. This chapter describes how to load data into your data store; how to remotely sort, group, and filter stores; and how to sync (save) multiple records to a server. You will implement sorters, groupers, and filters for the FindACab app.

Chapter 10, *Offline Storage (Client Proxies)*

Client proxies are part of the Sencha data package. This chapter describes how to save data locally on your device, using Local Storage, Session Storage, and Web SQL (local databases). This chapter will also cover how to work with the cache manifest file, to cache assets such as images. You will come up with a strategy for how to sync online data offline, and you will implement it into the FindACab app.

Chapter 11, *View Components*

This chapter describes how to implement messageboxes, tool and title bars, panels, buttons, lists, overlays, and charts. This chapter will also cover how to implement a Google Map. Finally, the FindACab app will get a face.

Chapter 12, *Forms*

This chapter describes how to implement a form (formpanels, fieldsets, fields, and buttons) and how to handle, validate, and submit forms. You will implement a formpanel for the FindACab app, and validate and submit user input.

Chapter 13, *Themes and Styles*

This chapter describes the out-of-the-box themes that ship with Sencha Touch. You'll learn how to create your own custom Sass themes. This chapter will also cover how to incorporate custom fonts and icons into your theme. You will see how a custom Sencha Touch theme is built for the FindACab app.

Chapter 14, *Builds*

This chapter describes how to create deployment builds for test, production, or native mobile environments. This chapter will also describe how to create builds with Phone-Gap. The FindACab app can be built as a test, production, and native package.

Appendix A

This appendix contains additional help with setting up iOS certificates and provisioning.

Appendix B

Appendix B contains the full stylesheet used for the FindACab app.

Conventions Used in This Book

The following typographical conventions are used in this book:

Italic
> Indicates new terms, URLs, email addresses, filenames, and file extensions.

`Constant width`
> Used for program listings, as well as within paragraphs to refer to program elements such as variable or function names, databases, data types, environment variables, statements, and keywords.

`Constant width bold`
> Shows commands or other text that should be typed literally by the user.

`Constant width italic`
> Shows text that should be replaced with user-supplied values or by values determined by context.

This element signifies a tip or suggestion.

 This element indicates a warning or caution.

 This element indicates a general note.

Safari® Books Online

 *Safari Books Online* is an on-demand digital library that delivers expert content in both book and video form from the world's leading authors in technology and business.

Technology professionals, software developers, web designers, and business and creative professionals use Safari Books Online as their primary resource for research, problem solving, learning, and certification training.

Safari Books Online offers a range of product mixes and pricing programs for organizations, government agencies, and individuals. Subscribers have access to thousands of books, training videos, and prepublication manuscripts in one fully searchable database from publishers like O'Reilly Media, Prentice Hall Professional, Addison-Wesley Professional, Microsoft Press, Sams, Que, Peachpit Press, Focal Press, Cisco Press, John Wiley & Sons, Syngress, Morgan Kaufmann, IBM Redbooks, Packt, Adobe Press, FT Press, Apress, Manning, New Riders, McGraw-Hill, Jones & Bartlett, Course Technology, and dozens more. For more information about Safari Books Online, please visit us online.

How to Contact Us

Please address comments and questions concerning this book to the publisher:

O'Reilly Media, Inc.
1005 Gravenstein Highway North

Sebastopol, CA 95472
800-998-9938 (in the United States or Canada)
707-829-0515 (international or local)
707-829-0104 (fax)

We have a web page for this book, where we list errata, examples, and any additional information. You can access this page at *http://bit.ly/hands-on-sencha-2*.

To comment or ask technical questions about this book, send email to *bookques tions@oreilly.com*.

For more information about our books, courses, conferences, and news, see our website at *http://www.oreilly.com*.

Find us on Facebook: *http://facebook.com/oreilly*

Follow us on Twitter: *http://twitter.com/oreillymedia*

Watch us on YouTube: *http://www.youtube.com/oreillymedia*

Acknowledgments

This book wouldn't exist without the help of some amazing people. Therefore I would like to thank:

- Simon St. Laurent and Meghan Blanchette at O'Reilly for their help with the production of this book. Thanks also to my editor Brian Anderson; English is not my native language, so I am sure he had a lot of work with this book!

- My coworkers at Sencha: Jeff Hartley, David Marsland, Kevin Jackson, Max Rahder, and the rest of the training team. Although everyone on the training team is located in the United States, I also have some great coworkers in the Amsterdam office who are always there for me to discuss or share great Sencha ideas and concepts: Miro Bojic, Rob Dougan, Simon Brunel, and Tommy Maintz.

- I am very thankful to the experienced reviewers who spent their time and shared their knowledge for this book. Special thanks to Paul Carstens at EA Games and my coworkers and friends Kevin Jackson and Max Rahder of Sencha.

- Special thanks also to Anke v.d. Berg and Audra Marshall. Not only are you great friends, but your help in the background for this book is also appreciated.

- Last but not least, I would like to thank my partner Michele, my dad, and all my friends for their love and support. There were many times that I had to bail on fun events because I had to work on finalizing this book. Now there will be plenty of time to catch up!

Sencha Touch Essentials

The first part of this book will discuss the Sencha Touch essentials—everything you need to know before you can start developing real-world mobile web applications the object-oriented programming (OOP) way.

In this part, you'll learn about:

- The Sencha Touch framework and Sencha Inc.
- How to set up your development environment
- The fundamentals to start developing Sencha Touch
- The class system to learn OOP development for real-world apps
- The layout manager to create mobile interfaces

Let's get started!

## CHAPTER 1

Introduction to Sencha Touch

With the Sencha Touch framework, developers can create native-like mobile app experiences by building an HTML5 web application. Sencha Touch uses MVC design patterns to establish best practices for clean code creation. Your app can look like a native mobile iOS, Android, Windows, or BlackBerry application, but it's also possible to create your own look and feel. No native languages like Java, Objective-C, or C++ are required, just client-side technologies such as JavaScript, CSS3, and a bit of HTML5.

Like Ext JS, the Sencha Touch framework contains lots of GUI/widgets, but its focus is on touch devices. Think of toolbars, sheets, form elements, lists, CSS transitions, and touch events (like tap, swipe, pinch).

You can access Sencha Touch applications with any modern browser, but it is also possible to package them (with Sencha's own packaging tools or PhoneGap) to distribute them to an app store.

Licenses

Sencha Touch is available for free, and you may create an unlimited number of mobile applications with it. When you want to download Sencha Touch for commercial use (for distribution to Apple's App Store or Google Play), you'll need to register your email address first. For open source projects, Sencha Touch is also available for free under the GPLv3. If you want to read more about Sencha Touch licenses, visit the online Sencha License documentation (*http://bit.ly/sencha-license*).

Bundles

It is also possible to purchase Sencha Touch in one of the Sencha bundles. Each bundle comes with Sencha Touch, as well as some handy tools and support. See Table 1-1 for an overview of what's included.

Table 1-1. Sencha bundles

Sencha Complete	Sencha Touch bundle
Sencha Touch[a]	Sencha Touch
Touch Charts	Touch Charts
Sencha Architect	Sencha Architect
Eclipse Plugin	Eclipse Plugin
Sencha Mobile Packaging	Sencha Mobile Packaging
Sencha Support Package	Sencha Support Package
Ext JS	-
Enterprise Data Connectors	-

[a] The Sencha Touch commercial version, which is included in the bundles, contains the *Touch Grid*—a grid component (like Ext JS grid), optimized for Touch—as an extra.

For more information, see the Sencha Products page (*http://www.sencha.com/prod ucts*) and the page for Sencha Touch bundles (*http://bit.ly/touch-bundle*).

This book will use the (free) open source version of Sencha Touch.

Touch Charts

With Sencha Touch Charts (see Figure 1-1), you can visualize complex charts and datasets such as Cartesian charts (i.e., charts with two axes, such as bar, column, and line charts) or polar charts (e.g., pie, radar, and gauge charts). All charts will be rendered in the HTML5 canvas and utilize hardware acceleration for optimized performance. Charts can contain animations, events, legends, and/or tool tips.

Touch Charts are included within the Sencha Touch Bundle and Sencha Complete Bundle. There is also a GPL open source version of Touch Charts; this one won't require a license, though it will display a small logo/watermark at the bottom of each chart.

This book will use the (free) Sencha Touch open source version of Touch Charts.

Sencha Cmd

Sencha Cmd (Sencha Command) is a command-line tool that makes it quick and easy to do several application-development tasks. It is used in all facets of your project from scaffolding to minifying and deploying your application to production. Sencha Cmd can be used for both Ext JS and Sencha Touch frameworks. For a more detailed overview, see Table 1-2.

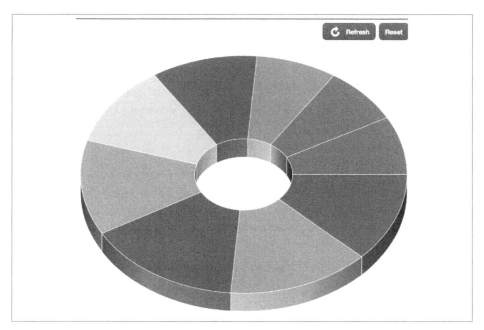

Figure 1-1. Touch Charts

Table 1-2. Sencha Cmd 4 or higher overview of functionality

Name	Description
Code generation tools	Code generation tools to generate entire applications and extend those applications with MVC components for Sencha Touch and Ext JS.
JS compiler	A framework-aware JavaScript compiler that knows the semantics of Sencha frameworks and produces minimal-footprint builds from your source.
Web server	Provides a (Jetty 1.8.7) web server that serves files from localhost.
Packaging	Native packaging to convert a Sencha Touch app into a mobile app that has access to device APIs and can be distributed in app stores. Sencha Touch native packaging also supports Apache Cordova APIs and packaging.
Management system	Distributed package management system for easy integration of packages (e.g., Ext JS Themes) created by others (e.g., the Sencha Market) or from the Sencha Package Repository.
Build scripts	Generated build script for applications and packages with "before" and "after" extension hooks so you can customize the build process to fit your own needs.
Tuning tools	Powerful code selection tools for tuning what is included in your application's final build, determining common code across pages, and partitioning shared code into packages.
Workspace management	Assists in sharing frameworks, packages, and custom code between applications.
Image capture	Converts CSS3 features (e.g., `border-radius` and `linear-gradient`) into sprites for legacy browsers (Ext JS).

Name	Description
Flexible configuration system	Enables defaults to be specified for command options at the application or workspace level or across all workspaces on a machine.
Logging	Robust logging to help you understand the inner workings of commands and facilitate troubleshooting.
Third-party software	Sencha Cmd includes a compatible version of Compass, Sass, and Apache Ant.
Code generation hooks	Can be specific to one page or shared by all pages in the workspace (e.g., to check coding conventions or guidelines as new models are generated).

Sencha Network

I have introduced you to some of the Sencha (Touch-related) products and tools to you. Did you know there are many more Sencha gadgets? Together, they are bundled as the *Sencha Network*. To benefit from the Sencha Network, you will need to have a Sencha account. You can register for free on one of the network sites.

With a Sencha Network account, you will have access to the following sites:

- Sencha Network
- Sencha website
- Sencha forum
- Sencha Try
- Sencha Market
- Sencha Devs
- Sencha.io Src

We'll go over the last four in the following sections.

Sencha Try

On Sencha Try (*http://try.sencha.com*) (Figure 1-2), there are thousands of Sencha examples available for you to learn from, find inspiration in, and experiment with. You can try them out online without setting up your environment. You can download somebody else's code or contribute your own.

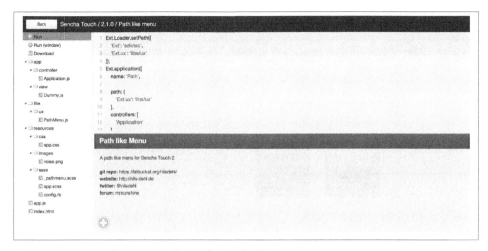

Figure 1-2. Learn from examples with Sencha Try

Sencha Market

In the Sencha Market (*http://market.sencha.com*) (Figure 1-3), you can find and share Sencha Extensions. There are lots of components, tools, and themes for Ext JS or Sencha Touch that you can download. You can also list or sell your own extension.

Sencha Devs

Sencha Devs (*http://www.senchadevs.com*) has a definitive list of Sencha developers from all over the world to help you promote your skills or find development partners. With a Sencha account, you can easily set up your profile and share your skills.

Sencha.io Src

Originally, Sencha.io was a set of cloud services that could interact with each other. It had an image service (to dynamically resize images), cloud hosting, and login features, and it was possible to push JSON messages to subscribed phones. Unfortunately, Sencha chose to stop supporting Sencha.io and focus on a new product: Sencha Space (*http://www.sencha.com/products/space/*), a secure wrapper with an API you can use for all your HTML5 apps. Right now, what is left of Sencha.io is the image service, Sencha.io Src.

You probably don't want your app to download an image that's too large for your screen. Sencha.io Src can control that for you, as you can see in Figure 1-4.

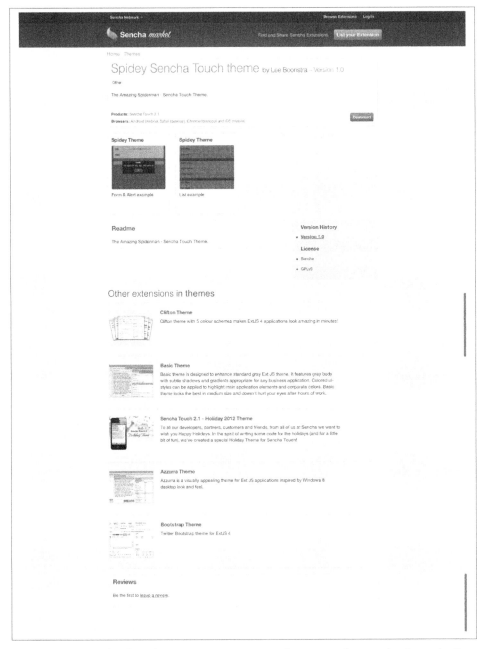

Figure 1-3. Download or share great components, themes, and examples from the Sencha Market

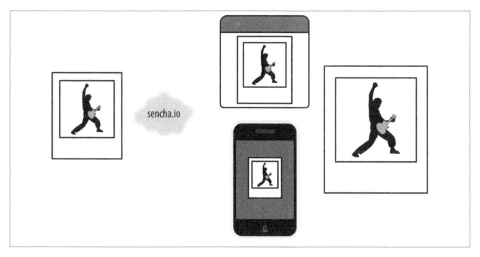

Figure 1-4. Sencha.io Src resizes images

Where to Find Help

Do you want to learn Sencha Touch and need help? There are several ways to get started with learning Sencha Touch, and of course step one is this book. But you could also choose to get Sencha Touch training at your own location or visit an open (virtual) training. You can also learn a lot from the community at one of the online Sencha forums or in the online training center. Beyond all this, Sencha also provides support packages to help you out with your project.

Learning Center

There are great online guides, tutorials, and screencasts categorized by difficulty, that will help you to learn Sencha Touch. Whether it is a basic "how to start" walkthrough or a whole showcase of "how to distribute your app," you can find it all in the Sencha learning center (*http://www.sencha.com/learn/touch/*).

Sencha Forums

Sencha has a huge, active, and growing developer community. The Sencha forum (*http://www.sencha.com/forum/*) is the perfect place to get in touch with the Sencha team or other developers. Every Sencha technology is categorized with its own board. When you are facing problems, have questions, or want to share plug-ins, usually you'll get a response within a few hours. Learning Sencha Touch is much more fun when you do it with others, and you'll help the technology to grow.

Sencha Trainings

Sencha offers training programs for all Sencha products. The Sencha Touch hands-on course includes advanced sections on MVC, theming, Sencha Touch Charting, optimizing for production, and deploying Sencha Touch applications to an app store with Sencha Cmd. This course also includes designing and prototyping MVC Sencha Touch apps with Sencha Architect 2.

Training is available both at your location and through open enrollment sessions. For an overview of standard courses, browse the Sencha training site (*http://www.sencha.com/training/*).

Buy Support

Sometimes you will just need the help of a Sencha expert. Sencha Touch support is already available for $299 per developer pack. With a standard support subscription, you will have access to public releases, and you will get free upgrades to the next major releases. You will also get a premium forum support account. When you are subscribed to premium support, you will get telephone support and emergency bug fixes in addition to the standard offerings. For more information, check out the Sencha support center (*http://www.sencha.com/store/touch/*).

The Sencha Support Package is also included in the Sencha Complete and Sencha Touch bundle.

API Documentation

The API documentation for Sencha Touch is available online (*http://docs.sencha.com/touch.2.3.1/*) and is also included in the framework package after you download the Sencha Touch package. When you're not connected to the Internet, you can find the docs in the downloaded package by opening the *index.html* file in the *docs* folder. Now what's the difference between the online and package versions? Well (and I think this is really great), the online documentation has commenting features, so you can comment on API methods—for example, to ask questions or share examples and tips.

Usually when I am developing Sencha Touch (or Ext JS) code, I keep the API documentation open. It's really powerful. All of the available Sencha Touch classes are listed by package name or inheritance. You don't know the package name? You can search methods and classes with the search box. Every Sencha class has example code, which you also can edit and preview (see Figure 1-5). This is really handy when you just want to try something out before using it in your project. Within a class, you can quickly navigate to class configs, properties, methods, events, or CSS mixins. Can't see the forest for the trees? You could also filter out properties, methods, or events by inheritance.

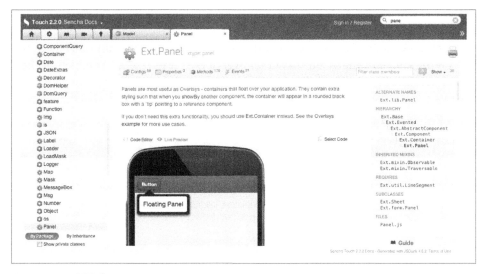

Figure 1-5. API documentation

But there's more! There are tabs with guides (these are tutorials that teach you important aspects of Sencha Touch), videos (of SenchaCon, the annual Sencha conference, with nice presentations), and Sencha Touch app examples. Of all the examples, I like the Kitchen Sink (Figure 1-6) the most.

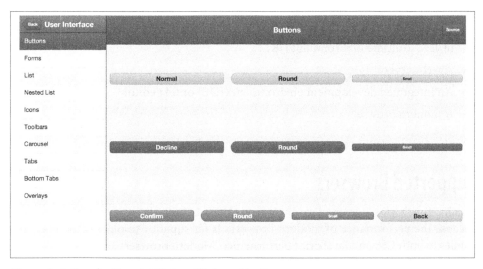

Figure 1-6. Sencha Touch Kitchen Sink application

Kitchen Sink

When framework developers talk about the "kitchen sink," they usually don't mean the sink on the kitchen counter but rather an overview of features and examples of their framework. The Sencha Touch Kitchen Sink is an easy-to-browse collection with components and code snippets. See Table 1-3 for a complete overview of what's included.

Table 1-3. The Kitchen Sink

Category	Definition
User Interface	All view components like buttons, forms, nested lists, icons, toolbars, carousels, bottom tabs, and overlays.
Animations	Transitions like slide, fade, cover, reveal, pop, and flip animations.
Touch Events	Touch events and gestures like touchstart, touchmove, touchend, dragstart, drag, dragend, tap, singletap, doubletap, longpress, swipe, pinch, and rotate.
Data	Loading of data such as JSONP, YQL, and AJAX.
Media	Media components like video and audio.
Graphics	Vector examples like the drawing API to draw vector images and Cartesian and polar charts.

Required Software

You will need the following software to set up your development environment to work with Sencha Touch:

- The Sencha Touch framework
- Sencha Cmd—and for its installation, Ruby and a Java SE Development Kit (JDK7) or Java Runtime Environment (JRE)
- A web server
- An integrated development environment (IDE) or text editor
- A modern browser

Chapter 6 will help you set up your Sencha Touch development environment.

Supported Browsers

Sencha Touch works in modern browsers; this is because it requires CSS3, but also because the performance of modern browsers is far superior to older browsers. This applies to both CSS and JavaScript performance. Modern browsers are also maintained and constantly updated.

Here's a selection of modern browsers that support Sencha Touch (some browsers have experimental support, which means that Sencha is working on it, but it's not 100% yet):

- Safari
- Google Chrome
- WebKit
- Microsoft Internet Explorer 10+
- BB10 Browser
- Android Browser
- Tizen Browser
- Opera Mobile (experimental support)
- Firefox 21 (experimental support)

Summary

As you can see, Sencha wants to make the life of a (Sencha) developer easier by providing frameworks, tools and services. This chapter explained all the tools and services of Sencha, and I've listed all the modern browsers which are currently supported by Sencha Touch.

## CHAPTER 2

Installation

To start developing Sencha Touch codes, you will need to install the following:

- An integrated development environment (IDE) or text editor
- Modern browser
- Ruby
- Java
- Sencha Cmd 4 or higher
- Web server
- Sencha Touch 2.3

Optionally, there's an extra set of software that might come in handy. In this chapter, I will explain why you might want these:

- Sass and Compass
- NodeJS
- Adobe PhoneGap and Apache Cordova
- Development SDK

This might look like a long list, but honestly it's not that complicated and you might have already installed some of them. Let's take a look at each item, one by one.

Some steps require that you work with the command-line interface (CLI):

- Windows users can open the Command Prompt (Start → Run), type **cmd**, and press OK.
- Mac users can open the Terminal Applications → Utils → Terminal.

Install the Required Software

Let's start with the essential software.

IDE or Editor

You will need an editor that has JavaScript syntax highlighting, validation, and formatting to develop Sencha code. I also recommend that your editor include JavaScript syntax checking—for example, JSLint or JSHint. Feel free to use the editor or *integrated development environment* (IDE) of your choice. Popular editors include Sublime Text, WebStorm, Aptana/Eclipse, and NetBeans. If you have no preference, use one of my favorites:

- Sublime Text (*http://www.sublimetext.com/*) for its simplicity
- WebStorm (*http://www.jetbrains.com/webstorm/*) because it has code completion for Sencha frameworks

 Are you deeply in love with Sublime Text like I am? I have created some Sencha Ext JS and Touch code snippets/templates, available on Github (*http://bit.ly/sublime-bits*). You will need to have package control installed.

Modern Browser

You will need a modern browser to preview Sencha Touch applications on your development machine. Modern browsers include Google Chrome, Safari, and Internet Explorer 10 (or higher). Currently, Mozilla Firefox 21 would work too, although it has experimental support.

If you have no preference, use Google Chrome.

 There are some really great Google Chrome browser extensions online or currently in development that can help you with developing Sencha code. These include Bruno Tavares's Sencha Inspector (*http://bit.ly/sencha-inspect*) and Illuminations (*http://bit.ly/illume-dev*).

Ruby

Sencha Cmd requires Ruby to compile Sass to CSS for your Sencha Touch app builds. Make sure Ruby is available to your class PATH variables. Here are some helpful tips:

- Ruby is automatically installed for Mac OS X users.

- Windows users can download the RubyInstaller (*http://rubyinstaller.org*) *.exe* file and run it.
- Unix users can use `sudo apt-get install ruby2.0.0` to download and install Ruby.

Java

Sencha Cmd is written in Java and needs the Java Runtime Environment 1.7 (*http://bit.ly/JRE-17*) or Java SE Development Kit 7 (*http://bit.ly/javakit-7*) to run (these are known as the JRE and JDK 7, respectively). JDK 7 is also used for running the command `sencha app watch`, which compiles the Sencha Touch application and your Sass stylesheet in the background every time you click Save. If you don't need this feature, and you want to build your application manually (with `sencha app build`) or compile your Sass themes with compass (`compass watch .`), then the JRE is sufficient.

 Be aware that JDK 7 disables Java in Google Chrome for Mac OS X users. Java 7 runs only on 64-bit browsers, and Chrome is a 32-bit browser on Mac OS X. In addition, note that installing the JDK also installs the JRE. The one exception is that the system will not replace the current JRE with a lower version. To install a lower version of the JRE, first uninstall the current JRE version.

Sencha Cmd

To develop Sencha Touch code, you will need to have a copy of Sencha Cmd on your machine. With Sencha Cmd you can start scaffolding a new project, minifying, and deploying your application to production.

This book will make use of version 4.x. or higher. If you have the old Sencha SDK tools installed, remove them before completing this book's examples.

Check whether you have the required version of Cmd by opening a terminal/command window and type the following command:

    sencha which

Sencha Cmd not installed?

If Sencha Cmd is not installed, you'll get a "command not found" message. If Cmd is installed, the response will list your version and install directory.

To install Sencha Cmd, download it and run the installer (*http://bit.ly/senchacmd-install*).

Remember where you installed the Sencha Cmd directory and the version number you are using. By default, the installation path is:

- For Windows users: *C:\Users\Me\bin\Sencha\Cmd{cmd-vers}*
- For Mac OS X users: *~/bin/Sencha/Cmd/4 or higher*
- For Unix users: *~/bin/Sencha/Cmd/4 or higher*

Wrong version of Sencha Cmd?

If Cmd is installed, but it's an earlier version, go to the terminal/command window and type:

```
sencha upgrade
```

Once you've upgraded Cmd, you can close the terminal/command window, restart it, and type:

```
sencha
```

This should display all the Sencha commands and options.

Manually adding Sencha Cmd to your system variables

Did you encounter problems while installing Sencha Cmd? Or are you not seeing the `sencha` command on the command line, but you are sure that you installed it? In that case, you will need to add Sencha Cmd (`sencha`) to your classpath/system variables manually.

Windows users:

1. Navigate to Start → Control Panel → Performance and Maintenance → System.
2. In your system properties, click the Advanced tab.
3. Click the Environment Variables button.
4. Edit the `classpath` variable or create a new variable called `classpath`.
5. Add the following value and save: *C:\Users\Me\bin\Sencha\Cmd\<cmd-vers>*. (Make sure you are entering the correct path and version number.)

Mac users:

1. Make hidden files visible by typing the following commands in your terminal:

   ```
   defaults write com.apple.finder AppleShowAllFiles TRUE
   killall Finder
   ```

   (Running these commands with `FALSE` will hide the files again).

2. Now open *~.bash_profile*. Add the following lines and save the file:

```
export PATH=/Users/username/bin/Sencha/_Cmd/{cmd-vers}:$PATH
```

(Make sure you are entering the correct path and version number.)

> Before Sencha Cmd version 4.0.1.x, Sencha Cmd was using Ruby 1.x.
> When you had Ruby 2.0 installed, you couldn't build applications
> with Sencha Cmd. In October 2013, Mac OS X launched the free 10.9
> (Mavericks) update. This update includes Ruby 2.0. When you're
> having problems building your app, and you're running a version
> lower than Sencha Cmd 4.0.1.x, you need to upgrade your Cmd to
> the latest stable version by typing **sencha upgrade** from the
> command line, or to the latest beta version by typing **sencha up
> grade -b**.

Web Server

You will need a web server on your development system to preview Sencha Touch applications on your development machine. Sencha Cmd comes with a built-in web server (Jetty 8.1.7), which you can use for Sencha Touch, or you can install/use your own web server.

Use the built-in web server

To start the built-in web server, run the following command from the CLI:

```
sencha fs web -p 80 start -map /path/to/htdocs/
```

Point to the folder that contains your web projects and then the *touch* folder, which will become the web server root.

> Mac OS X users might need to prefix the preceding command with
> sudo to get admin rights.

If everything works, you should see something like this in the console/terminal:

```
sencha fs web -port 80 start -map ~/htdocs
Sencha Cmd v4.0.1.45
[INF] Starting shutdown listener socket
[INF] Listening for stop requests on: 53194
[INF] Mapping http://localhost/ to /Users/someuser/htdocs...
[INF] Starting http://localhost
[INF] jetty-8.1.7.v20120910
[INF] NO JSP Support for /, did not find org.apache.jasper.servlet.JspServlet
[INF] started o.e.j.w.WebAppContext{/,file:/Users/someuser/sencha/}
[INF] started o.e.j.w.WebAppContext{/,file:/Users/someuser/sencha/}
```

```
[INF] Started SelectChannelConnector@0.0.0.0
[INF] Started http://localhost
```

Use a different web server

Do you have your own preference for a web server? You're welcome to use any one you like. If you have no preference, I would advise an Apache web server, such as XAMPP.

XAMPP (*http://bit.ly/get-xampp*) is an Apache distribution containing MySQL, PHP, and Perl; it's really easy to install and use—just download, extract, and start.

Sencha Touch

Of course, you will need the Sencha Touch framework (*http://bit.ly/sencha-framew*). Follow these steps:

1. Extract the framework and copy the folder to your *htdocs* folder.

2. Rename the framework folder to *touch* (e.g., *htdocs/touch*).

3. The framework will be available via your localhost. Test whether you can access the Sencha Touch Kitchen Sink demo (using a modern browser) via the following URL: *http://localhost/touch/docs/#!/example/kitchen-sink*.

Install the Optional Software

By now, you should have a working Sencha Touch environment installed. The next sections cover some additional setup instructions to make your Sencha Touch dev environment a little more powerful.

Sass and Compass

Sencha Touch makes use of Sass and Compass to style a Sencha Touch app. Sass is a preprocessor. You will need to compile Sass to CSS so the browser can understand it. Sass and Compass are included in the Sencha Cmd build process. This means when you build your application from the CLI (via `sencha app build` or `sencha app watch`), Sencha Cmd will compile the stylesheet and you will not need to install Sass or Compass separately.

However, if you would rather compile Sass by yourself (e.g., with the command `compass watch .`), you will need to have Sass and Compass installed on your development machine. To install both, you will need to have Ruby installed to run the following commands from the CLI:

```
gem install compass
gem install sass -v 3.1.1
```

Wait until each process is completed. It will take a few minutes before the command completes and the command prompt returns.

> Mac OS X users might need to prefix the preceding command with sudo to get admin rights.

Verify that Sass and Compass are installed with the following commands, which should prompt you with a version number:

```
compass -v
sass -v
```

Install NodeJS

When you want to make use of Adobe PhoneGap or Apache Cordova to create a native build of your Sencha Touch app, you will need to have NodeJS (*http://nodejs.org/*) version 0.9.9 or higher installed.

After running the wizard, node should be available on the CLI. Type the following command on the CLI, which should output the latest version:

```
node -v
```

Install PhoneGap and Cordova

You will need to have Adobe PhoneGap or Apache Cordova installed to package your mobile apps to a native (hybrid app) build. Apache Cordova is the free, open source, community-driven version of Adobe PhoneGap. Apache Cordova requires a development kit such as XCode or Android Tools to be installed on your machine, while Adobe PhoneGap can also build via the cloud web service (*http://build.phonegap.com*). To build via the cloud, you will need a (free) Adobe ID and PhoneGap account.

Make sure NodeJS is installed, and the node command is available on the CLI. Run the following command from the CLI to install Adobe PhoneGap:

```
npm install -g phonegap
```

Run the following command from the CLI to install Apache Cordova:

```
npm install -g cordova
```

> Mac OS X users might need to prefix the preceding command with sudo to get admin rights.

After a successful installation, check for the latest version to verify that PhoneGap is correctly installed and available on the CLI:

```
phonegap -v
```

or

```
cordova -v
```

 Mac OS X users who want to create a native package for iOS, and want to test their app in the simulator, will need to install ios-sim, the CLI launcher for the iOS simulator:

```
sudo npm install -g ios-sim
```

Also, you will need to have the latest iOS Simulator up and running. Go to XCode and click the XCode → Preferences → Download tab. Update/download the latest iOS 6 simulator and CLI tools.

To create a PhoneGap account, first visit the PhoneGap build website (*https://build.phonegap.com/*). You will need these account details for building a PhoneGap project from the CLI. There is a free and a paid plan; both plans work the same. Next, choose how you want to log in; for CLI use, you will need to log in with an Adobe account. However, you can choose to create an account with GitHub and later hook up the Adobe ID.

Log in to the PhoneGap build on the CLI:

```
phonegap remote login -u myemailadress@gmail.com -p mypassw0rd
```

To log out, use `phonegap remote logout`.

Development SDK

When you are using Apache Cordova or the local build option of Adobe PhoneGap, you will need to install the SDK of the particular device. Here are the most common options:

- Mac OS X, with XCode 5 for iOS development (*http://bit.ly/apple-xcode*)
- Android Developer Tools for Android development (*http://bit.ly/sdkandroid*)
- BlackBerry 10 SDK for BlackBerry 10 development (*https://developer.blackberry.com/*)
- Windows 8 Pro with Visual Studio for Windows Phone development (*http://developer.windowsphone.com/*)
- Tizen SDK for Tizen development (*http://bit.ly/tizen-sdk*)

To create a native package for iOS, Windows Phone, or BlackBerry, you will also need a signed developers account. For BlackBerry this is free, but for iOS and Windows Phone you will need to pay a yearly fee. See their websites for additional information.

Do you want to set up an Android emulator? Check out Patrick Chu's blog post on the subject (*http://bit.ly/setup-st-droid*). If you need help with iOS provisioning and certificates, check out Appendix A for a short and simple guide.

Summary

This chapter explained how to install the necessary software for developing Sencha Touch code. Assuming you already have an environment with an IDE/editor and your browser of choice installed, the most important pieces are Sencha Cmd and the Sencha Touch framework. Sencha Cmd requires an installation of Ruby and Java (JRE or JDK), and it includes a web server.

If you are planning to create Sass stylesheets for Sencha Touch and you want to compile these by yourself, you may install Sass and Compass separately. When you want to build a native/hybrid app of a Sencha Touch app, you can install Adobe PhoneGap or Apache Cordova on top of NodeJS, and/or the device development SDK of your choice.

For a more complete guide on how to set up your Sencha environment for different operating systems, see my blog post on the subject (*http://bit.ly/setupsencha*).

Everything ready and set? All right, now we can start diving into the Sencha Touch code!

## CHAPTER 3

The Fundamentals

Before we create a real-life Sencha Touch application, let's focus on the fundamentals. This chapter will cover all the Sencha Touch basics: how to create a component, how to reference it (creating a selector), and how to listen to their events.

All of the Sencha Touch visual components (like panels, lists, and toolbars) extend from the `Ext.Component` class. This base class gives every component the ability to set certain standard layout-related properties, such as `height`, `width`, `margin`, `padding`, and `style`, or set content with the `html` or template (`tpl`) configs. Every component in Sencha Touch can be rendered to the DOM.

In this chapter, you'll learn:

- How to instantiate a basic component
- How to implement templates
- How to make references to components
- How component traversing works
- How to make references to DOM nodes
- How to fire and remove events using event handling

 You can test the examples in this chapter from my GitHub repo (*http:// bit.ly/essentials-ex*) or you can open a Sencha Fiddle (*https:// fiddle.sencha.com*) and try it out yourself. (When using the Sencha Fiddle, make sure you choose the Sencha 2.3.x framework.)

Instantiating a Basic Component

The first technique we'll discuss is how to instantiate and configure a basic component. In Sencha Touch 2 (and in Ext JS 4), this works a little different than how you do it with native JavaScript code.

In native JavaScript, you use the new operator to create a new object instance:

```
var helloworld = new Object();
helloworld.html = "Hello World!";
```

JavaScript is a prototype-based language that contains no class system, as opposed to OOP-based languages such as C++ or Java. Because there is no class system in JavaScript, you could write JavaScript the object-oriented way, by creating a function. Let's assume I defined a new class called Component and I want to create an instance c from it:

```
//function Component(html) { this.html = html }
var c = new Component('Hello World!');
```

Let's do the same with Sencha code. You can create an instance of a Sencha Touch view component (a defined Sencha Touch framework class) as follows:

```
var c = Ext.create('Ext.Component', {
    //key value pairs here, i.e.
    html: 'Hello World!'
});
```

As you can see, in Sencha Touch you use a method, Ext.create(), to create a new object instance (in this case, Ext.component). This is because Sencha Touch has a built-in class system and class loader.

In this example, I create an Ext.Component and I pass in a *configuration object* with class properties (html:"Hello World!"). It is just a plain object with key/value pairs. (Yes, it looks like JSON, although in JSON you need to specify the key/value pairs as strings.)

 What about the new operator? In native JavaScript, you would use the new operator to instantiate objects—for example: var obj = new Object(). While developing with Sencha Touch, you will rarely use the new operator (although you could). The reason is because the new operator won't inform the Sencha loader to load the required classes in the background (which would cause runtime errors), and thus you would need to take care of any dependencies yourself.

A much simpler way to render components to the DOM is what we call *object literal notation* (or *lazy instantiation*). You will probably use this more often when building real-world applications:

```
var c = {
    xtype: 'component',
```

```
   html : 'Hello World'
}
```

Wait a minute! What is an xtype? An xtype is an alias that stands for the following key/value pair: alias: widget.<some-component>. You would normally use an xtype in these two situations:

- When you define your own custom class (a blueprint for objects you create), you set an alias name to this component so you can easily refer to it later.
- To create a component instance in the object literal notation, use the xtype defined in the class blueprint (as above).

 In the next chapter, I will discuss how to create your own custom class.

Every Sencha view component has an xtype name, which can be found in the API docs. Usually, the name of the xtype is the class name without Ext, dots, or capital letters, such as Ext.List versus xtype: 'list', or Ext.navigation.View versus xtype: 'navigationview'.

 When you use Sencha Architect for building Sencha Touch or Ext JS apps and you are creating an interface, xtype has a different name. You will need to look for the setting *useralias*. In the code that it generates, Sencha Architect will use alias: widget.<useralias-name>. So, in other words, xtype: <useralias-name> is equivalent to alias: widget.<useralias-name>.

When you instantiate components (and you are not using the *sencha-touch-all.js/sencha-touch-all-debug.js* frameworks), you will need to tell the Sencha Ext.Loader to load the corresponding Sencha class into memory. The Ext.Loader is a mechanism that loads all the correct classes and dependencies for you in the right order. (If you are familiar with Java, you can compare it to the import lines at the top of your class.) When you define your own classes and you are nesting xtypes, you can tell the Ext.Loader to load the required Sencha classes by putting them into the requires array. When instantiating components with Ext.create(), you can load these classes by adding them to the Ext.require() method; for example, Ext.require("Ext.List"); or requires: ["Ext.List"],. When would you use the Ext.create() method? It is generally used for testing purposes or prototyping.

Configuration objects can be nested within each other. This is a declarative approach, which lets you describe the object as you create it. Of course, you can't remember every config setting from each component, which is why it's important to always have the API docs with you.

When you are prototyping these examples with the Sencha Fiddle, or when you are using my GitHub examples, you will notice that I do not use Ext.require(*Ext.Component*). This is because in this example I make use of the *-all.js* version of the framework, which includes all Sencha classes and therefore has no dynamic loading.

Let's look at another example. This is a runnable example you can test yourself. Here I use Ext.create() to create a simple red box and render it to the DOM:

```
Ext.onReady(function() {

    Ext.create('Ext.Component', {
        html: 'Hello World!',
        style : { background: 'red' },
        cls: 'box',
        width: 300,
        height: 100,
        renderTo: Ext.getBody()
    });

});
```

In this example, the component will be created when the DOM is ready after loading and executing the Sencha Framework; see Ext.on Ready(). (You can compare Ext.onReady with $(document).ready in JQuery, but note this is not the same as window.onload() in Java-Script, which will be fired after the DOM is ready *and* all images and resources are loaded.)

Ext.create() creates the component instance and, with the renderTo property, places the component (which is technically a set of HTML <div> tags) into the body of the HTML page; see Ext.getBody().

As we saw in the example earlier, these components have a hardcoded html property. That's helpful for prototyping as well, but you will probably not use it often in production apps. In that case, you want to push dynamic content into the component before rendering or while running. We'll discuss this next.

Implementing Templates

In the previous examples, I hardcoded data in the view components. Obviously that is not ideal. You will probably want to make it dynamic. We will use templates for this. In Sencha Touch, templates are little predefined HTML snippets with placeholders. You can dynamically inject these HTML snippets with data.

To define such a template, you will use the `Ext.XTemplate` class:

```
Ext.create('Ext.Component', {
    tpl: Ext.create('Ext.XTemplate','<h1>{name}</h1><p>{description}</p>'),
    data: {
        name: 'Template',
        description: 'This is an example of how to configure a basic template.'
    }
});
```

As you can see, `Ext.Component` enables you to assign an `Ext.XTemplate`. This is very nice because it allows you to inject dynamic content.

Let's check out some runnable examples. You will define a template and inject it with data. First, you need to declare a custom object, `data`, which has the keys `name` and `description`. When the DOM is ready, the data will be loaded into the template:

```
Ext.onReady(function() {

    var data = {
        name: 'Taxi Amsterdam',
        description: 'The only taxi in Amsterdam that does not circle around'
    };

    Ext.create('Ext.Component', {
        tpl: '<h1>{name}</h1><p>{description}</p>',
        data: data,
        styleHtmlContent: true,
        cls: 'box',
        renderTo: Ext.getBody()
    });

});
```

Changing the Data at Runtime

Now let's take a look at an example that uses the `setData()` method to change the data at runtime:

```
var data = {
    name: 'Taxi Amsterdam',
    description: 'The only taxi in Amsterdam that does not circle around.'
};
```

```
var c = null;

Ext.require('Ext.Component');
Ext.onReady(function() {

    c = Ext.create('Ext.Component', {
        tpl: '<h1>{name}</h1><p>{description}</p>',
        data: data,
        styleHtmlContent: true,
        cls: 'box',
        renderTo: Ext.getBody()
    });

    data.description = "We like tourists a lot!";

    c.setData(data);
});
```

In the previous code, you can see that the template (tpl) renders the data with the description "The only taxi in Amsterdam that does not circle around." in the DOM, but at runtime this text will be immediately changed to "We like tourists a lot!" because of the setData() method.

In this example, I used two global variables: an object named c and an object named data. I did this so that I can edit the data object from elsewhere in my code. For example, if I open my debugger console and change the data.name to Tourists Taxi (data.name = "Tourists Taxi"), followed by the setData() method c.setData(data), I would modify the header title to "Tourists Taxi."

Organizing Template Snippets

I can imagine that you don't want to save all these HTML snippets into your JavaScript view code. Instead, you can use template snippets (Ext.XTemplate) and save those in different files. Such a template can be assigned to the tpl property:

```
Ext.require('Ext.Component');
Ext.onReady(function() {

    var data = {
        name: 'Taxi Amsterdam',
        description: 'The only taxi in Amsterdam that does not circle around.'
    };

    var myTpl = Ext.create(
        'Ext.XTemplate','<h1>{name}</h1><p>{description}</p>');

    Ext.create('Ext.Component', {
        tpl: myTpl,
        data: data,
        styleHtmlContent: true,
```

```
        cls: 'box',
        renderTo: Ext.getBody()
    });

});
```

The myTpl variable contains the Ext.XTemplate snippet. It's just a variable, so I could move it over to any other file to get (global) access to it. Notice the new Ext.XTem plate() class. Here a template is assigned to the variable myTpl, which will be configured in the component tpl config.

In real-world applications you could decide to save all HTML templates in a custom separate (singleton) class, instead of saving it globally (Example 3-1). (See the examples in "Defining Singletons and Static Members" on page 51.)

Example 3-1. utils/Template.js

```
Ext.define('Utils.utils.Template', {
    statics: {
        MY_TPL: Ext.create('Ext.XTemplate','<h1>{name}</h1><p>{description}</p>');
    }
});
```

Implementing Advanced Templates

Let's get a bit more advanced. Now you don't want to save the data in just a random object, but rather you want to push it from a data store (such as CabStore) to the template, as shown in Example 3-2.

Example 3-2. Advanced templates

```
Ext.application({
    requires: ['Ext.dataview.DataView', 'Ext.data.Store', 'Ext.Component'],
    launch: function() {

        //create a data store with id: CabStore.
        Ext.create('Ext.data.Store', {
            id:'CabStore',
            fields: ['name', 'description'],
            data : [
                { name: "Taxi Amsterdam", description: "The best taxi service" +
                    "of Amsterdam."},
                {   name: "Cab & Co", description: "Always fast."}
            ]
        });

        var myTpl = Ext.create('Ext.XTemplate', '<tpl for=".">',
                '<div class="row">',
                    '<h1>{name}</h1><p>{description}</p>',
                '</div>',
            '</tpl>'
```

```
    );

    Ext.create('Ext.DataView', {
        itemTpl: '<h1>{name}</h1><p>{description}</p>',
        store: 'CabStore',
        styleHtmlContent: true,
        cls: 'box',
        fullscreen: true,
        height: 250
    });

  }
});
```

In the previous example, I have created a new data store with the id `CabStore`. It contains the `name` and `description` fields with two rows of data. I have used the `myTpl` `XTemplate` like you have seen before, only this time I created `<tpl for=".">` looping tags, which loop through the root (.) of all the data records. This `<tpl>` tag sets the template markup for every row of data.

Instead of an `Ext.Component`, I have created a `dataview` instance because `Ext.Data View` handles multiple template rows. Because a `dataview` consists of one or more items, it doesn't require a single `tpl` property anymore but rather an `itemTpl`, which sets the HTML template for every item in the `dataview`. Last but not least, I have set a `store` with a lookup to *look up* the `CabStore` id. I don't need an array with `data` anymore, because the data store contains the data from now on.

What else can you do with templates? `XTemplate`s are very powerful. You can run conditional expressions, basic math functions, built-in variables, custom member functions, and loops into templates. Check the API documentation (*http://bit.ly/ext-docs*) to discover more options for `XTemplate`s.

I discussed how to instantiate components and inject them with custom templates. When working with components, you might also want to reference them. Let's talk about this basic technique next.

Making References to Components

When you are working with components, you might want to select them, or you might want to make a reference or selector to them. Maybe you are familiar with other JavaScript frameworks such as jQuery or MooTools, where you can make selectors to DOM elements.

Sencha Touch can also make references to DOM elements, as we'll discus in "Making References to DOM Nodes" on page 35. In practice, however, you will make references to components more often than to DOM elements, because Sencha Touch uses components instead of DOM elements.

The best practice to make references to a view component is by using a `ComponentQuery`:

```
Ext.ComponentQuery.query('selector');
```

The `ComponentQuery` searches components through the `Ext.ComponentManager`. It will return an array with components (even when only one component is found). In the component query, you pass in a string with the `xtype`:

```
var cars = Ext.ComponentQuery.query('car');
```

Or to search and select for multiple components:

```
var carsAndCabs = Ext.ComponentQuery.query("car, cab");
```

 An alternative way of creating references to components is by using a `refs` object in the controller. Don't worry about this now; I will discuss this topic in Chapter 6.

It's also possible to retrieve components with a component query for `id` or `itemId`, by passing in the string `id` name, prefixed with a `#`. As `itemIds` are not globally unique, it is a better practice to use them instead of `ids`.

```
Ext.ComponentQuery.query('#mybutton');
```

Using the get Component Method

In Sencha Touch version 1 or Ext JS version 3, you could use the `get` component method: `Ext.getCmp(id)`. That's an easy way of creating a reference to a component with an `id`. The `getCmp()` method is a shorthand notation for `Ext.ComponentMgr.get(id)`; you pass in the string `id` of a component and it will return an `Ext.Component`. If the component is not found, it will return `undefined`. For example, the following component query makes a reference to a component that has an `id` of `mybutton`:

```
Ext.getCmp('mybutton');
```

There might be use cases for using `Ext.getCmp()`. However, it is bad practice to set an `id` in a custom component. The issue with `ids` is that they need to be globally unique. That means that you can't reuse your custom components in your apps; if you do so, strange things may happen. The trick is to use component queries with `xtype` or `item Id` instead.

You can even make your component query more complex by passing in CSS-like selectors. For example, you can select components with certain attributes by using bracket notation. In this case, I select all panels that have the attribute `title="Test"`:

```
Ext.ComponentQuery.query('panel[title="Test"]');
```

Or we can select only child elements from a component:

```
Ext.ComponentQuery.query('formpanel > button');
```

It's also possible to walk up and down by retrieving components (*traversing* nested components). The next section will discuss this concept.

Traversing Components

In the previous section, you saw component queries that look like this:

```
Ext.ComponentQuery.query("formpanel > button");
```

This component query walks through the components and selects all the child elements that match the selector. (In this case, direct `button` items of `formpanel` xtypes.) We call this *traversing*. For example, say you have a reference to a `formpanel` and you want to drill down to retrieve a particular form field.

To traverse components, you can use the `up()` and `down()` methods to retrieve the first parent or first child component:

```
//get first parent
myComponent.up(el);

//get first child
myComponent.down(el);
```

Sencha has the `up()` and `down()` traversing methods. All components have an `up()` method. All containers have a `down()` method (and also an `up()` method, because containers extend from `Ext.Component`).

`myComponent.up()` finds the parent component. `myComponent.down()` finds the child component:

```
var form = myButton.up('formpanel');
var input = form.down('textfield[name="lastname"]');
```

Now that you know how to select and traverse Sencha components by using the component query, you might be curious how to select DOM elements. We'll look into that in the next section.

Be aware that when `Ext.ComponentQuery.query("formpanel but ton")` returns an array with components, the `up()` or `down()` method returns the first parent or child that it finds.

To illustrate, take a look at this code snippet, which runs in the browser developer console, while previewing the example on Git-Hub (*http://bit.ly/refs-trav*):

```
> Ext.ComponentQuery.query('button')
[Class, Class]

>Ext.Viewport.down('button')
Class {onInitializedListeners: Array[0],
initialConfig: Object, id: "mybutton",
getId: function, element: Class…}
```

Making References to DOM Nodes

Earlier we discussed how to make references to Sencha components. But how can you select DOM nodes? Sencha works with components, so you would think that you don't need to point to DOM nodes. That's not completely true; especially when you are creating custom components and plug-ins yourself, you might need to work with the DOM.

Creating custom components or plug-ins in Sencha Touch is beyond the scope of this book. It's an advanced technique that requires an understanding of the Sencha class system, DOM, and custom styling. If you are interested in custom components, take a look at the Sencha Market (*http://market.sencha.com*), where a lot of plug-in developers share their components and plug-ins for free.

Sencha provides three ways to retrieve the DOM:

- Getting Sencha's version of a DOM element.
- Getting a collection of multiple direct DOM elements.
- Getting the direct DOM node.

When you are working with the Sencha Fiddle, you can select the *resources* button to edit the *index.html* page.

Let's create an HTML snippet that contains the following:

```
<h2 id="title">Taxi Amsterdam</h2>
<div id="description">
    <p>Taxi description</p>
    <p>Taxi description2</p>
</div>
```

Next we'll cover a couple of techniques for retrieving DOM elements.

Ext.get()

`Ext.get(el)` is the trick you use to retrieve the `Ext.dom.Element`, which is a kind of wrapper that encapsulates a DOM element, adding simple DOM manipulation facilities and normalizing for browser differences.

You can pass in the following:

- An ID to the node
- A DOM node
- An existing `Ext.Element`

See the following example from my browser developer console while previewing the *essentials/refs-domelements/* example from my GitHub repo (or by using the Sencha Fiddle):

```
Ext.onReady(function() {
        var title = Ext.get('title');
    console.log(title);
});
```

This returns the `Ext.dom.Element`:

```
Class {dom: h2#title, id: "title", self: function,
superclass: Object, defaultConfig: emptyFn}
```

 Ext.get() is the shorthand notation for Ext.dom.Element.get().

Ext.select()

Now, let's see how to select multiple DOM elements. For this, we can use `Ext.se lect(selector)`.

You can pass in a CSS-like selector (with an `xtype`, `itemId`, or CSS class), and it returns an `Ext.dom.CompositeElementLite`, which is a collection of DOM elements providing methods to filter members or to perform actions upon the whole set.

Let's reuse the code we used for the `Ext.get()` example, but use `Ext.select()` instead. Here, `Ext.select("p")` selects all paragraph DOM elements and returns it as a composite:

```
> var pars = Ext.select("p");
Class {elements: Array[2], el: Class, self: function,
superclass: Object, defaultConfig: emptyFn}
```

Once we have the composite, we can select the first DOM node:

```
> var firstPar = Ext.select("p").elements[0];
<p>Number one taxi in Amsterdam.</p>
```

In vanilla JavaScript, you would use the following line of code to retrieve an array of DOM nodes by a tag name:

```
var pars = document.getElementsByTagName('p');
```

Ext.getDom()

Finally, you can also request the true DOM with Ext JS by using `Ext.getDom(el)`.

You can pass in the following:

- An ID to the node
- A DOM node
- An existing `Ext.Element`

Let's reuse the code we used before, but now we'll use `Ext.getDom()` instead. Here, `Ext.getDom("title")` returns the DOM element:

```
> var title = Ext.getDom('title');
<h2 id="title">Taxi Amsterdam</h2>
```

In vanilla JavaScript, you would use the following line of code to retrieve a DOM node by an `id`:

```
var title = document.getElementById('title');
```

The previous examples showed you how to retrieve the `Ext.dom.Element` (Sencha's version of a DOM element with extras), the `Ext.dom.CompositeElementLite` (a collection of DOM elements that you can filter), and the DOM node as it's generated in the DOM tree.

Now that you know all the possible ways of retrieving DOM elements and Sencha components, let's see how you can actually *do something* with these references (hint: we'll need to listen to events).

Handling Events

Event handling is done via the `Ext.util.Observable` mixin. A *mixin* is a technique to support (multiple) inheritance. See Chapter 4 to read more about mixins. By adding (mixing) the `Ext.util.Observable` class to another Ext JS class, you are able to fire events. Under the hood, observable objects basically have a map that associates them to an event name. The `Ext.Component` class uses the `Ext.util.Observable` mixin, which means that all components are able to respond to events, because `Ext.Component` is the base class for every view component in Sencha Touch.

There are three types of events:

System events
> Events invoked by the framework—for example, loading data with the `load` event.

Lifecycle events
> Events invoked by the framework lifecycle—for example, painting a view with the `painted` event.

User events
> Events invoked by the user—for example, a `tap` event.

This section will focus on user events, although the code for system events or lifecycle events is almost the same.

User events are events that occur when the user interacts with the mobile app. Examples include a click event (`mousedown`) or tap event (`touchstart` and `touchend`).

Touch events are a bit like mouse events, but there are some very important differences:

- Clicking on a button with a mouse is much more accurate than a finger tap. The mouse arrow is precise compared to the size of your fingertips on the tap surface area. This is the reason for the design guideline that buttons and links on touch components should have a size of at least 44×44 points.

- There is no mouseover or hover equivalent.

- A touch is very hard to keep steady, whereas a mouse can stay at a fixed position. When your fingertips touch the surface area, a `touchstart` event occurs; it can directly detect a `touchmove` event when you move your finger, while a mouse has a `mousedown` event and must move for the `mousemove` event to be detected.

Firing Events

When you want to listen to a tap event, in native JavaScript code, your code could look like this:

```
function myEventHandler(ev) {
    //do something
}

element.addEventListener('touchend', myEventHandler);
```

In Sencha Touch, when you want to fire an event from a component, you can define an event listener that listens to a certain event, such as the tap event:

```
listeners : {
    tap: 'myEventHandler'
}
```

You handle events by passing a callback function to the component you're observing. Some people call the callback function a *listener*, while other people call it a *handler*. When it comes to Sencha Touch, you can use either term; the handler syntax is just an alternative syntax for the listener code but only for buttons. Actually, there are additional ways to listen to events. You can use the handler or listeners configs, or you can add the events later with the on() or addListener() methods on the component instances.

Let's add some event listeners. They all listen to the tap event, but they each use a different approach.

The first approach is what we have seen so far—the listeners configuration directly into the component class:

```
Ext.define('BookTaxiBtn', {
    extend: 'Ext.Button',
    xtype: 'booktaxibtn',
    config: {
        text: 'Book a Taxi - listeners',
        margin: 5,
        listeners: {
            tap: 'bookTaxiEventHandler'
        },
    },
    bookTaxiEventHandler: function(b){
        console.log('You tapped the ' + b.getText() + 'button');
    }
});
```

The next approach uses the handler config. It invokes the callTaxiEventHandler() function on a button tap. The handler works only on the Ext.Button:

```
var callTaxiBtn1 = Ext.create('Ext.Button', {
    text: '1: Call a Taxi - handler',
    margin: 5,
```

```
        handler: callTaxiEventHandler
    });
```

The next approach is the addListener() method. It takes the event name and the function-to-execute name as arguments:

```
var callTaxiBtn2 = Ext.create('Ext.Button', {
    margin: 5,
    text: '2: Call a Taxi - addListener'
});
callTaxiBtn2.addListener('tap', callTaxiEventHandler);
```

Here we use the short version of the addListener() method: the on() method. It takes the event name and the function-to-execute name as arguments:

```
var callTaxiBtn3 = Ext.create('Ext.Button', {
    margin: 5,
    text: '3: Call a Taxi - on'
});
callTaxiBtn3.on('tap', callTaxiEventHandler);
```

Feel free to test the preceding buttons. You'll just need to wrap each button in an Ext.application.launch() method:

```
Ext.application({
    name: 'Events',
    requires: ['BookTaxiBtn'],

    launch: function() {

        var callTaxiEventHandler = function(b) {
            console.log('You tapped the ' + b.getText() + 'button');
        };

        var callTaxiBtn1 = Ext.create('Ext.Button', {
            text: '1: Call a Taxi - handler',
            margin: 5,
            handler: callTaxiEventHandler
        });

        var callTaxiBtn2 = Ext.create('Ext.Button', {
            margin: 5,
            text: '2: Call a Taxi - addListener'
        });
        callTaxiBtn2.addListener('tap', callTaxiEventHandler);

        var callTaxiBtn3 = Ext.create('Ext.Button', {
            margin: 5,
            text: '3: Call a Taxi - on'
        });
        callTaxiBtn3.on('tap', callTaxiEventHandler);

        //Display the buttons, for testing purposes
```

```
Ext.create('Ext.Container', {
    fullscreen: true,
    padding: 10,
    items: [
        callTaxiBtn1,
        callTaxiBtn2,
        callTaxiBtn3,
        { xtype: 'booktaxibtn'}
    ]
});

    }
});
```

All of the available events for each component are listed in the API docs. If you want to read more about Touch gestures in mobile web applications, check out the W3C spec (*http://bit.ly/touch-int*).

Removing Events

Just as you can add listeners at any time, you can remove them too. You will use the removeListener() method for this. To remove a listener, you need a reference to its function. In case you want to remove event listeners, it's a good practice to not write event-handler function bodies inline in the code. You should always assign functions to a variable; otherwise, it will be hard to reference the function to remove (from outside the function body).

In native JavaScript, your code could look like this:

```
element.removeEventListener('touchend',myEventHandler,false)
```

To remove an event listener, use the removeListener() method, pass in the event name you want to remove, and pass a reference to the event function that will be invoked when the event occurs:

```
button.removeListener('tap', myEventHandler);
```

The next example creates a callTaxi button with a tap listener that invokes callTaxiEventHandler. This function removes the tap listener from the callTaxi button because it knows the reference to it (var callTaxiEventHandler):

```
Ext.application({
    name: 'Events',

    launch: function() {

        var callTaxiEventHandler = function(b) {
            console.log('You tapped the ' + b.getText() + 'button');
```

```
        this.removeListener('tap', callTaxiEventHandler);
        console.log('From now on, you can not call again.');
    };

    var callTaxi = Ext.create('Ext.Button', {
        text: 'Call the Taxi',
        margin: 5,
        listeners: {
            tap: callTaxiEventHandler
        }
    });

    //just for testing purposes
    Ext.create('Ext.Container', {
        fullscreen: true,
        padding: 10,
        items: [callTaxi]
    });

    }
});
```

After removal, it shows a log message telling you that you cannot invoke the same function again (because the listener is removed).

 Just as the on() method is a shorthand version for addListener(), there is a shorthand version for the removeListener() function un(). So, instead of:

```
button.removeListener('tap', myEventHandler);
```

you can use:

```
button.un('tap', myEventHandler);
```

Firing Custom Events

Imagine you developed a nice interface with buttons. I will talk about code structure and MVCs later, but for now let's say you coded all the event handlers in a separate JavaScript class (e.g., the Sencha Touch controller). Then the lead designer comes in and wants to change the interface—no more buttons but instead a list with menu items. Hmm, that's a bummer. Now you have to change your code in two places. You have to edit the interface and the separate class with the event handler (the controller).

For situations like this, Sencha has the fireEvent() method, which you can code in your view component.

The taxiview component fires a custom calltaxi event with the fireEvent() method:

```
listeners : {
   tap: function(e){
      this.up('taxiview').fireEvent('calltaxi', e);
   }
}
```

With this method, you can fire custom event names. The idea is that you pass (*fire*) events to another view component. From anywhere else in your code (e.g., in the controller), you'll listen to this custom event name and execute the logic after it is fired:

The controller listens to the custom `calltaxi` event:

```
Ext.define('TaxiController', {
    extend: 'Ext.app.Controller',

    config: {
        control: {
            'taxiview': {
                calltaxi: 'onCallTaxi'
            }
        }
    },
    onCallTaxi: function() {
        console.log("Call the Taxi");
    }
});
```

You will learn how controllers can listen to events in Chapter 6.

Summary

By now you know the Sencha Touch fundamentals: configuring components, creating templates for injecting data, and making references to components. I've also showed you how to create references to DOM nodes, although this is a less common practice because Sencha Touch works with components instead of DOM elements. At the end of the chapter, I discussed component event handling (i.e., how to fire and remove events).

In the next chapter, we will take a deeper look into the Sencha class system, specifically how to define a class and how class inheritance works in Sencha.

## CHAPTER 4

The Class System

In the previous chapter, you learned how to instantiate components from existing component classes and reference them. Within Sencha Touch you can also define your own *custom* component classes by extending from Sencha Touch base classes. The next examples will show you how to instantiate a component and how to define your own classes.

In this chapter, you'll learn:

- How to define your own custom class
- How to define getters and setters
- How to define singletons and static members
- How inheritance works (extending)
- How multiple inheritance works (mixins)

 You can test the examples in this chapter from my GitHub repo (*http://bit.ly/host2-ch4*) or you can open a Sencha Fiddle (*https://fiddle.sencha.com*) and try it out yourself. (When using the Sencha Fiddle, make sure you choose the Sencha 2.3.x framework.)

Defining Your Own Custom Class

Now that you know how to instantiate a class definition for view components, let's discuss how the Sencha class system works and how to define your own blueprints to define a class.

Let's make a blueprint containing a variable, `myVar`, and a method, `myMethod`. Using `Ext.define()`:

```
Ext.define('AppName.packagename.ClassName', {
    //class configuration object
    myVar: 1,
    myMethod: function(name){
        //console.log("Log: " + name);
    }
},function(){
    //optional callback
});
```

In the code example from Chapter 3, I instantiated a few components: a simple Hello World component and an XTemplate component. It's important to know that components in the Sencha framework are, in fact, classes.

Officially, JavaScript is a prototype-oriented language; it has no class system. The most powerful feature of JavaScript is its flexibility. This comes at a price: JavaScript might be hard to understand, reuse, or maintain.

This makes it different from object-oriented languages like Java or C++. These come with code standards and well-known patterns. This imposes structure and forces developers to adhere to standards.

Sencha, however, allows you to create classes within JavaScript. This should allow you to take advantage of the flexibility of JavaScript and the structure that object-oriented programming provides.

 Object-oriented programming (OOP) is a programming paradigm that represents concepts as *objects* that have data fields (properties that describe the object) and associated procedures known as *methods*. A good book about OOP coding patterns in JavaScript is *JavaScript Patterns* by Stoyan Stefanov.

To create a class definition, you will use the Ext.define method. In this method, you pass in the first argument, a class name (which is a string); and as a second argument, you pass in a config object to configure and initialize the component. The third argument is optional: you can assign a callback function. This might be handy for logging, but I rarely use it.

In general, the string class name consists of the following parts: AppName.package name.ClassName. For example, the following class maps to the file *app/view/ListView.js*:

```
Ext.define('MyDemoApp.view.ListView', {
    //class configuration object
});
```

In the preceding code, note the following:

- The app name, `MyDemoApp`, maps to the *app* folder in your project root and should be written in the upper CamelCase notation (wherein each word begins with a capital letter).

- The package name, `view`, maps to the package folder in the *app* folder; package names are always written in lowercase.

- The class name, `ListView`, should also be written in the upper CamelCase notation. The class name should contain the same name as the JavaScript filename (*List-View.js*); therefore, it's not possible to put multiple Sencha Touch classes in a single JavaScript file.

Because you pass the class name as a string, the namespace doesn't need to exist before you assign the reference. This is great, because you won't need to worry about the order of execution. The framework does this. It's asynchronous, and dependencies will automatically load through the load mechanism (`Ext.Loader`). For example, if a child class requires a parent class, the `Ext.Loader` will make sure that class will be in memory. String class names are also handy for debugging because Sencha classes know their class name. When there is a bug in your code, it will show you a nice stack trace with readable class names to help you easily find your bug.

The second argument takes a class configuration object. This is where you can set properties and methods. This makes total sense when you are defining a custom component, like in Example 4-1.

Example 4-1. Class definition for a custom component

```
Ext.application({
    name: 'DemoApp',
    launch: function() {


        /* Start class definition code: */

        //Create a class definition
        Ext.define('DemoApp.view.DemoComponent', { //❶
            //❷
            extend: 'Ext.Component',
            config: {
                html: 'Hello World' //❸
            }
        }, function() {
            console.log("class is created"); //❹
        });


        //Create a class instance
        Ext.create('DemoApp.view.DemoComponent', { //❺
```

```
        fullscreen: true
    });


  }
});
```

❶   As you can see, I have defined a single class. `DemoApp.view.DemoComponent` maps to a single file, *app/view/DemoComponent.js*.

❷   This definition takes the following configurations: `extend` and a `config` object. Don't worry at this point what `extend` and `config` stand for. I will discuss them in the next couple of sections.

❸   What is important for now is that a default `html` string for the `DemoComponent` was set.

❹   Also, I have created an optional callback function that will log after the class definition is created.

❺   The `DemoComponent` will be created after it is instantiated. The only thing that my `DemoComponent` does is display an HTML string.

Do you like the Sencha class system? There is a lot more to it—autogeneration of getters and setters (magic methods), and multiple inheritance. Read on to find out about more nice features of the Sencha class system.

 Are you looking for more information about the Sencha class system? Check out the SenchaCon presentation by Jacky Nguyen (*http:// bit.ly/senchacon*) or read the book *JavaScript Patterns* about OOP design patterns in native JavaScript. Another great book about native JavaScript design patterns is Addy Osmani's ebook *Learning Javascript Design Patterns* (*http://bit.ly/learn-js-dp*).

Defining Getters and Setters

In object-oriented programming, properties aren't accessed directly very often; it's better to use accessors and mutators (get and set methods) instead. One benefit of this approach is that if you have a set method, you can add a business rule or fire an event as the mutator is run.

You probably won't be very happy when you have to create a get method and a set method for every property. Luckily, the Sencha class system can automatically create accessors and mutators (known as *magic methods*) for you.

It is very easy to create getter and setter methods to access or mutate a class property; they will be automatically generated for you. That is why some people call them *magic*.

To autocreate magic getter and setter methods, set a property in the class config:

```
config: {
  myProperty: "some value"
}
```

The config object autocreates the getter and setter methods as follows:

```
getMyProperty: function(){
  return this.myProperty; //returns "some value"
}
setMyProperty: function(x){
  this.myProperty = x;
}
```

You don't need to add these functions by yourself. This reduces repetitive code.

Besides getter and setter methods, it also automatically creates *apply* and *update* methods. These methods are handy to change the process, before and after you set a value:

```
applyMyProperty: function(x){
  //runs before this.myProperty changes.
  //for example validation
}
updateMyProperty: function(x){
  //runs after this.myProperty was changed.
}
```

Validation is an area where these methods can be implemented. Figure 4-1 shows the entire process of getting and setting values. Let's say we have a class config, driver, set to the default value "John Doe" (config: { driver: "John Doe" }). You can retrieve the driver with the getter getDriver(), and it returns the current value John Doe. You can set the driver to a new value, setDriver("Lee Boonstra"), and before the value gets changed it will run applyDriver(), at which point you can run a validator check. If all goes well, it will change the value and afterward will run updateDriver(); you can add some additional logics or logging at this time.

Example 4-2 provides the accompanying code to Figure 4-1. It defines a Cab class with configs. Note that getDriver(), setDriver(), applyDriver(), and updateDriver() are automatically generated. To create some validation, you would override the apply Driver() function; and to add some functionality after changing the driver, you could override the updateDriver() function.

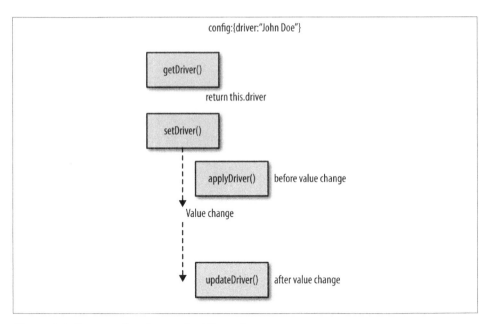

Figure 4-1. Process of getting and setting values

Example 4-2. Configs in a class that generate magic methods

```
Ext.define('VehicleApp.vehicle.Cab', {
    // The default config
    config: {
        driver: 'John Doe',
        driver2: {
          firstName: 'John',
          lastName: 'Doe'
        }
    },

    constructor: function(config) {
        this.initConfig(config);
    },

    applyDriver: function(newVal){
      if(newVal === 'The Pope') {
        console.log(newVal + " is an invalid taxi driver.");
        return;
      }
      return newVal;
    },
    updateDriver: function(newVal, oldVal){
      console.log('The owner has been changed from ' + oldVal + ' to ' + newVal);
    }
});
```

Because the previous code example does not extend from a Sencha component, I had to initialize the config settings in my constructor:

```
constructor: function(config) {
    this.initConfig(config);
},
```

The `config` object sets some default values. When you are not extending from an `Ext.Component`, you have to call the `initConfig(config)` method once by yourself (e.g., in the base class), which will initialize the configuration for the class that was passed in while creating the objects.

After you instantiate the class, you have access to the getters and setters in the prototype. They have been *magically* generated:

```
var taxi = Ext.create("VehicleApp.vehicle.Cab", {
    driver: "John Doe"
});
alert(taxi.getDriver()); //alerts 'John Doe';

taxi.setDriver('The Pope');
alert(taxi.getDriver()); //alerts 'John Doe' because 'The Pope' is invalid.

//changes the driver from 'John Doe' to 'Lee Boonstra'
taxi.setDriver('Lee Boonstra');
alert(taxi.getDriver());
```

You can even use magic getter and setter methods to access complex objects. For example, let's change the code in Example 4-2 and define a `config` with a complex object:

```
config: {
  driver: {
    firstName: "John",
    lastName: "Doe"
  }
}
```

I can get access to its properties with the line `taxi.getDriver().firstName`.

The `config` object in a class definition is very useful for class instances. Sometimes you don't want to instantiate a class; for example, you may just want to run some default common utility functions. Singletons and static members would do the trick. We'll discuss them in the next section.

Defining Singletons and Static Members

In software engineering, the singleton pattern is a design pattern that restricts the instantiation of a class to one object. This is useful when exactly one (global) instance of a class is needed to coordinate actions across the system.

To get access to a function or a property of the class itself (without instantiating an object), you would need to define a class as a singleton or static member—for example, a common utility function such as converting the speed of a car from miles per hour to kilometers per hour, or a static property that tells me the version number of the application. You don't need an object for that; you just want to run a generic used function or retrieve a common used constant from anywhere in your app.

It is pretty simple to define a class as a singleton—just set the config `singleton` to `true`:

```
Ext.define('Utils.common.Functions', {
    singleton: true,
    //key value pairs here
});
```

A singleton class definition *can't* create objects (technically it can't create more than one object, because the singleton itself gets instantiated once), but you can get access to all the methods and properties in the class itself. This is very handy for when you want to get access to generic functions or properties used as constants:

```
Ext.define('Utils.common.Logger', {
    singleton: true,

    version: "1.02",
    log: function(msg) {
        console.log(msg);
    }
});
```

You can call the `log()` function by invoking `Utils.common.Logger.log()` directly from the class, and retrieve the `version` property by calling `Utils.common.Logger.ver sion` from the class.

Singletons also can contain `config` objects, and therefore generate magic getters and setters from properties. For example:

```
Ext.define('Utils.common.Version', {
    singleton: true,

    config: {
      version: "1.03",
    }
});
```

The previous code will generate a getter: `getVersion()`. Now, from anywhere in my application I can get access to this property with `Utils.common.Version.getVer sion()`.

A nice alternative for singletons are classes with a `statics` object defined. To set up a class with a `statics` object, you only need to define a `statics` object with key/value pairs. (Note that you can't set a `config` object within a `statics` object.)

Here we define `statics` with the `VehicleApp.utils.Commons` class:

```
Ext.define('VehicleApp.utils.Commons', {
        statics: {
                YELP_API: 'http://api.yelp.com/business_review_search?',
                YELP_KEY: 'ftPpQUCgfSA3yV98-uJn9g',
                YELP_TERM: 'Taxi',
                LOCATION: 'Amsterdam NL',

                getUrl: function() {
                        return this.YELP_API + "term=" + this.YELP_TERM +
                                "&ywsid=" + this.YELP_KEY
                                + "&location=" + this.LOCATION;
                },
        }
});
```

You *can* create objects of a class that has `statics` defined, but these objects cannot get access to its properties and methods without invoking it from the class itself with the dot notation. In other words, requesting properties and methods from an instance via `this` will not work, but calling the full namespace (i.e., `VehicleApp.utils.Commons.LO CATION`) will:

```
var mySettings = Ext.create('VehicleApp.utils.Commons');
//It is possible to create an instance of a class with static members:
console.log(mySettings);
//But getting access to a static member from an object fails:
mySettings.getUrl();
  //Uncaught TypeError: Object [object Object] has no method 'getUrl'
```

Inherit from a Single Class

Inheritance is when a child class receives functionality from a parent class. Inheritance is known as *extending* in Sencha Touch. To create single class inheritance, you extend from a parent class by setting the `extend` config:

```
Ext.define('AppName.packagename.ClassName', {
    extend: 'AppName.packagename.SomeClassName'
});
```

The following code examples illustrate the concept of single class inheritance. Example 4-3 defines the base class, `Vehicle`, while Example 4-4 defines the class `Car`, which inherits behavior from the parent. Example 4-5 creates instances of both classes.

Example 4-3. Define a parent class

```
Ext.define('VehicleApp.vehicle.Vehicle', {
    unit: "mph",
    drive: function(speed) {
        console.log(this.$className + ": Vrrroom: " + speed + " " + this.unit);
```

```
    }
});
```

In Example 4-3, the `VehicleApp.vehicle.Vehicle` class is the parent class. It has a `unit` property set and a method, `drive()`.

Example 4-4. Define a child class and implement inheritance

```
Ext.define('VehicleApp.vehicle.Car', {
    extend: 'VehicleApp.vehicle.Vehicle',
    drive: function(speed) {
        console.log(this.$className + ": Vrrroom, vrrroom: " + speed + this.unit);
    }
});
```

In Example 4-4, the `VehicleApp.vehicle.Car` class inherits both the `unit` property and the `drive()` method. However, it has its own `drive()` method, and therefore this method will be overridden. (Although it still has access to the `unit` property!)

Example 4-5. Create instances

```
var vehicle = Ext.create("VehicleApp.vehicle.Vehicle");
vehicle.drive(40); //alerts "Vrrroom: 40 mph"

var car = Ext.create("VehicleApp.vehicle.Car");
car.drive(60); //alerts "Vrrroom, vrrroom: 60 mph"
```

As with any object-oriented language, if you need to do further initializations upon creation, you code a constructor. It makes sense to code an `initConfig(config)` method in a constructor.

The `initConfig(config)` method initializes the configuration for this particular class. Whether you initialize default config values or pass in config values as an argument while creating an object, this method will override and merge them all together and create an instance with these default settings. When you are inheriting from other classes, you don't need to rewrite the `initConfig` method. It's inherited, so the functionality is already there, but it does need to exist. Typically, the best place to include it would be in your base class.

Another powerful method is `callParent([arguments])`. It also makes sense to write this call in the constructor, although you don't have to. You can run this from any other method, as shown in Example 4-6, which I will discuss shortly.

The `callParent(arguments)` method calls the `ancestor` method, in this case the `drive()` function in the parent `VehicleApp.vehicle.Motor` class. When you invoke this method from the constructor, it will call the parent's constructor. Object-oriented languages used to force developers to write this call in the constructor. It's important to have this call in your custom classes, because you always want to initialize the config settings from every parent. Maybe in the future you will change some base class config properties, in which case you will want your child classes to have access to them.

But you are free to call the parent from whatever method you are in. This can be handy for overriding functionality. In Example 4-6, I want to override the drive() function that is inherited from the Vehicle class in order to customize it specifically for a Motor class.

Example 4-6. Class inheritance

```
Ext.define('VehicleApp.vehicle.Motor', {
    extend: 'VehicleApp.vehicle.Vehicle',

    config: {
        nrOfWheels: 2 //❶
    },

    constructor: function (config) {
        this.initConfig(config); //❷
    },

    drive: function(speed) { //❸

        if(this.getNrOfWheels() < 3) { //❹
            console.log(this.$className +
                ": Vrrroom, vrrroom on " + this.getNrOfWheels() +
                    " wheels.");
        } else {
            this.callParent([60]); //❺
        }
    }
});
```

❶   The config object that needs to be initialized.

❷   The initialization of the config object. An even better practice would be to put this constructor and initConfig method into the base class, which would be Vehicle.js, but for demo purposes, I'll leave the code here.

❸   You use the same drive() signature so the drive() method will contain the override. This override will contain an additional check.

❹   When an instance passes in a nrOfWheels property that is smaller than three, it will populate a specific log message.

❺   When an instance does not pass in the nrOfWheels property, or the property is larger than four, then it will display the default behavior, which we can retrieve by calling the parent (Vehicle) class.

I can run this code by creating an instance of the Motor class.

```
var motor = Ext.create('VehicleApp.vehicle.Motor', {
    //nrOfWheels: 4
});
motor.drive();
```

Component inheritance works the same way, because at the end a component is a Sencha class. Use the `extend` property within the configuration of the class definition. You will pass in the string name of the parent Sencha component (e.g., `Ext.Component`. This maps to the *<sencha-touch-framework-folder>/src/Component.js* component. But you can also find the component class names (as well as the `xtype` names) in the API docs.

Constructors aren't used with components. If you subclass `Ext.Component`, you probably won't use a constructor. Instead, components are initialized in a method named `initialize()`.

Inheritance is a very powerful concept. What about multiple inheritance? Sometimes you need to inherit functionality from multiple classes. Let's check out the next section.

Inherit from Multiple Classes

When would you want to use multiple inheritance? In some cases, you might want a class to inherit features from more than one superclass. When you want to implement multiple inheritance of classes, you need *mixins*. A mixin object does exactly what the name implies: it mixes in functionality. "Take a little bit of this, use a little bit of that…" For example, take a method of class X, take a method of class Y, implement it in class Z.

Let's say we have two vehicle classes, a normal car and a monster 4-wheeler. Both vehicles can inherit the methods to brake and to drive. Only the monster 4-wheeler can also jump, however; the normal car can't.

Take a look at Figure 4-2. The code corresponding to this diagram is written in Example 4-7.

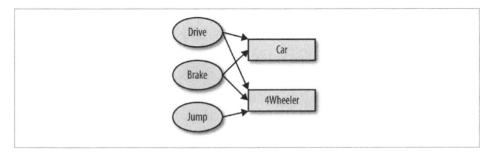

Figure 4-2. Inheriting multiple classes

Now, let's define three classes, each with its own functionality to share `drive()`, `brake()`, and `jump()`. Later you will define two vehicle classes that inherit from these classes and mix in those methods.

Example 4-7. Define classes with the methods you will mix in

```
Ext.define('VehicleApp.mixins.Drive', {
  drive: function(){ //the method to share
    console.log(this.$className + ": Vrrrrooom");
  }
});
Ext.define('VehicleApp.mixins.Brake', {
  brake: function(){
    console.log(this.$className + ": Eeeeekk");
  }
});
Ext.define('VehicleApp.mixins.Jump', {
  jump: function(){
    console.log(this.$className + ": Bump");
  }
});
```

Finally, you can define the two `Vehicle` classes with the mixin implementations. Again, these are just normal class definitions, but with a `mixins` object. You can list all the mixins underneath one another. They are used from one place without copying code over.

Example 4-8 shows the `Car` class with mixins to inherit the `drive()` and `brake()` functionalities.

Example 4-8. Define a Car class with mixin implementations

```
Ext.define('VehicleApp.vehicle.Car', {
  mixins: {
    canBrake: 'VehicleApp.mixins.Brake',
    canDrive: 'VehicleApp.mixins.Drive'
  }
});
```

Example 4-9 shows the monster `FourWheeler` class with mixins to inherit the `drive()`, `brake()`, and `jump()` functionalities.

Example 4-9. Define a FourWheeler class with mixin implementations

```
Ext.define('VehicleApp.vehicle.FourWheeler', {
  mixins: {
    canBrake: 'VehicleApp.mixins.Brake',
    canDrive: 'VehicleApp.mixins.Drive',
    canJump: 'VehicleApp.mixins.Jump'
  }
});
```

With the implementation of Examples 4-8 and 4-9, the drive() and brake() methods are available to the Car class, and the drive(), brake(), and jump() methods are available to the FourWheeler class. You can just execute those methods with the following code:

```
var mercedes = Ext.create('VehicleApp.vehicle.Car');
var honda = Ext.create('VehicleApp.vehicle.FourWheeler');

mercedes.drive();
mercedes.brake();

honda.drive();
honda.jump();
honda.brake();
```

The mixin identifier canBrake matches the prototype, and therefore you can run the brake() method on the FourWheeler and Car classes.

Summary

Vanilla JavaScript by its nature has no class system, as JavaScript is a prototype-based language. To mimic the ideas of object-oriented programming, you can write your JavaScript functions in an object-oriented way:

```
function Cab(driver, passenger) {
  this.driver = driver;
  this.passenger = passenger;
}
```

To create an instance of this Cab class, you can create a new object with the new operator:

```
var mercedes = new Cab('John Doe', 'The president');
```

For every object that you create, you need to make sure the class definition is loaded in the memory. It is possible to create inheritance or define singletons—the functionality's just not there out of the box.

Sencha Touch has a built-in class system that ships with inheritance, magic methods, and singleton strategies. Example 4-10 is the Sencha version of the previous Cab class.

Example 4-10. app/view/Cab.js

```
Ext.define('TaxiApp.view.Cab', {
  extend: 'Ext.Component',
  config: {
    driver: '',
    passenger: ''
  }
});
```

Sencha has strict naming conventions. The class that you define needs to contain an application name in upper CamelCase notation (TaxiApp) that maps to the *app* folder. Packages are subfolders in the *app* folder and are written in lowercase. The class name should contain the same name as the filename, and should also be written in CamelCase notation (Cab). The class TaxiApp.view.Cab maps to *app/view/Cab.js* and it can contain only a single class definition. These naming conventions are required by the Sencha loading mechanism. The Ext.Loader will make sure that every class definition is loaded in the right order.

With the extend class configuration, it is possible to inherit from a single class. In this example we will need it, so we do not need to write a constructor.

To create an instance of this Sencha Cab class, you can create a new object, but without the new operator:

```
var mercedes = Ext.create('TaxiApp.view.Cab', {
  driver: 'John Doe',
  passenger: 'The president'
});
```

When you run mercedes.getDriver(), it will return the name John Doe. This is because the config object in Example 4-10 automatically generates magic methods, like get Driver() and setDriver()—as well as applyDriver() and updateDriver().

Now that you know everything about the Sencha class system and the Sencha fundamentals, we are almost ready to build our application.

There is just one topic I would like to discuss first: how to create layouts for your Sencha applications and components. In the next chapter, we'll explore the layout system.

## CHAPTER 5

The Layout System

In Sencha Touch there are two basic building blocks: *components* and *containers*. When you instantiate both with no configuration, they look the same. However, there is one important difference: containers can *contain* components (or other containers):

```
var container = Ext.create('Ext.Container', {
    items: [{
        xtype: 'component',
        html: 'Nested component'
    }, {
        xtype: 'container',
        items: [{
            xtype: 'component',
            html: 'Nested container with component'
        }]
    }]
});
```

Usually when containers hold other components, you want to think about how to position these multiple components. Maybe you want to position the components on top of each other, or maybe next to each other. In other words, you want to give the container a *layout*.

Under the hood, Sencha Touch uses the CSS3 flexbox layout. This is different from Ext JS 4, which uses JavaScript to dynamically calculate absolute CSS positions. The reason for the difference is because Ext JS needs to support old legacy browsers (IE6, ouch!). CSS3 flexbox layouts work only in modern browsers, and even here, there are multiple implementations required to support multiple browsers. To understand CSS3 flexbox layouts, take a look at "A Complete Guide to Flexbox" (*http://bit.ly/flexbox-css*).

While implementing layouts in Sencha Touch (and in Ext JS), you do not need to worry about the underlying CSS techniques—the framework takes care of it. That said, some concepts, like *flexing* boxes in Sencha Touch (dynamic sizing), are similar to the CSS3 flexbox techniques.

`Ext.Component` is the base class for any Sencha Touch view component (widget). `Ext.Container` is the base class for any Sencha Touch component that may visually contain other components. The most commonly used container classes for Sencha Touch are `Ext.Panel`, `Ext.tab.Panel`, and `Ext.form.Panel`. Containers handle the basic behavior for containing, inserting, showing, removing, and hiding items. Speaking of containing items, you might want to position items next to each other, or even on top of each other. Some items should be bigger than others. You might want to give those a fixed width and height, or even better, a height and width relative to the screen size. You can achieve all of this while working with layouts. To make this concept clear, we'll see some screenshots of all the different layout types. The next examples explain all the different layout types provided by the layout package.

In this chapter, you'll learn:

- How to implement a horizontal layout
- How to implement a vertical layout
- How to implement a full screen (fit) layout
- How to implement a card layout
- How to implement the default layout (no layout)
- How to dock components

Implementing a Horizontal Layout

When you want to position components horizontally, use the horizontal box layout. The layout type `hbox` positions items next to each other.

At the top of your container view class, you will require `Ext.layout.HBox`, so the `Ext.Loader` knows to load the `hbox` framework class first. Next, you will create a `lay out` object that sets the type to `hbox`. Follow up by creating an array with `items`; this array can contain all the items that need to be positioned next to each other. Here's the full example:

```
Ext.define('MyApp.view.MainInterface', {
    extend: 'Ext.Container',
    requires: ['Ext.layout.HBox'],
    layout: {
        type: 'hbox',
    },
    items: [{
        xtype: 'component',
        html: 'box 1'
    },{
        xtype: 'component',
        html: 'box 2'
```

```
    }]
});
```

If you want to learn more about nesting components, see "Instantiating a Basic Component" on page 26.

You can set the `align` config to position items vertically on the screen. The options for the `align` config are `start` (top), `center` (middle), `end` (bottom), and `stretch`. The last option stretches a component to give it the full container height. Then there is the `pack` config—`start` (left), `center` (middle), and `end` (right)—which positions the set of items horizontally on the screen.

Here are some of the `hbox` layouts, each of which is followed by its corresponding illustration (Figure 5-1 through Figure 5-7).

```
layout: {
    type: 'hbox',
    align: 'start',
    pack: 'start'
},
items: [{
    xtype: 'component',
    html: 'width: 150'
    width: 150
},{
    xtype: 'component',
    html: 'width: 150'
    width: 150
}]
```

Figure 5-1. Layout type: hbox; (vertical) align: start; and (horizontal) pack: start

```
layout: {
    type: 'hbox',
    align: 'center',
    pack: 'center'
},
items: [{
    xtype: 'component',
```

```
        html: 'width: 150'
        width: 150
    }, {
         xtype: 'component',
        html: 'width: 150'
        width: 150
    }]
```

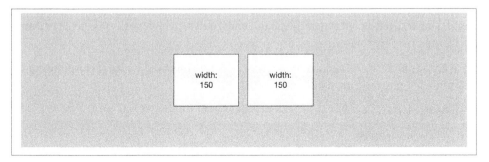

Figure 5-2. Layout type: hbox; (vertical) align: center; and (horizontal) pack: center

```
    layout: {
        type: 'hbox',
        align: 'center',
        pack: 'end'
    },
    items: [{
        xtype: 'component',
        html: 'width: 150'
        width: 150
    },{
        xtype: 'component',
        html: 'width: 150'
        width: 150
    }]
```

Figure 5-3. Layout type: hbox; (vertical) align: center; and (horizontal) pack: end

```
layout: {
    type: 'hbox',
    align: 'end',
    pack: 'start'
},
items: [{
    xtype: 'component',
    html: 'width: 150'
    width: 150
},{
     xtype: 'component',
    html: 'width: 150'
    width: 150
}]
```

Figure 5-4. Layout type: hbox; (vertical) align: end; and (horizontal) pack: start

```
layout: {
    type: 'hbox',
    align: 'stretch',
    pack: 'start'
},
items: [{
    xtype: 'component',
    html: 'width: 150'
    width: 150
},{
     xtype: 'component',
    html: 'width: 150'
    width: 150
}]
```

Figure 5-5. Layout type: hbox; (vertical) align: stretch; and (horizontal) pack: start

The preceding examples used a `width` config for every item. When you want more dynamic sizes, you can use the `flex` config. *Flexing* means that you divide the available area based on the `flex` of each child component. The next example, illustrated in Figure 5-6, shows a horizontal `flex` layout:

```
layout: {
    type: 'hbox',
},
items: [{
    xtype: 'component',
    flex: 2,
    html: 'flex: 2',
},{
    xtype: 'component',
    flex: 1,
    html: 'flex: 1',
}]
```

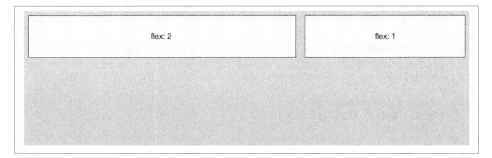

Figure 5-6. Layout type: hbox, and items with flexes

This is a container with two items; the left item takes one-third of the container, and the right item takes two-thirds. This would be translated with the following `flex` setup: left item has `flex:1`, and right item has `flex:2`. (Because the total of both flexes, 1+2, equals 3.)

Now let's say you have three items. The first item has `flex: 2`, the second item has `flex:1`, and the third item has a fixed pixel width, `width: 100px`. How will the layout be calculated? First, the 100px will be subtracted from the 100%. The remainder will be divided into two-thirds and one-third (see Figure 5-7).

```
layout: {
    type: 'hbox',
},
items: [{
    xtype: 'component',
    flex: 2,
    html: 'flex: 2',
},{
    xtype: 'component',
    flex: 1,
    html: 'flex: 1',
},{
    xtype: 'component',
    width: 100,
    html: 'width: 100'
}]
```

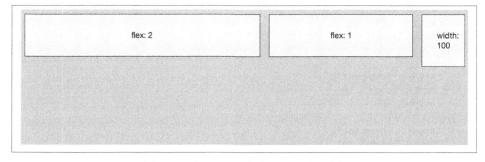

Figure 5-7. Layout type: hbox, and items with flexes and widths

Implementing a Vertical Layout

When you want to position components vertically, you will use the vertical box layout. The layout type `vbox` positions items on top of each other.

At the top of your container view class, you will require `Ext.layout.VBox`, so the `Ext.Loader` knows to load the vbox framework class first. Next, you will create a `lay out` object that sets the type to `vbox`. Follow up by creating an array with `items`; this array will contain all the items that need to be positioned on top of each other. Here's the full example:

```
Ext.define('MyApp.view.MainInterface', {
    extend: 'Ext.Container',
    requires: ['Ext.layout.VBox'],
```

```
        layout: {
            type: 'vbox',
        },
        items: [{
            xtype: 'component',
            html: 'box 1'
        },{
            xtype: 'component',
            html: 'box 2'
        }]
});
```

You can set the align config to position items horizontally on the screen. The options for the align property are start (left), center (middle), end (right), or stretch. The last option stretches a component to give it the full container width. Then there is the pack property—start (top), center (middle), and end (bottom)—which positions the set of items vertically on the screen.

Here are some of the vbox layouts, each of which is followed by its corresponding illustration (Figure 5-8 through Figure 5-14):

```
layout: {
    type: 'vbox',
    align: 'start',
    pack: 'start'
},
items: [{
    xtype: 'component',
    html: 'height: 50'
    height: 50
},{
    xtype: 'component',
    html: 'height: 50'
    height: 50
}]
```

Figure 5-8. Layout type: vbox; (horizontal) align: start; and (vertical) pack: start

```
layout: {
    type: 'vbox',
    align: 'center',
    pack: 'center'
},
items: [{
    xtype: 'component',
    html: 'height: 50'
    height: 50
},{
    xtype: 'component',
    html: 'height: 50'
    height: 50
}]
```

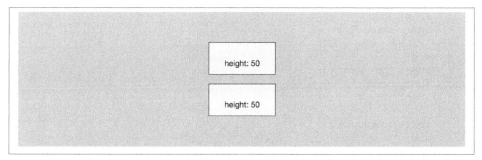

Figure 5-9. Layout type: vbox; (horizontal) align: center; and (vertical) pack: center

```
layout: {
    type: 'vbox',
    align: 'center',
    pack: 'end'
},
items: [{
    xtype: 'component',
    html: 'height: 50'
    height: 50
},{
    xtype: 'component',
    html: 'height: 50'
    height: 50
}]
```

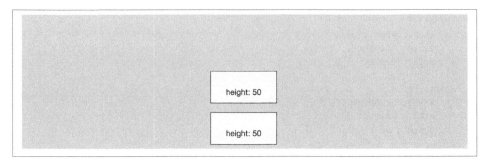

Figure 5-10. Layout type: vbox; (horizontal) align: center; and (vertical) pack: end

```
layout: {
    type: 'vbox',
    align: 'end',
    pack: 'start'
},
items: [{
    xtype: 'component',
    html: 'height: 50'
    height: 50
},{
    xtype: 'component',
    html: 'height: 50'
    height: 50
}]
```

Figure 5-11. Layout type: vbox; (horizontal) align: end; and (vertical) pack: start

```
layout: {
    type: 'vbox',
    align: 'stretch',
    pack: 'center'
},
items: [{
    xtype: 'component',
    html: 'height: 50'
    height: 50
```

```
},{
    xtype: 'component',
    html: 'height: 50'
    height: 50
}]
```

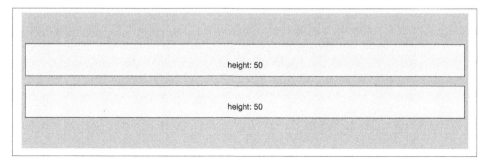

Figure 5-12. Layout type: vbox; (horizontal) align: stretch; and (vertical) pack: center

If you want to set a fixed height for one of the items, you use the height config. When you want more dynamic sizes, you use the flex config. *Flexing* means that you divide the available area based on the *flex* of each child component. The next example, illustrated in Figure 5-13, shows a vertical flex layout:

```
layout: {
    type: 'vbox',
},
items: [{
    xtype: 'component',
    html: 'flex: 1',
    flex: 1
},{
    xtype: 'component',
    html: 'flex: 3',
    flex: 3
}]
```

Figure 5-13. Layout type: vbox, and items with flexes

This is a container with two items; the top item takes one-quarter of the container, and the bottom item takes three-quarters. This would be translated with the following flex setup: top item has flex:1, and bottom item has flex:3. (Beause the total of both flexes, 1+3, is 4.)

Now let's say you have three items. The first item has flex: 1, the second item has flex:3, and the third item has a fixed pixel height, height: 50px. How will the layout be calculated? First, the 50px will be subtracted from the 100%. The remainder will be divided into one-quarter and three-quarters (see Figure 5-14):

```
layout: {
    type: 'vbox',
},
items: [{
    xtype: 'component',
    html: 'flex: 1',
    flex: 1
},{
    xtype: 'component',
    html: 'flex: 3',
    flex: 3
},{
    xtype: 'component',
    html: 'height: 50',
    height: 50
}]
```

Figure 5-14. Layout type: vbox, and items with flexes and widths

Implementing a Full-Screen (Fit) Layout

When you want to position a component full screen, you use the fit layout. The layout type `fit` makes a child item fit to the full size of its parent container.

```
layout: 'fit',
items: [{
    html: 'Item 1'
}]
```

At the top of your container view class, you will require `Ext.layout.Fit`, so the `Ext.Loader` knows to load the `fit` framework class first. Next, you will create a `lay out` object that sets the type to `fit`. Follow up by creating an `items` array; this array can contain only one item. Here's the full example (see Figure 5-15):

```
Ext.define('MyApp.view.MainInterface', {
    extend: 'Ext.Container',
    requires: ['Ext.layout.Fit'],
    layout: {
        type: 'fit',
    },
    items: [{
        xtype: 'component',
        html: 'layout: fit'
    }]
});
```

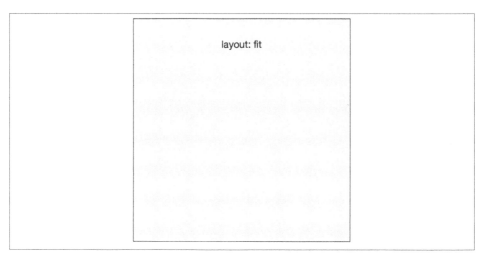

Figure 5-15. Layout type: fit; the container has dimensions of 400×400px

The container has a height and width of 400×400 pixels. The nested item (component) takes the full width and height that has been set in the parent container, so it has the same 400×400 pixel dimension.

Here's another example of the same fit layout. The container has a 400×400px dimension, but this time the nested component has a margin of 25px on each side (see Figure 5-16):

```
layout: {
    type: 'fit',
},
items: [{
    xtype: 'component',
    margin: 25,
    html: 'layout: fit'
}]
```

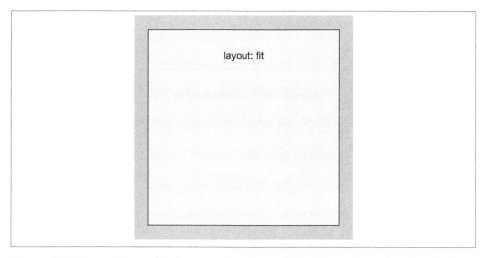

Figure 5-16. Layout type: fit; the container has a 400×400px dimension, but the item has a margin of 25px on each side

Implementing a Card Layout

You can create a more complex layout by using cards. A card layout allows you to fit multiple components in one space, and show only one at a time, just like a stack of cards. To do this, set the layout type to card .

At the top of your container view class, you will require Ext.layout.Card, so the Ext.Loader knows to load the card framework class first. Next, you will create a lay out object that sets the type to card. Follow up by creating an array with items; this array can contain all the items that need to be positioned as a stack of cards.

Here's the full example (see Figure 5-17):

```
Ext.define('MyApp.view.MainInterface', {
    extend: 'Ext.Container',
    requires: ['Ext.layout.Card'],
    layout: {
        type: 'card',
    },
    items: [{
        xtype: 'component',
        html: 'card 1'
    },{
        xtype: 'component',
        html: 'card 2'
    },
    {
        xtype: 'component',
        html: 'card 3'
```

```
        }]
});
```

stacked card 3: .setActiveItem(2)

Figure 5-17. Layout type: card

This layout has the same visual look as a fit layout; it also takes the size of the container. But there is one important difference with this layout type. When the container contains multiple items, they will be stacked on top of each other, like a deck of cards. See Figure 5-18.

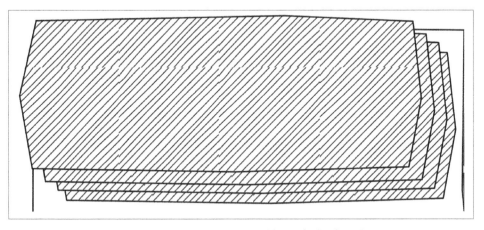

Figure 5-18. Layout type: card; this layout resembles a deck of cards

With the method setActiveItem(), you can set the item to be displayed at the top of the cards stack. All the other items won't be visible. Carousels (a Sencha Touch component for cards that you can slide with your fingers) and tabpanels (a Sencha Touch component for cards that you can activate with tabs) both use a card layout.

`Ext.Container.setActiveItem(activeItem)` and `Ext.Contain` `er.getActiveItem()` set or return an `activeItem` number. The number 0 points to the first container item, the number 1 to the second container item, and so on. For example, `stack.setActiveItem(2)` displays the third container item and hides all the other items.

A nice extra that comes with the card layout is the ability to add an animation while changing the active slide. You can set an `animation` object with a `type` and a `direction`. The supported types are:

- `slide` (`Ext.fx.layout.card.Slide`)
- `fade` (`Ext.fx.layout.card.Fade`)
- `cover` (`Ext.fx.layout.card.Cover`)
- `reveal` (`Ext.fx.layout.card.Reveal`)
- `pop` (`Ext.fx.layout.card.Pop`)
- `flip` (`Ext.fx.layout.card.Flip`)
- `scroll` (`Ext.fx.layout.card.Scroll`)
- `cube` (`Ext.fx.layout.card.Cube`)

Here's an example of how you can include an animation for a page transition in a card layout. Please note the animation subject:

```
layout: {
    type: 'card',
    animation: {
        type: 'slide',
        direction: 'left'
    }
}
```

Android 2 supports only `scroll` and `fade`; otherwise, it forces the animation to `slide`.

Implementing the Default Layout

When you do not want to set a layout or you want to fall back to the default browser behavior, you can use the default/auto layout.

When you do not specify the layout object, or you set the layout to auto or default, your design will take the Ext.layout.Default layout. Maybe you are using this layout for a reason. For example, say you want to design your own custom layouts with self-written CSS. In that case, you might set this layout purposely to improve readability/maintainabily. When you read it back later, you will understand why you set it.

At the top of your container view class, you will require Ext.layout.Default, so the Ext.Loader knows to load the default framework class first. Next, you will create a layout object that sets the type to auto or default. Follow up by creating an array with items; this array can contain all the items that you can position by yourself. Here's the full example (see Figure 5-19):

```
Ext.define('MyApp.view.MainInterface', {
    extend: 'Ext.Container',
    requires: ['Ext.layout.Default'],
    layout: {
        type: 'auto',
    },
    items: [{
        xtype: 'component',
        cls: 'component1',
        html: 'component 1'
    },{
        xtype: 'component',
        cls: 'component2',
        html: 'component 2'
    }]
});
```

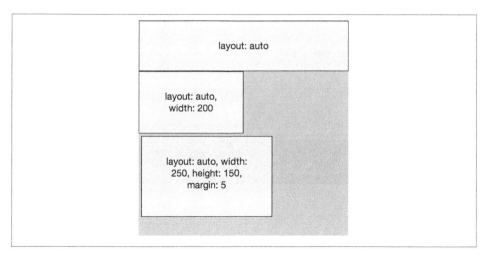

Figure 5-19. Layout type: default, like the default browser block-level behavior

This layout tiles your elements directly beneath each other. It takes the full available width to fill its parent container unless a width is set. If no height is set, it will expand naturally to fit itself or its child items. It's the same behavior as how a browser positions block-level elements.

 Impressive Webs has a helpful article (*http://bit.ly/block-inline*) about browser block-level elements versus inline-elements.

All other layouts inherit from Ext.layout.Default, and the default layout also supports docking items, which we'll cover next.

Docking Components

Instead of using the layout system, you can also *dock* a component so it "sticks" to one side. To dock a component, add the docked variable; it works in combination with any layout type.

With docking, you can set an item to dock left, top, right, or bottom from its container. A good example is a toolbar that is docked to the top of the screen. (Some people call this a *sticky header*.)

Here's a full example where I dock the toolbar to the top of the screen (see Figure 5-20):

```
Ext.define('MyApp.view.MainInterface', {
    extend: 'Ext.Container',
```

```
    items: [{
        docked: 'top'
        html: 'docked: top',
    },{
        html: ''
    }]
});
```

Figure 5-20. A panel docked to the top of the screen

You must use an HTML5 doctype for a docked bottom to work. To do this, simply add the following code to the top of the HTML file: `<!doctype html>`.

Let's take a look at the other `docked` settings, each of which is followed by its corresponding illustration (Figures Figure 5-21 through Figure 5-23):

```
Ext.define('MyApp.view.MainInterface', {
    extend: 'Ext.Container',
    items: [{
        docked: 'left'
        html: 'docked: left',
    },{
        html: ''
    }]
});
```

Figure 5-21. Layout type: a panel docked to the left side of the screen

```
Ext.define('MyApp.view.MainInterface', {
    extend: 'Ext.Container',
    items: [{
        docked: 'right'
        html: 'docked: right',
    },{
```

```
        html: ''
    }]
});
```

Figure 5-22. Layout type: a panel docked to the right side of the screen

```
Ext.define('MyApp.view.MainInterface', {
    extend: 'Ext.Container',
    items: [{
        docked: 'bottom'
        html: 'docked: bottom',
    },{
        html: ''
    }]
});
```

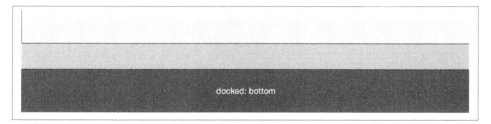

Figure 5-23. Layout type: a panel docked to the bottom of the screen

 For more information (and a video tutorial), check out the Sencha 2.3 docs (*http://bit.ly/sencha-23*).

Summary

As you can see, there are many ways to position components in Sencha Touch. The best way of creating interfaces is by prototyping the application before you implement it in your app. You could do this with code, as with the code snippets in this chapter, or you could use Sencha Architect, Sencha's visual design tool.

The Sencha layout system supports the following layout types: hbox (horizontal box layout), vbox (vertical box layout), fit (take the size of the container layout), card (stacked layout), and default, the browser's, block-level layout. All of these types have a set of additional configurations, such as align, pack, and animation.

What about layouts for different devices? What about responsive design? Sencha Touch 2 doesn't need a responsive design, like the HTML5/CSS3 responsive layouts we are familiar with for the Web (e.g., media queries). Sencha Touch sizes your layouts/UI to the full viewport.

The Ext.Viewport is an instance created when you use Ext.application(). Ext.Viewport extends from Ext.Container, so it has a layout (which defaults to the card layout). This means you can add items to it at any time, from anywhere in your code. The viewport fullscreen configuration is true by default, so it will take up your whole screen, and thus it matches any device to its screen size.

However, I imagine you would like the main layout for your tablet to be different from that of your phone. Sencha Touch handles this with *device profiles*, which create different mobile experiences. With a device profile, you can share code (like layouts and views, but also logics and controllers) between device types, to customize the appearance, behavior, or workflows for each device. Device profiles can be generated with Sencha Cmd. These classes will be stored in the *app/profile* directory. For more information about device profiles, read the online guide (*http://bit.ly/sencha-231-docs*).

Now that we've covered some of the fundamentals of Sencha Touch, including its class system and layout system, we're finally ready to start building a real-world application: the FindACab app.

In the next part of the book, you can read more about the MVC pattern, how to start building our application, and working with a lot of code.

## PART II

Building the FindACab App

This part will be the starting point for building a real-world application, the FindACab app.

The FindACab app is a touch application for tablets that can be used to browse through nearby taxi services (provided by Yelp). This MVC app uses all the techniques covered in this part—creating the application architecture, requesting live data through the Yelp API web service, saving data offline, handling forms, theming your app, and creating production/native device builds.

If you want to create a Sencha Touch application without using Sencha Architect (Sencha's visual design tool), you'll need to use Sencha Cmd, command-line tools for generating and building a Sencha Touch app. As depicted in Figure II.1, the first important step is to generate your folder structure with Sencha Cmd. It's important to use Sencha Cmd, because it also saves metadata in a hidden *.sencha* folder that is required for building your application later. Step 2 is to write your application logic and classes, using the coding editor or IDE of your choice. Step 3, the last step, is to build your application. You need to build the application to create a minified package before going to production.

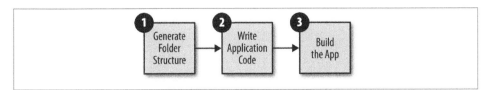

Figure II.1. The process for writing a Sencha Touch application

This part focuses on all three steps of this process, and you'll learn:

- How to structure your code
- How to implement data models
- How to make remote connections by implementing server proxies
- How to implement data stores
- How to save data offline by implementing client proxies
- How to work with view components like maps, lists, and floating panels
- How to implement and handle forms
- How to create a custom theme
- How to create production and native builds

I'll kick off with Step 1, how to generate the structure with Sencha Cmd. We will end this part with Step 3, how to create production and native builds (Chapter 14).

## CHAPTER 6

Structured Code

If you work in software development, you probably will recognize the following situation: your manager comes in and drops a bombshell. Your coworker, the lead developer of the FindACab app, is ill. The app needs to go live today, but there's a huge bug in it. The app doesn't display any results. "Can you help fix this?" your boss asks (read: demands).

Together with the project manager, you review the application in Google Chrome. When you click on the Network tab, you see that the AJAX request returns no results. Digging deeper, you learn that this is because the parameters in the URL are incorrect. "Piece of cake," you say, "there's something wrong with the request URL. Just give me an hour." But, once you open your coworker's project file, you see that the entire project exists as one single JavaScript file. There is no structure in it at all. What should have taken one hour suddenly turns into five. Wouldn't it be better if there were a bit more structure in the code?

Design Patterns

Another expression for building *structure* in code is creating a *design pattern*. When you are working with a large code base, you're probably also working with a team. When working with teams, you'll have to create standards because you don't want to deal with a different coding style for every team member.

As of the release of Sencha Touch version 2.0, Sencha solves this challenge with the Model-View-Controller (MVC) pattern. The benefits of using this pattern are scalability, maintainability, and flexibility. Once your code is broken into smaller chunks, bugs are easier to find and fix. This improves code maintainability—which means that it will be that much easier if your manager asks you to implement the ability to find clubs in the Find-a-Bar app. The MVC pattern improves teamwork too, because it's much easier for multiple developers to work on the app because they can all work on different parts simultaneously (and at the end of the day, you will like your coworkers better!).

In the previous scenario with the Find-a-Bar app, you noticed that there was something wrong with the AJAX request. With an MVC pattern, you don't need to search in your whole project—you'll know that there's a bug in the application logic, so you just need to open the controller. The whole functionality wherein the application creates Sencha Touch view components may be a black box for you. Figure 6-1 shows such a schema.

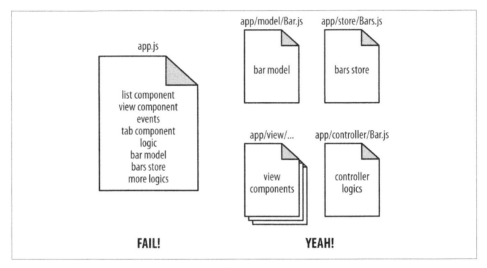

Figure 6-1. On the left, a fail scenario: all the code is in one single file. On the right, how it should be: a nice structured way. If there is a bug in the app logic, it's much easier to find because you don't have to open and read all the UI-related code files.

Let's start with an overview of the MVC pattern to get a more in-depth understanding of design patterns in general.

The MVC Pattern

The more functionality your app gains, the more code you'll have to write. More code means your app will be harder to maintain. If you don't prepare for that larger code base in advance, you can end up with a hard-to-read, maintenance headache.

In server-side technologies, MVC is a common pattern, used in such popular frameworks as Ruby on Rails, Django, Spring MVC, and the Zend Framework for PHP. As web applications have become more and more advanced, JavaScript frameworks are implementing MVC ideas too. The *traditional* MVC design pattern decouples the design of the application into three important components: the data model (*model*), the data presentation (*view*), and the application logic (*controller*). With this pattern, code can easily be reused and changes in the interface (view) won't mess up the model (and vice versa). See Figure 6-2 for an illustration of this pattern.

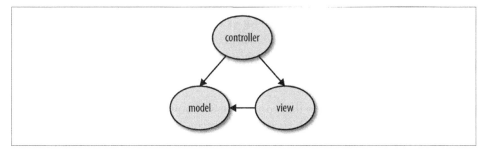

Figure 6-2. An overview of the classic MVC pattern: the controller updates the model and view. The view can update the model.

There are several JavaScript frameworks that have implemented the core ideas of the MVC pattern. Some examples are Ext JS, KnockOut JS, YUI, Backbone JS, and, the focus of this book, Sencha Touch.

Sencha MVC

Sencha Touch and Ext JS have their own implementation of the MVC design pattern. Although it is partly based on the traditional MVC design pattern, the Sencha Touch MVC design pattern differs a bit from the familiar server-side MVC pattern. First of all, Sencha Touch apps are single-page applications (SPAs), meaning they have one HTML page instead of multiple HTML pages. This is because most mobile web apps load content in the screen instead of surfing to a real URL. This is very common for mobile web applications. With server-side MVC, you could have one controller file that dispatches events to the correct page URL. Although Sencha Touch applications have only one HTML page, you can have multiple views and you could also have multiple controllers that can listen to user input.

Beyond this, there is one other way in which the Sencha Touch MVC differs from the traditional (or server-side) MVC; in the traditional MVC, the term *model* is a general term, encompassing application data. In Sencha Touch (and also in Ext JS), model is more clearly defined, comprising a model class definition (which contains the application data structure), and two other class definitions: store (the data pool) and record (the actual data).

The following explains what these terms stand for:

- The model (`Ext.data.Model`) is a class definition that represents some object—for example, a `TaxiService`. Like a database table, it describes the structure of the data.

A model can contain *fields* (Ext.data.Field); for example, the TaxiService has an id, a name, and a phonenumber field.

- A record (Ext.data.Record) could be a specific TaxiService Model object, or the instance of the TaxiService class—for example, the record with the name "Taxi Amsterdam" and phone number "020xxxxxxx."

- The Ext.data.Store is the whole set of model objects, a client-side cache of all records together. Figure 6-3 illustrates this.

Sencha Touch's *views* are classes that contain view components—basically, any Sencha component that you can see on the screen. All Sencha Touch view components extend from Ext.Component; therefore, every component has a certain set of configurations, like to set an html string, or to hide() and show() components. We will discuss Sencha Touch views in Chapter 11.

Sencha Touch's *controller* (Ext.app.Controller) is like the glue between the model and the view. Controllers are responsible for responding to events that occur within your app. You can compare the Sencha Touch controller with a helpdesk—for example, the helpdesk of an Internet provider to call when your Internet is down. In my experience, usually the person who answers my call does not understand the Internet service at all, but she knows who I am because I am a customer in the database, and she can forward my call to a technical support person who can help me out. That is exactly how the controller in Sencha Touch works: it doesn't know much about the application, but it has *references* to view components and it can access the data. It works as a dispatcher, listening to (user, system, or lifecycle) events and forwarding to some method. See Figure 6-3. Now, you can choose to write down all your (business) logic within the controller, or you choose to keep the controller clean and small, and forward to a static or singleton method in a separate class.

Once you have defined all the class definitions for your models, stores, views, and controllers, there needs to be one certain place to hook it all up and kickstart the application. This is what happens in the *app.js* file that defines Ext.application; it is the entry point for every MVC in Sencha Touch.

A Sencha Touch application can consist of multiple models, stores, views, and controllers. In the upcoming chapters, you will build the FindACab app. This application will also make use of the Sencha MVC, and its architecture will look like Figure 6-4.

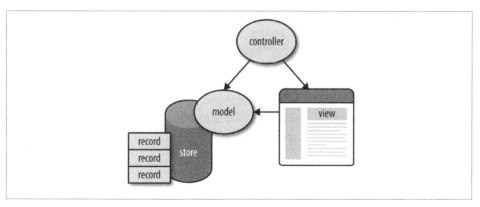

Figure 6-3. An overview of the Sencha MVC pattern: the term "model" encompasses a model, store, and record class definition.

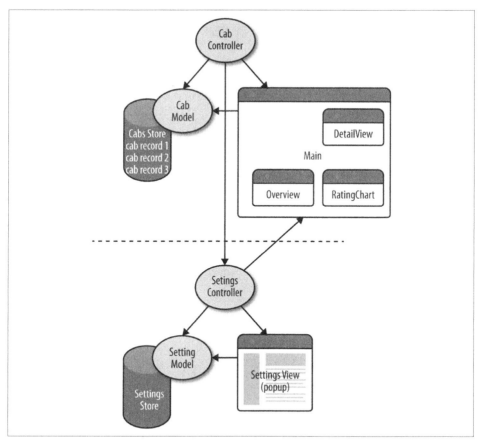

Figure 6-4. The architecture of the FindACab app

The FindACab app has a main view, which contains an overview list with all the `Cab` items (names of `TaxiServices`). The overview list is hooked up to the `Cabs` store, to display all items. When you select a `TaxiService` from the list, it will show a detail screen with a rating chart. Both views (the chart and the detail view) get populated by a record selected from the `Cabs` store. The `Cab` controller will take care of that. From the main view you can open the Settings view, which is a pop-up window that contains a form. The user can enter a location, and the `Settings` controller will make sure that this information will be saved in the `Settings` store.

Now that you have a sense of the MVC pattern and how this concept translates to a Sencha MVC pattern, you probably want to know where to start. Well, honestly, it is very easy; with Sencha Touch in combination with Sencha Cmd, you can generate the Sencha Touch MVC application and folder structure. Let's begin with the first step: generating an application with Sencha Cmd to start developing.

What Is Sencha Cmd?

Sencha Cmd is a tool to design, develop, and deploy Sencha desktop and touch applications based on design standards with good performance. This cross-platform command-line tool provides many automated tasks around the full lifecycle of your applications, from generating a new workspace, MVC application, or form, to deploying an application for a production, test, or native environment.

As mentioned, Sencha Cmd is a tool that runs on the command line. To make sure it's installed, enter **sencha** in the terminal or command prompt. When Sencha Cmd is correctly installed, it will output the version number and an overview of all the available Sencha commands. If it's not correctly installed, consult Chapter 2 for installation instructions. Figure 6-5 shows how Sencha Cmd should look.

The Sencha documentation (*http://bit.ly/senchacmd-doc*) is a great online resource that tells you all the information you need about Sencha Cmd. Also, typing the command `sencha help` will tell you which options are available for Sencha Cmd.

Is Sencha Cmd correctly installed? Yes? OK, let's start!

In this chapter, you'll learn:

- How to generate an application with Sencha Cmd
- How to generate a model with Sencha Cmd
- How to implement a data store
- How to implement a view

- How to generate a controller with Sencha Cmd
- How to reference a component from a controller
- How to listen to events from a controller
- How to implement the MVC entry point
- How to load external classes

```
Options
  * --cwd, -cw - Sets the directory from which commands should execute
  * --debug, -d - Sets log level to higher verbosity
  * --nologo, -n - Suppress the initial Sencha Cmd version display
  * --plain, -pl - enables plain logging output (no highlighting)
  * --quiet, -q - Sets log level to warnings and errors only
  * --sdk-path, -s - The location of the SDK to use for non-app commands
  * --time, -ti - Display the execution time after executing all commands

Categories
  * app - Perform various application build processes
  * compass - Wraps execution of compass for sass compilation
  * compile - Compile sources to produce concatenated output and metadata
  * fs - Utility commands to work with files
  * generate - Generates models, controllers, etc. or an entire application
  * io - Create, deploy and manage applications on the Sencha.io cloud platform
  * iofs - Manage Files stored in the Sencha.io cloud platform
  * manifest - Extract class metadata
  * package - Manages local and remote packages
  * repository - Manage local repository and remote repository connections
  * theme - Commands for low-level operations on themes

Commands
  * ant - Invoke Ant with helpful properties back to Sencha Cmd
  * build - Builds a project from a legacy JSB3 file.
  * config - Load a properties file or sets a configuration property
  * help - Displays help for commands
  * js - Executes arbitrary JavaScript file(s)
  * upgrade - Upgrades Sencha Cmd
  * which - Displays the path to the current version of Sencha Cmd
```

Figure 6-5. Sencha Cmd running on the command line.

Generating an Application with Sencha Cmd

When you generate an MVC application with Sencha Cmd, it generates the folder structure and all the files for you.

Make sure Sencha Cmd is installed and sencha is added to your classpaths. Open your terminal/command prompt and on the command line navigate to the Sencha Touch sdk (framework) folder.

(If you followed Chapter 2, it will be the *touch* folder.)

The following command generates a new application with the namespace `FindACab` to the *findacab* folder in your web root:

```
cd /path/to/sencha-touch-2-sdk
sencha generate app -name <namespace> -path ../<appfolder>
```

This preceding line generates the MVC folder structure for the FindACab app as follows:

- *.sencha/*
- *touch/*
  - *app/*
    - *sencha.cfg*
    - *plugin.xml*
- *app/*
  - *controller/*
  - *model/*
  - *profile/*
  - *store/*
  - *view/*
- *app.js*
- *app.json*
- *bootstrap.js*
- *bootstrap.json*
- *build.xml*
- *index.html*
- *packager.json*
- *resources/*
  - *css/*
    - *app.css*
  - *sass/*
    - *app.scss*
  - *icons/*
    - *...*
  - *loading/*

— ...

— *images/*

Here's a description of each folder:

The hidden .sencha folder

The hidden *.sencha.* folder contains config/meta files and Ant scripts for build processes with Sencha Cmd. These are settings such as the paths to the namespace (in this case, *FindACab*) and references to the Sencha Touch folder and folders that are outside the *app* folder. If you are not going to add new folders outside the *app* MVC folder structure, you probably don't need to edit the *sencha.cfg* file. But if you *are* adding new folders outside the *app* folder, you will have to add the new folder paths to the app classpath in *.sencha/app/sencha.cfg* to make sure your build processes won't fail.

What else is in the *.sencha* folder? Lots of Ant build scripts. You can use these to figure out what's going on during the build, but in general you shouldn't change them. If you want to change the build process (e.g., to copy additional folders over to a production folder), you would change the *build.xml* file that's located in the root of your project folder.

 Apache Ant is a software tool for automating software build processes. It requires the Java platform, and it uses XML to describe the build process and its dependencies. By default, the XML file is named *build.xml*.

Ant is open source software, and is released under the Apache Software License. For more information about Apache Ant, check out the Ant manual (*http://bit.ly/ant-dirtask*).

The app folder

The `generate app` command generates the *app* folder. This folder contains the MVC folder structure—folders for the models, views, controllers, stores, and profiles. We will discuss all the MVC folders in this chapter. For now, it autogenerates a single view: *app/view/Main.js*. This displays the demo application, a tabpanel with two panels: the welcome tab and the video tab. (Go ahead, you can test it in your modern browser; just open *http://localhost/findacab*.) See Figures 6-6 and 6-7.

Figure 6-6. The generated FindACab app; it contains a tabpanel with a demo view like the welcome tab

The resources folder

The *resources* folder contains subfolders with files for CSS, Sass, and app assets such as icons and splash screens.

The touch folder

If the application is generated without a workspace, there will be a *touch* folder. When the application is generated in a workspace, this *touch* folder will be located one folder up. The *touch* folder is a copy of the Sencha Touch sdk. All the necessary framework files, Sencha documentation, and example applications are not included in this copy.

The other files

Then there are some files in the root of the folder. *app.js* is the starting point of your MVC application. *app.json*, *packager.json*, and *build.xml* contain settings and instructions for building or distributing your application. The *bootstrap.js* and *bootstrap.json* files are required for development purposes. They contain metadata (things like aliases, alternate class names, and filepaths) for the dynamic loader to make sure that your application will load the correct files in the correct order.

The index.html file

This is just the HTML index page you browse to in order to load the application. It contains the references to the Sencha Touch framework, the JavaScript start point (the *app.js*), and the stylesheet.

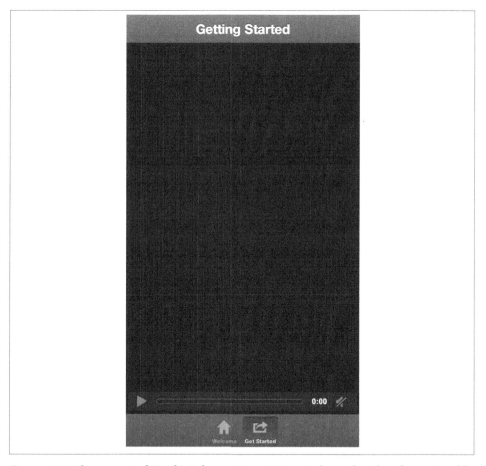

Figure 6-7. The generated FindACab app; it contains a tabpanel with a demo view like the video tab

Review the folder structure in Figure 6-8.

.DS_Store	Today, 10:27 AM	6 KB	Document
▼ .sencha	Today, 10:25 AM	--	Folder
▶ app	Today, 10:25 AM	--	Folder
▶ workspace	Today, 10:25 AM	--	Folder
▼ app	Today, 10:25 AM	--	Folder
▶ controller	Today, 10:25 AM	--	Folder
▶ form	Today, 10:25 AM	--	Folder
▶ model	Today, 10:25 AM	--	Folder
▶ profile	Today, 10:25 AM	--	Folder
Readme.md	Today, 10:25 AM	224 bytes	Markdown
▶ store	Today, 10:25 AM	--	Folder
▶ view	Today, 10:25 AM	--	Folder
app.js	Today, 10:25 AM	2 KB	JavaScript
app.json	Today, 10:25 AM	5 KB	JSON
bootstrap.js	Today, 10:25 AM	35 KB	JavaScript
bootstrap.json	Today, 10:25 AM	423 bytes	JSON
▶ build	Today, 10:25 AM	--	Folder
build.xml	Today, 10:25 AM	3 KB	XML Document
index.html	Today, 10:25 AM	2 KB	HTML
packager.json	Today, 10:25 AM	5 KB	JSON
▶ packages	Today, 10:25 AM	--	Folder
▶ resources	Today, 10:25 AM	--	Folder
▶ touch	Today, 10:25 AM	--	Folder

Figure 6-8. Sencha Touch application folder structure

 There is a shorter version of the `generate app sencha g a FindA Cab ../findacab`. There is only one command in Sencha Cmd that starts with a `g` (for *generate*), and within the `generate` command, there is only one thing you can generate that starts with an `a` (app).

Generating Workspaces

If you want to create multiple Touch applications that share the Sencha Touch framework, or maybe even share code, the correct procedure would be to generate a workspace. (It's even possible to host a copy of Ext JS—Sencha's framework for rich desktop applications—in a workspace.) To generate a workspace, run the following command:

```
sencha generate workspace <../myworkspacefolder>
```

The `generate workspace` command will generate workspace metadata in the hidden *.sencha* folder, which contains the workspace classpath. It will copy the *touch* framework folder in the root of the workspace folder. (This is a little different than when generating just an app because in that case the *touch* folder would be located in the application root folder.) The `generate workspace` command will also create two new (empty) folders: a *packages* folder, in case you want to download Sencha plug-ins, and a *build* folder, which will be the location where your build packages will be created and stored.

Once you have a workspace, generating apps is the same as before:

```
cd <../myworkspacefolder>
cd touch
sencha generate app -name <namespace}> -path <../appfolder>
```

Figure 6-9 shows the folder structure of a Sencha Touch workspace.

.DS_Store	Today, 10:27 AM	6 KB	Document
▶ .sencha	Today, 10:25 AM	--	Folder
▶ build	Today, 10:26 AM	--	Folder
▼ myapp	Today, 10:26 AM	--	Folder
▶ sencha	Today, 10:26 AM	--	Folder
▼ app	Today, 10:26 AM	--	Folder
▶ controller	Today, 10:26 AM	--	Folder
▶ form	Today, 10:26 AM	--	Folder
▶ model	Today, 10:26 AM	--	Folder
▶ profile	Today, 10:26 AM	--	Folder
Readme.md	Today, 10:26 AM	224 bytes	Markdown
▶ store	Today, 10:26 AM	--	Folder
▶ view	Today, 10:26 AM	--	Folder
app.js	Today, 10:26 AM	2 KB	JavaScript
app.json	Today, 10:26 AM	5 KB	JSON
bootstrap.js	Today, 10:26 AM	35 KB	JavaScript
bootstrap.json	Today, 10:26 AM	426 bytes	JSON
build.xml	Today, 10:26 AM	3 KB	XML Document
index.html	Today, 10:26 AM	2 KB	HTML
packager.json	Today, 10:26 AM	5 KB	JSON
▶ resources	Today, 10:26 AM	--	Folder
▶ packages	Today, 10:25 AM	--	Folder
▶ touch	Today, 10:25 AM	--	Folder

Figure 6-9. Sencha Touch workspace folder structure

 If you want to upgrade to a newer version of Sencha Touch, you can download the latest version from the website and let Sencha Cmd update your folder structure. Here's an example of how to upgrade the app (or workspace) from the command line:

```
sencha app upgrade ../path-new-sdk-folder
```

When upgrading your framework, you don't need to worry—it won't touch your self-written classes. It basically just copies a newer version of the sdk in your application root or workspace, and it might change some metadata in the hidden *.sencha* folder. However, it's also possible that it will need to update the *app.js*, *app.json*, or *bootstrap.js* files.

Now that you have all the files, you can start modifying the generated application, to build your own Touch application. But before doing so, let's take a deeper look into all the layers of the Sencha MVC. Let's inspect the data model first. For more detailed information about Sencha Cmd, check out the Sencha Guide (*http://bit.ly/sencha-23*).

Generating a Model with Sencha Cmd

To create the model definition, you create a new JavaScript file and save it in the *app/ model* directory. But a better choice is to have Sencha Cmd generate it for you.

Here's the general syntax for implementing the model definition for a Sencha MVC application. On the command line, navigate to the *app* folder and run the following command:

```
sencha generate model <MyModelName> <fieldstring>
```

Make sure you already have an MVC application generated with Sencha Cmd. To generate our FindACab app model, navigate to your project folder and type the following:

```
sencha generate model Cab id:auto,name:string,latitude:float,longitude:float,
address1:string,phone:string,state_code:string,zip:string,city:string,
userinput:string,country_code:string,avg_rating:float,distance:float
```

Sencha Cmd will generate the code shown in Example 6-1.

Example 6-1. app/model/Cab.js

```
Ext.define('FindACab.model.Cab', {
    extend: 'Ext.data.Model',

    config: {
        fields: [
            { name: 'id', type: 'auto' },
            { name: 'name', type: 'string' },
            { name: 'latitude', type: 'float' },
            { name: 'longitude', type: 'float' },
            { name: 'address1', type: 'string' },
            { name: 'phone', type: 'string' },
            { name: 'state_code', type: 'string' },
            { name: 'zip', type: 'string' },
            { name: 'city', type: 'string' },
            { name: 'userinput', type: 'string'},
            { name: 'country_code', type: 'string' },
            { name: 'avg_rating', type: 'float' },
            { name: 'distance', type: 'float' }
        ]
    }
});
```

That's pretty impressive, eh? Sencha Cmd has created the full data model for you. Now you don't need to type it all yourself (although you could).

The code in our newly generated JavaScript file defines the model `Cab.js`. Usually, the name of a model is a noun, because it has the namespace: *FindACab.model.Cab* translates to *app/model/Cab.js*. It makes this class behave like a model class because it extends all its properties from `Ext.data.Model`. Furthermore, this model has a lot of fields. Every field name has a `type`; for example, the field name `phone` has a type `string`. The possible field types for a model are `string`, `int`, `float`, `boolean`, and `auto`. The type `auto` means there is no type conversion at all. This might be handy when the model field represents an object (or array—note that an array in JavaScript is an object too).

Now that you have the model in the *model* folder, it should be linked somehow to the application. (For now, in the FindACab app, you will create a reference to the model in the *app.js* file. Later, you will move these references to a corresponding controller.) In `Ext.application()`, create a `models` array, and assign the `Cab` model to it:

```
models:[
    'Cab'
],
```

Connect a Model or Store to app.js or to the Controller?

A model can be hooked up to MVC architecture via the *app.js* `models` array or via the corresponding controller `models` array, as long as the corresponding controller is hooked up to the *app.js* `controllers` array. But which way is better? Honestly, it is an architecture choice. Imagine you have `Cab` and `Car` functionalities. Both have `Cab` and `Car` models, stores, and controllers. Say we hook up all `Cab` models and stores to a `CabController` and all `Car` models and stores to a `CarController`, and next week we decide to release the app but without the `Car` functionality. That would be just a simple matter of decoupling the `CarController`, whereas otherwise we would have had to go through all our code. So the choice is up to you!

The application knows where to find *app/model/Cab.js* because `Cab` in the `models` array defaults to the `<NAMESPACE>.model.<MODELNAME>` (`FindACab.model.Cab`), which again maps to the folder structure.

Now that you have built the model, you can start creating the data store.

Implementing a Data Store

Unfortunately, there is no command in Sencha Cmd that can generate stores. You have to create a JavaScript file yourself in the *app/store/* directory:

```
Ext.define('NameSpace.store.MyStore', {
    extend: 'Ext.data.Store',
});
```

The next code snippet defines the `Cabs` data store for the FindACab app. In this case, you have to create a new JavaScript file in the *app/store/* folder that is called *Cabs.js*. Write the following in your new JavaScript file:

```
Ext.define('FindACab.store.Cabs', {
    extend: 'Ext.data.Store',
});
```

The Sencha convention for naming the store class is to take the model class name (usually a noun) and make it plural. This model is called `Cab`, so the name of your data store will be `Cabs`. Once you know the store name, you can easily define a class; the format is the namespace plus the package name `store` plus the store filename (`<NAME SPACE>.store.<STORENAME>`), so in this case it's `FindACab.store.Cab`. It makes this class behave like a store class because it extends all its properties from the `Ext.data.Store`.

A data store can be linked to a model. The FindACab app uses the `FindACab.mod el.Cab` model to define the data structure of `Cab` data. Let's edit the *app/store/Cabs.js* file:

```
Ext.define('FindACab.store.Cabs', {
    extend: 'Ext.data.Store',
    config: {
        model: 'FindACab.model.Cab',
        autoLoad: true
    }
});
```

The model is written within a `config` object, and therefore you can use getter and setter methods later on. `Store.getModel()` would retrieve an `Ext.data.Model` object (in this case, a `Cab` model). `Store.setModel()` could set the string name of a model.

There is another important config you will set: the `autoLoad`. This setting makes sure the store will load its data automatically after creation.

 For now, there is no data in the `Cabs` store. That's fine; you will create it in Chapter 8 after setting a proxy on the model.

After you create the data store, the store should be linked to the MVC architecture. For now, in the FindACab app, you will create a reference to the store in the *app.js* file. (Later, you will need to move these references to a corresponding controller.) To create a reference, go to `Ext.application()`, create an array called `stores`, and assign the `Cabs` store to it:

```
stores:[
    'Cabs'
],
```

The application knows where to find the *app/store/Cabs.js* file because `Cabs` in the `stores` array defaults to the `<NAMESPACE>.store.<STORENAME>` (`FindA Cab.store.Cabs`), which again maps to the folder structure. After everything is done, you can start coding a view.

Stores can be written without models. You can write the model in-line in the store by just defining a `fields` array.

Implementing a View

As is the case with models, you need to manually create view class definitions. You create them in the *app/view/* folder. I will not go into detail here about all the different views that are possible; you can read about this in Chapter 11.

Create in the *app/view/* folder a new JavaScript file and write the view component:

```
Ext.define('NameSpace.view.MyView', {
    extend: 'Ext.Container',
});
```

When you define a view, you just define a custom Sencha class definition (see Chapter 4) that extends from some view component that in turn extends from `Ext.Compo nent`, which again extends from `Ext.Base`.

Although it's very basic, the `Ext.Container` is a component and therefore it extends from the `Ext.Component` class. If you changed the `extend` to `Ext.Component` instead of `Ext.Container`, you might not see a difference while running it in the browser, but there is one. A container component can nest other components inside; it can even add or remove child components at runtime. Those child components (let's call them *items*) can be positioned next to each other, underneath each other, or on top of each other. You specify this positioning with the `layout` config. If you want more information about components and layouts, check out Chapters 4 and 5. For now, it's important that you know how to extend from a container, so you can nest multiple child items to your class definition. That's the trick for creating entire interfaces.

Using the FindACab app, you can create an empty container as a simple view. Create the *Main.js* view component in the *app/view* folder:

```
Ext.define('FindACab.view.Main', {
    extend: 'Ext.Container',
    config: {
        html: 'Here comes the view.'
    }
});
```

The code example shows a basic `Container` component, the `FindACab.view.Main` class, and an `xtype` that has been set to refer to this view component later. The `html` string is just for stubbing out the interface. I do this all the time when I create new views. Before specifying all its properties, I just set the `html` property so I end up with a whole click-through with just…yep, placeholders.

After the view is created, it should be linked to the `Ext.application()` `views` array. In `Ext.application()`, create an array called `views` and assign the `Main` view to it:

```
views:[
    'Main'
],
```

The application knows where to find the *app/view/Main.js* file because `Main` in the `views` array defaults to the `<NAMESPACE>.view.<VIEWNAME>` (`FindACab.view.Main`), which again maps to the folder structure. The next time your application loads the file, it knows where to look for this class.

After the model, store, and view, you can work on the controller. While the model is the data and the view is the way the data is presented, the controller is the way the data and the layout interact (see Figure 6-10). Let's create one next.

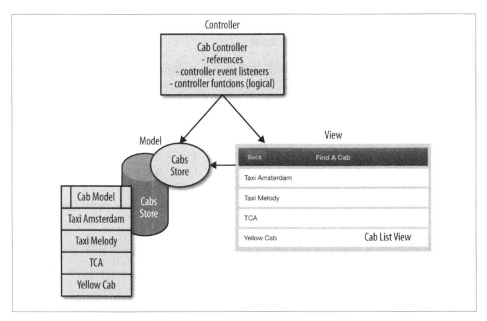

Figure 6-10. A general overview of MVC for the FindACab app

Generating a Controller with Sencha Cmd

To create the controller definition, you create a new JavaScript file and save it in the *app/controller* directory. But a better choice is to have Sencha Cmd generate it for you.

On the command line, navigate to the *app* folder and run the following command:

```
sencha generate controller <MyController>
```

In your console, navigate to the FindACab project folder and type the following command:

```
sencha generate controller CabController
```

which generates the code shown in Example 6-2 for the FindACab app.

Example 6-2. app/controller/CabController.js

```
Ext.define('FindACab.controller.CabController', {
    extend: 'Ext.app.Controller',

    config: {
        models: ['Cab'],
        stores: ['Cabs'],

        refs: {

        },
        control: {

        }
    },

    //called when the application is launched; remove if not needed
    launch: function(app) {

    }
});
```

Let's go quickly through this code. Sencha Cmd defines a class called `CabController`, which is subclassed from the Sencha Touch class `Ext.app.Controller`. It stubs out a `config` object, which includes the objects `refs` and `control`. Both objects are empty, but you can use the `refs` object later to enter references to view components, such as form elements or buttons. The `control` object dispatches events that belong to certain view components to custom methods.

Sencha Cmd already generated one (empty) function for you: the `launch()` method. This function does not need a `control`; it will automatically be run by the controller, immediately after the launch of the application (`Ext.application()`). This method is usually a good place to run any logic that has to run after the app UI is initialized.

It is also possible to create an `init` method in the controller. Like the `launch()` method, this function will also be automatically called by the controller. However, while the `launch()` method runs after the whole application is started, the `init()` method is called during the application initialization.

As with models, stores, and views, all controllers need to be linked to the application. You should create a reference to the controller in *app.js*. In `Ext.application()`, create a `controllers` array and assign the `CabController` controller to it:

```
controller:[
    'CabController'
],
```

The application knows where to find the *app/controller/CabController.js* file because `CabController` in the `controllers` array defaults to the `<NAMESPACE>.control` `ler.<CONTROLLERNAME>` (`FindACab.controller.CabController`), which again maps to the folder structure.

Let's look more into the controller methods that will run after being invoked by an user or data event, such as a button tap or data change. In this case, you will need two additional steps. The first step is to create a reference, and the second step is to dispatch events. The next sections will dive into that.

Referencing a Component from a Controller

When you want to create a reference from the Sencha MVC controller to a component, you can either use `refs` or you can use the component query, (see Chapter 3).

Controller `refs` are available only in (of course) the controller, as demonstrated in Example 6-3.

Example 6-3. Defining a Controller reference

```
refs: {
    myRef: 'somextype'
}
```

The component query can be used anywhere in your code:

```
Ext.ComponentQuery.query('somextype');
```

References leverage the component query syntax, and you can create as many as you want. You define a reference, and you pass in a (CSS-like) selector to locate a view component on your page. Every `ref` that is created will automatically generate a getter. In Example 6-3, then, `this.getMyRef()` would find the component that has the `xtype:` `"somextype"`.

Example 6-4 shows the `Cab` controller, which hooks up the `Cab` data model and the `Cabs` data store. We'll write down some log messages to see the order of execution.

Example 6-4. app/controller/CabController.js

```
Ext.define('FindACab.controller.CabController', {
    extend: 'Ext.app.Controller',
```

```
    config: {
        models: ['Cab'],
        stores: ['Cabs'],

        refs: {
            main: 'mainview'
        }
    },

    init: function(){
        console.log("On init app found "
            + Ext.ComponentQuery.query('mainview').length
            + " mainviews: ",
            Ext.ComponentQuery.query('mainview'));
        console.log("On init app found the reference: ",
            this.getMain());
    },

    launch: function(app) {
        console.log("On launch app found "
            + Ext.ComponentQuery.query('mainview').length
            + " mainviews: ",
            Ext.ComponentQuery.query('mainview'));
        console.log("On launch app found the reference: ",
            this.getMain());
    }
});
```

I have created one ref; it maps to the xtype name mainview, which is defined in the
FindACab.view.Main class. I can access this component with this.getMain() or with
Ext.ComponentQuery.query("mainview"). In the init() method of the controller, the
controller can't find the component. That makes sense, because the components are not
there yet and they need to be loaded; and they will, but after the controller is loaded.
On the launch() method of the controller, the components are present. When I use the
query() method, I will retrieve an array of mainview xtypes. (Yes, you can reuse your
component somewhere else in the app.) When I use the this.getMain() getter generated by the controller, it will return the first component found.

> A ref needs to be specific enough that it fetches only the compo-
> nents that you really want. But be careful! When it's too specific, if
> you ever decide to move a component, it's possible that the ref won't
> find anything.

Now that we've created component references in the controller, our next step is to bind
events to the components. Let's take a look.

Listening to Events from a Controller

When you want to control events in the Sencha MVC controller, add a `control` object to the controller's `config` object. This `control` object contains a reference to a component (in this example, `myref`) and adds an event listener with some event that dispatches to `myFunction`:

```
control: {
    'myref' : {
        <event>: 'myFunction',
    }
},
```

Once you have a reference to a component, you can bind an event to it. The trick is the `control` object, which listens to key/value pairs. For the key, you enter the reference name (the CSS-like selector, or it could also be the `xtype`); this key has another object as a value. This object accepts the name of the event as a key (for example, `tap` or `initialize`) and as a value, the string name of controller function that should be called after the event has happened.

See Example 6-5 for how this works in the FindACab app.

Example 6-5. app/controller/CabController.js

```
Ext.define('FindACab.controller.CabController', {
    extend: 'Ext.app.Controller',

    config: {
        models: ['Cab'],
        stores: ['Cabs'],

        refs: {
            main: 'mainview'
        },
        control: {
            'mainview': {
                initialize: 'onInitMain',
            },
            'button[action=press]': {
                tap: 'onTapMain'
            }
        }
    },

    onInitMain: function() {
        console.log("Initialize mainview");
    },
    onTapMain: function() {
        console.log("Tapped a button in mainview");
    }
});
```

In this example, the reference `main` will execute the controller method `onInitMain()` while initializing the view. The CSS-like selector `button[action=press]` invokes the controller method `onTapMain()`, which listens to all button `xtypes` that have the config `action: press` set.

When you're working with events, it is always handy to open the API docs (*http://bit.ly/ sencha-23*), which describe all the available events with signatures for every component.

Now you know how to create models, stores, views, and controllers, but how does this all work together? How are all the classes loaded? The good news is that Sencha maintains this all for you. Next, we'll check out how to implement the Sencha MVC entry point.

Implementing the MVC Entry Point

After you create models, stores, views, and controllers (and profiles), you have to hook them up to implement the Sencha MVC entry point for setting up the Sencha architecture.

In your *app.js* file, set up the `Ext.app.Application` to define your application:

```
Ext.application();
```

`Ext.app.Application()` is the entry point for every MVC app. It sets your namespace with the `name` property, and it could define the sets of models, stores, views, controllers, and profiles to automatically load all these dependencies.

The `Ext.Application()` does more nice things for you. Take a look at Example 6-6.

Example 6-6. app.js

```
/*
    This file is generated and updated by Sencha Cmd. You can edit this file as
    needed for your application, but these edits will have to be merged by
    Sencha Cmd when it performs code generation tasks such as generating new
    models, controllers, or views and when running "sencha app upgrade".

    Ideally, changes to this file would be limited and most work would be done
    in other places (such as Controllers). If Sencha Cmd cannot merge your
    changes and its generated code, it will produce a "merge conflict" that you
    will need to resolve manually.
*/

// DO NOT DELETE - this directive is required for Sencha Cmd packages to work.
//@require @packageOverrides

//<debug>
Ext.Loader.setPath({
    'Ext': '../../touch/src',
    'FindACab': 'app',
```

```
    'Utils': 'utils'
});
//</debug>

Ext.application({
    name: 'FindACab',

    requires: [
        'Ext.MessageBox',
        'Utils.Commons'
    ],

    views: ['Main'],

    controllers: [
        'CabController'
    ],

    icon: { //❶
        '57': 'resources/icons/Icon.png',
        '72': 'resources/icons/Icon~ipad.png',
        '114': 'resources/icons/Icon@2x.png',
        '144': 'resources/icons/Icon~ipad@2x.png'
    },

    isIconPrecomposed: true, //❷

    startupImage: { //❸
        '320x460': 'resources/startup/320x460.jpg',
        '640x920': 'resources/startup/640x920.png',
        '768x1004': 'resources/startup/768x1004.png',
        '748x1024': 'resources/startup/748x1024.png',
        '1536x2008': 'resources/startup/1536x2008.png',
        '1496x2048': 'resources/startup/1496x2048.png'
    },

    launch: function() { //❹
        // Destroy the #appLoadingIndicator element
        Ext.fly('appLoadingIndicator').destroy(); //❺

        // Initialize the main view
        Ext.Viewport.add(Ext.create('FindACab.view.Main')); //❻
    },

    onUpdated: function() { //❼
        Ext.Msg.confirm(
            "Application Update",
            "This application has just successfully been updated" +
                " to the latest version. Reload now?",
            function(buttonId) {
                if (buttonId === 'yes') {
                    window.location.reload(); //❽
```

```
            }
          }
        );
      }
});
```

❶   The `icon` object can set the icon that will be bookmarked on your phone's home screen for various sizes. By default, Sencha Cmd generates references to four different icons for mobile phones and tablets. You have to create the icons yourself, though.

❷   `isIconPrecomposed` is set to the boolean value `true`, for *not* having a glossy effect applied by the OS by default (which is currently only the case with iOS devices).

❸   The `startupImage` object does almost the same as the `icon` object: it saves references to the startup splash images. These images will be shown once the app is bookmarked and launched from the home screen (currently only on iOS devices).

❹   The `launch()` method is an optional function that overrides the `launch()` method on the controller. The app will call this function when all the dependencies are loaded. Usually this method is used to draw the screen. That is also what Sencha Cmd generated for you.

❺   Did you see the nice loading animation when you ran the FindACab app in your browser? The image and the styles are set in the inline stylesheet directly in the *index.html*; these are the first objects that are available in the DOM (therefore you also don't move it to a stylesheet, because then it needs to be downloaded). Once the Sencha dynamic loader has loaded all your dependencies, this `launch()` method will search for an HTML element with the `id` `#appLoadingIndicator` (which displays the loading animation) and destroy it.

❻   Then it will draw the `FindACab.view.Main` view class to the screen by adding it to the `Ext.Viewport`.

❼   The `onUpdated()` method is magic! Sencha Touch has a mechanism that can automatically check versions of your app and only download the updated code. (When building for production, it saves differences in the *deltas* folder.) Sencha Cmd generates the `onUpdated()` method for you; when the `onUpdated()` method is fired, it will show a confirmation messagebox.

❽   When you accept this box, it will refresh the page. The Sencha framework will do the rest and show you the updated version of the app.

It is also possible to specify application dependencies from outside your application. This can be handy when you share code between multiple applications. I will discuss this next.

When you use Sencha Cmd 3.1.1.x, this version of the tool will automatically add models, stores, controllers, and views to the `Ext.application()` for you. This is handy, but note that this happens every time you use Sencha Cmd for generating code. When you add this code manually, look out for merge errors in the *app.js* file. Such a merge error might look like:

```
<<<<<<< Generated
        'MyStore1',
        'MyStore2',
        'MyStore3'
= = = = = = =
        'MyStore1', 'MyStore2'
>>>>>>> Custom
```

As you can see, every magic trick comes with a price. In this case, it is easy to solve, though, by removing the <, =, > characters and the duplicated code.

Loading External Classes

Now that you know how to hook up models, stores, views, and controllers, you might want to hook up other classes that are not defined in the *app* MVC folders. This might not be so common if you decide to create all your business logic within a new directory within *app*. However, there might be occasions when you'd rather save your custom Sencha classes outside the *app* folder—for example, because you want to create two Sencha Touch applications in one workspace and you want to share code between both Sencha Touch apps.

This is how you can hook up Sencha classes that are not located in the *app* folder. In *app.js*, specify the paths to the classes in the `Ext.Loader`:

```
Ext.Loader.setPath({
    'Ext': '../touch/src',
    'FindACab': 'app'
    '<new namespace>': '<folder-to-point-to>'
});
```

The trick is to create a folder alongside your *app* folder and then configure the paths to the `Ext.Loader`. Let's do this for the FindACab app. We will create a new JavaScript folder and file, *utils/Commons.js*.

Let's add `"Utils":"utils"` to the `Ext.Loader` paths in the *app.js* file:

```
Ext.Loader.setPath({
    'Ext': '../touch/src',
    'FindACab': 'app'
    'Utils': 'utils'
});
```

This doesn't load anything in memory yet; it just tells the Sencha Touch loader where to find files that use the Utils namespace. You will use the Utils.Commons class in your app so the Sencha Touch loader needs to load the class in its memory. Therefore, you add Utils.Commons to the requires array in the *app.js*.

The Utils.Commons class is just a class with static members. I can access the defined properties from anywhere in my code. For example, in the FindACab app, I will need to have global access to the YELP_API URL. If I add it to the Utils.Commons class, I can access it from anywhere in my code by calling Utils.Common.YELP_API. The code for Utils.Commons will look like Example 6-7.

Example 6-7. utils/Commons.js

```
Ext.define('Utils.Commons', {
    statics: {
        YELP_API: 'http://api.yelp.com/business_review_search?',
        YELP_KEY: 'ftPpQUCgfSA3yV98-uJn9g',
        YELP_TERM: 'Taxi',
        LOCATION: 'Amsterdam NL',

        getUrl: function() {
            return this.YELP_API + "term=" + this.YELP_TERM +
                "&ywsid=" + this.YELP_KEY +
                "&location=" + this.LOCATION;
        }
    }
});
```

Using the Ext.Loader is really powerful. You no longer have to worry about loading scripts in the correct order. For example, in other frameworks, or in Sencha Touch version 1, you had to maintain this order yourself by including all the JavaScript in the <head> of your *index.html* file.

It's a really good thing that the Sencha Touch loader takes care of this. However, you do need to tell the Ext.Loader, "Hey loader, I require this class, so don't forget to load it." You can give this instruction by setting the requires array in a class (like how import works in Java). See the *app.js* file. It informs the loader to *require* Ext.MessageBox, which is used in the onUpdated() method.

When you're adding Sencha classes to your project and they are not saved within the *app* folder, you will also need to specify the paths to the classpath used for the build process; otherwise, your builds will fail.

There is an *app* and *workspace classpath*. The workspace classpath matters when you have multiple applications and you want to share code; in all other situations, the app classpath should be good enough.

In Chapter 14, you will add the *utils* folder to the app classpath in the hidden *.sencha/sencha.cfg* file so the FindACab app can be built:

```
app.classpath=${app.dir}/app.js,${app.dir}/app,${app.dir}/utils
```

You can forget to inform the `Ext.Loader` about your dependencies, or just ignore it. When you run your application in debug mode (you can enable it in the *app.json* file by loading the *sencha-touch-debug.js* framework with debug messages instead of *sencha-touch.js*), the console will throw some warnings and indicate which classes you need to require. When you ignore these warnings as well, strange things may happen. Sometimes parts of your app won't be visible, and you will certainly run into problems when building your app for production. So you'd better pay attention!

Summary

You should now be familiar with the MVC design pattern, and Sencha Touch's particular approach to MVC app development. With your new knowledge of Sencha MVC and Sencha Cmd concepts, you could also build Ext JS (rich desktop) applications. In that case, you need to generate an app from the Sencha Ext JS sdk.

We've completed the first step in the process of writing a Sencha Touch application—generating an application with Sencha Cmd. The next steps will be to start writing your custom classes, and at the end of the full process you will create a Sencha Touch build with Sencha Cmd.

If you've followed every step in this chapter, then you should have a fully set-up Sencha MVC pattern (Figure 6-11). It should have a model, a store, a controller, a view, and an *app.js* entry point. Of course, this app is only a skeleton. If you run the application now, you will see a blank page with the dummy text: `"Here comes the view."` The Chrome developer tools will show some log messages that describe the order of loading.

There is no interface yet and there is no data. I always prefer to start with writing the data first; after I have all the data in my application, I can think about how to display it in the view. So let's take this approach. In the next chapter, we will dive into data models to describe the data structure for the FindACab app.

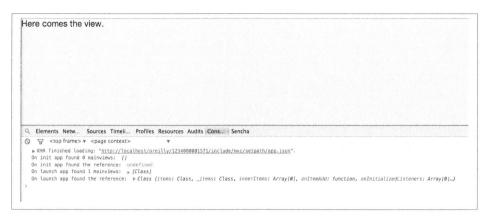

Figure 6-11. If you've followed every step in this chapter, you will see the skeleton of the FindACab app

## CHAPTER 7

Data Models

The model (`Ext.data.Model`) is a class that represents some object that your application manages. For example, you might define a model for users, products, cars, or any other real-world object that you want to model in the system.

The `Ext.data.Model` is part of the Sencha data package. As described in the preceding chapter, the Sencha architecture uses a pattern similar to MVC, but in the Sencha context the term *model* includes—besides the *model* itself (the structure of the data)—the layers *record* (the specific data) and *store* (a client-side cache of all records together). In this book, I will use the term *model* to refer to the `Ext.data.Model`.

A model contains fields to structure the data. For example, in the FindACab app, the `CabService` has three fields: `name`, `address`, and `total` number of cars. Each record (`Ext.data.Record`) is a specific `CabService` model object—for example, "Taxi Amsterdam," which has a total of 14 cars. The `Ext.data.Store` is the whole data pool full of records, otherwise known as the client-side cache.

The fields in a model use the `Ext.data.Field` class. Every field can be given a data type (see Table 7-1 for an overview of all data types). Data assigned to the field will be auto-converted to the default type. For example, when a field is set to `int` and the data `4.8` is passed, then the data will be converted to 5. When no datatype is specified, the datatype will be set to `auto`, which means there is no datatype conversion at all. This might be a solution for complex datatypes such as objects.

Table 7-1. Overview field datatypes

Type	Description	Example
auto	Complex data	`name: { first: "Lee", last: "Boonstra"}`
string	Text	`"Lee Boonstra"`
int	Numbers	`30`
float	Floating points	`30.2`
boolean	Boolean values	`true`
date	Date values; the data format can be specified	`16 June 2013`

Models may contain (optional) *validations* and *associations* (relations to other models). Both models and stores can have a *proxy* to send and retrieve data in JSON, XML, or JavaScript array notation.

Take a look at Figure 7-1. This is an example of how to retrieve data from some server-side service into a Sencha Touch data store. Later, the FindACab app will take a similar approach. It will retrieve data from the Yelp web service and save it into a store. To save (JSON) data in the store, it goes via a proxy first into a model and then into a store. Every data field will be parsed through a model field. When a model has validation rules you can manually validate the model before adding and syncing the data to the store.

In the case of the FindACab app, you will need a model for Cab objects. This object contains all taxi business instances retrieved from some external source (Yelp). The FindACab app needs another model to save and validate the user settings. For searching nearby taxis you will need at least a location (a city and a country) provided by the user. To implement this, you can set some validation rules on the Setting model of the FindACab app stipulating that every search for nearby cabs needs a location, so the city and country fields cannot be blank. Let's discuss this first: how to validate user input.

In this chapter, you'll learn:

- How to validate a model
- How to save a model to the server
- How to implement a model association

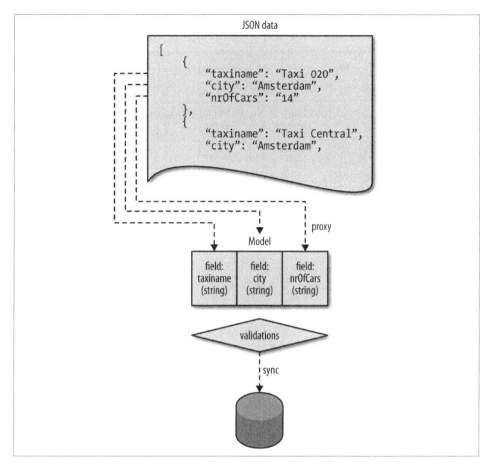

Figure 7-1. How to retrieve data from a web service into a model and store

Validating a Model

Before you want to save data to your store (e.g., user input), you might want to validate the data. For example, for the FindACab app, you will validate whether the user enters a city and a country when submitting a form.

In the model `config` object, you can set a `validations` array. This array contains validation objects:

```
validations: [
    {type: 'presence',  field: 'age'},
    {type: 'length',    field: 'name',     min: 2},
    {type: 'inclusion', field: 'gender',   list: ['Male', 'Female']},
    {type: 'exclusion', field: 'username', list: ['Admin', 'Operator']},
    {type: 'format',    field: 'username', matcher: /([a-z]+)[0-9]{2,3}/}
]
```

As you can see, there are different validation types. For example, you can validate fields on presence (if the data exists), on length (if a string has a min or max length of characters), inclusion (if the data string exists in a given list array), exclusion (if the data string does not exist in a given list array), and on format (if the data matches a regular expression, matcher).

Example 7-1 shows the validations in the Setting model for the FindACab app.

Example 7-1. model/Setting.js

```
Ext.define('FindACab.model.Setting', {
    extend: 'Ext.data.Model',
    requires: ['Ext.data.identifier.Uuid'],
    config: {
        idProperty: 'id',
        identifier: 'uuid',
        fields: [
            { name: 'id', type: 'auto' },
            { name: 'gps', type: 'boolean' },
            { name: 'city', type: 'string' },
            { name: 'country', type: 'string' }
        ],
        validations: [{
            type: 'presence',
            field: 'city',
            message: "Please provide a city."
        },
        {
            type: 'presence',
            field: 'country',
            message: "Please provide a country."
        }]
    }
});
```

Yes, I gave it the model name Setting (without the *s*) on purpose. It's a common naming convention to use singular names for models and plural names for stores. It's just a simple model scaffolded by Sencha Cmd with the following command:

```
sencha generate model Setting id,gps:boolean,city:string,country:string
```

This generates a Setting model with the following fields: id, gps (a boolean, to enable or disable geolocation), and the two fields, city and country, that accepts string values. I have created a validations array with two rules that check for presence. When a city or a country is not entered by the user, the model throws an error message, defined by the message setting.

Let's test this. Open the FindACab app in your modern browser. In your debug console, you can enter the code for creating a new model instance:

```
var setting = Ext.create('FindACab.model.Setting', { city: "Amsterdam"});
```

This creates a settings record, but it has a value only for `city`, not for `country`. Now you can validate your record with the following command in your console:

```
setting.validate();
```

Bam! After running the `validate()` method on the record, it will return an `Ext.da ta.Errors` object. Although the name is somewhat funny, it's actually a validation object. You can run the `isValid()` method on the `Ext.data.Errors` response object, to detect whether the record passed the validation.

When it returns `false`, it contains an `all` array with all the false fields. It collects the field name as an error message (see Figure 7-2). In the case of the FindACab app, the `country` field with the message: *Please provide a country*. Let's correct it; add the country code NL:

```
setting.set('country', 'NL');
```

Press Enter and run the `setting.validate()` again. You should notice that there are zero errors in the `all` error object. When you run `settings.get("country")`, you will see that the country is set to NL.

```
> setting.validate();
▼ Class {all: Array[1], items: Array[1], keys: Array[1], indices: Object, map: Object…}
    _autoFilter: true
    _autoSort: true
  ▼ all: Array[1]
    ▼ 0: Class
        _field: "country"
        _message: "Please provide a country."
      ▶ config: objectClass
      ▶ initConfig: function (){}
      ▶ initialConfig: Object
      ▶ __proto__: Object
        length: 1
    ▶ __proto__: Array[0]
  ▶ config: objectClass
  ▶ indices: Object
  ▶ initConfig: function (){}
  ▶ initialConfig: Object
  ▶ items: Array[1]
  ▶ keys: Array[1]
    length: 1
  ▶ map: Object
  ▶ __proto__: Object
>
```

Figure 7-2. A model validation error logged in the developer's console

After you have validated your model, you can send it to a server. The next examples will show you how to achieve this.

Saving a Model to the Server

You can save your data model server side by creating a reference to a model instance and running the save() method on it.

For this example, we can use the prototype I created in my GitHub account (*http://bit.ly/savingmodel*).

We will use a simple Car model that looks like this:

```
Ext.define('SaveTest.model.Car', {
    extend: 'Ext.data.Model',

    config: {
        fields: [
            { name: 'id', type: 'int'},
            { name: 'brand'},
        ]
    }
});
```

You will need a proxy object in the model. It should be set to type ajax or rest, and it should contain a server-side URL to post to. The following is an example of a rest proxy set on the model—the URL can be a nonexisting URL, because you will only be looking at the network traffic in the Network tab of your developer tools (such as the devtools of Google Chrome):

```
proxy: {
    type: 'rest',
    url : '/cars'
}
```

If you want to create readable rest URLs, you can edit the proxy as follows and use the api object. This allows you to differentiate data:

```
proxy: {
    type: 'rest',
    format: 'php', //❶
    api: { //❷
        create: 'cars/addcar', //❸
        update: 'cars/editcar', //❹
        read: 'cars/loadcar', //❺
        destroy: 'cars/deletecar' //❻
    }
}
```

❶   Optionally, set the format to a URL extension.

❷   Set the api object for readable URLs.

❸   The create URL (e.g., *addcar.php*).

❹ The update URL (e.g., *editcar.php*).

❺ The read URL (e.g., *loadcar.php*).

❻ The destroy URL (e.g., *deletecar.php*).

Now let's play around! First, let's create a car record. You can add this code to the *app.js* launch() method to prototype. Running this code in the Google Developers console would work too:

```
var car = Ext.create('SaveTest.model.Car', {
    brand: 'Mercedes'
});
```

Once you've created a record, you can save it to the server side with record.save():

```
car.save({
    success: function() {
        console.log('The car record is saved');
    },
    failure: function(){
        console.log('The car record could not be saved.');
    }
});
```

This returns a callback because there is no server side implemented; in our case, it's a failure callback. When you open the Network tab in your browser dev tools, you will see an HTTP POST call:

```
POST http://localhost/cars/addcar.php?_dc=1395177154251
404 (Not Found)
```

For the next step, let's edit the car record with an id equal to 1. You can change the brand from mercedes to BMW with the record.set() method and then again, save the record with record.save() again:

```
car = Ext.create('SaveTest.model.Car', {
    id: '1'
});
car.set('brand', 'BMW');
car.save({
    success: function() {
        console.log('The car record is edited');
    },
    failure: function(){
        console.log('The car record could not be edited.');
    }
});
```

Again, this returns a callback because there is no server side implemented; in our case, it's a failure callback. When you open the Network tab in your browser dev tools, you will see an HTTP PUT call:

```
PUT http://localhost/cars/editcar.php?_dc=1395177154251
404 (Not Found)
```

In addition to saving data to the server, you can also remove data from the server. `record.erase()` will result in a `DELETE` call to the server. You can try this with the following code:

```
car.erase({
    success: function() {
        console.log('The car record is removed');
    },
    failure: function(){
        console.log('The car record could not be removed.');
    }
});
```

When you open the Network tab in your browser dev tools, you will see an HTTP `DELETE` call:

```
DELETE http://localhost/cars/deletecar.php?_dc=1395177154251
404 (Not Found)
```

Last but not least, in order to load data from the server side via the model, you can use `record.load(id, callback)`. When there is no store available, the trick is to first request the model via the `ModelManager`:

```
Ext.ModelManager.getModel('SaveTest.model.Car').load(1, {
    success: function(car) {
        console.log("Load Car: " + car.getId());
    },
    failure: function(){
        console.log("The car could not be loaded");
    }
});
```

When you open the Network tab in your browser dev tools, you will see an HTTP `GET` call:

```
GET http://localhost/cars/loadcar.php?_dc=1395177154251
404 (Not Found)
```

 When you set the `proxy` type to `ajax` instead of `rest`, you can still use readable URLs. The only difference is the HTTP method. Adding, editing, and removing records will be an HTTP `POST` call. Loading records will be an HTTP `GET` call.

Cross-Domain Restrictions

The `record.save()` method (as well as the `Ext.Ajax` and `form.submit()` methods) transmit through the `XMLHttpRequest()` object, and therefore you might face security restrictions when posting to a different domain. These are known as *cross-domain restrictions*.

However, there is a way to save and post data to another server. It requires setting up special HTTP headers (Access-Control-Allow headers) on the web server. This technique is called CORS (cross-origin resource sharing), and it enables you to override the default restrictions that prevent a web server from making AJAX request to other domains. For more information, see Chapter 8 and the AJAX sections of this book, or check out the HTML5 Rocks website (*http://bit.ly/usingCORS*).

Models can also have relationships with other models. For example, a User model can have a relationship with multiple Order models, and one Order model can have just one relationship with one payment method. Sound confusing? The next examples will show you how model associations work.

Implementing a Model Association

Models can have relationships with one or more other models. The following model associations can request data through each other:

- Ext.data.association.HasOne
- Ext.data.association.HasMany
- Ext.data.association.BelongsTo

You can create two or more models and connect these to each other with the hasMany, hasOne, and belongsTo configs:

```
Ext.define('TaxiService', {
    extend: 'Ext.data.Model',

    config: {
        fields: ['id', 'name'],
        hasMany  : {
            model: 'Car', name: 'cars'
        }
    }
});

Ext.define('Car', {
    extend: 'Ext.data.Model',

    config: {
        fields: ['id', 'brand']
    }
});
```

When you want to use associations, you have to add these to the `requires` array at the top of your model class:

```
requires: [
    'Ext.data.association.HasOne',
    'Ext.data.association.BelongsTo',
    'Ext.data.association.HasMany'
]
```

Let's check out how this works. See Examples 7-2 and 7-3, and Figure 7-3, the UML representation of these examples.

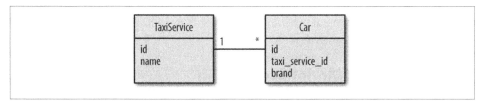

Figure 7-3. A TaxiService can have multiple Cars

When you want to display the different brands of `Cars` per `TaxiService`, you could express the relationships between both models. One `TaxiService` may contain many different types of `Car` records. You can define this relationship by specifying the `hasMany` property into the `TaxiService` model, so later you can request `Car` information via the `TaxiService` model.

You will need a `foreignKey` on the owner model that links to the associated model. By default, it takes the lowercase name of the owner model plus `_id`. For example, the `TaxiService` model would create `taxiservice_id` as the foreign key.

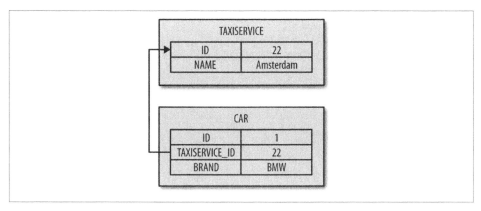

Figure 7-4. How the taxiservice_id field maps to the id field with a foreignKey

Example 7-2 shows how the `hasMany` association looks in the first model, *TaxiService.js*.

Example 7-2. model/TaxiService.js

```
Ext.define('AssociationsTest.model.TaxiService', {
    extend: 'Ext.data.Model',

    requires: ['Ext.data.association.HasMany'],

    config: {
        fields: ['id', 'name'],
        hasMany  : { //❶
                model: 'AssociationsTest.model.Car', //❷
                name: 'cars', //❸
                foreignKey: 'taxiservice_id' //❹
        }
    }
});
```

❶　Create the `hasMany` relationship.

❷　One `TaxiService` model has many `Car` models, so hook up the `Car` model.

❸　Set a name, which will be used to create a virtual store.

❹　Assign a `foreignKey` that links the associated model to the owner model.

As with every relationship, their connection can be confirmed; the `Car` model answers its relationship by confirming it `belongsTo` the `TaxiService` model. This `belongsTo` association allows me to request the `TaxiService` information via the `Car` model.

Example 7-3 shows how the `belongsTo` association looks in the second model, *Car.js*.

Example 7-3. model/Car.js

```
Ext.define('AssociationsTest.model.Car', {
    extend: 'Ext.data.Model',
    requires: ['Ext.data.association.BelongsTo'],
    config: {
        fields: [{
            name: 'id', //❶
            type: 'int'
        }, {
            name: 'brand'
        }, {
            name: 'taxiservice_id',
            type: 'int' //❷
        }],
        belongsTo: {
            model: 'AssociationsTest.model.TaxiService'
        },
        proxy: {
            type: 'ajax',
```

```
        reader: {
            rootProperty: 'cars'
        },
        url: 'app/data.php'
    }
}
});
```

❶ The id of the Car record.

❷ The id of the TaxiService record.

And now comes the fancy stuff: requesting all the records that have a relationship through the parent model. As covered in Chapter 6, many records are saved in a store —the set of all records together. When specifying the hasMany association, you will point to the relating hasMany model and set a name (cars). The association will dynamically create a virtual store and the name that is set in the association will become the store name. You can call this store by running the cars() method on the TaxiService model. Remember, creating a store will not autoload the data, so you will need to load() the virtual store manually.

Let's take a look at the next code snippets. First, create two TaxiService records, each of which will contain Car records. A TaxiService model has a hasMany relationship with the Car model:

```
var taxiAmsterdam = Ext.create('AssociationsTest.model.TaxiService', {
    id: 1,
    name: 'Taxi Amsterdam'
});

var yellowCab = Ext.create('AssociationsTest.model.TaxiService', {
    id: 2,
    name: 'Yellow Cab'
});
```

The Car records know that they belong to the TaxiService parent model (see previous code) because of the belongsTo relation (in Example 7-3). It has a property, model, that points (belongs) to the TaxiService model. The TaxiService model has a hasMany relationship to the Car model and it has a property: foreignKey (again, see Example 7-2).

Now let's create some Car records:

```
var bmw = Ext.create('AssociationsTest.model.Car', {
    id: 1,
    brand: 'BMW'
});

var mercedes = Ext.create('AssociationsTest.model.Car', {
    id: 2,
```

```
    brand: 'Mercedes'
});

var vw = Ext.create('AssociationsTest.model.Car', {
    id: 3,
    brand: 'Volkswagen'
});
```

To get access to all the Car records from the TaxiService record, you can call the cars()
method to create a virtual store:

```
var taxiAmsterdamStore = taxiAmsterdam.cars();
var yellowCabStore = yellowCab.cars();
```

The add() and sync() lines in the next piece of code just add the particular Car records
to each TaxiService store. You will read more about stores in the next two chapters:

```
//add new cars to the Store
taxiAmsterdamStore.add(mercedes);
taxiAmsterdamStore.add(vw);
taxiAmsterdamStore.sync();
yellowCabStore.add(bmw);
yellowCabStore.sync();
```

After the sync, check both stores to see the data they contain (and to test the hasMany
relation):

```
console.log("TaxiAmsterdam has the following Cars:",
    taxiAmsterdamStore.getData());
console.log("YellowCab has the following Cars:",
    yellowCabStore.getData());
```

To request the TaxiService data from a Car record (and to test the belongsTo relation),
you can use the autogenerated getter getTaxiService(). Now, let's request the Taxi
Service data for the first record in the taxiAmsterdamStore:

```
console.log(taxiAmsterdam.cars().first().getTaxiService());
```

Remote Associations

You can also request Car records from the server side. To do so, you would need to add
a remote proxy to the Car model:

```
proxy: {
    type: 'ajax',
    reader: {
        rootProperty: 'cars'
    },
    url: 'app/data.php'
}
```

After you add the records and sync the `taxiAmsterdamStore` and `yellowCabStore`, this proxy will POST the messages shown in Examples 7-4 and 7-5 to *app/data.json*.

Example 7-4. taxiAmsterdam

```
{cars: [{id:1, brand:BMW, taxiservice_id:1}, {id:2, brand:BMW, taxiservice_id:1}]}
```

Example 7-5. yellowCab

```
{cars: [{id:1, brand:BMW, taxiservice_id:2}]}
```

On your server side, you could code a script that takes these objects and adds them to a database.

When you want to load data from the remote, you can run the following command:

```
taxiAmsterdamStore.load(function(records){
    console.log(records);
});
```

Here, you are loading data into the `taxiAmsterdamStore`, which has a model with associations hooked up. Therefore, it will fire a GET request, with the following parameters:

```
filter:[{"property":"taxiservice_id","value":1}]
```

 When the remote store is loaded, the store is automatically filtered so that only records with a matching foreign key are included in the resulting child store. You can override this by specifying the `filter` Property.

On your server side, you could code a script that filters for the `taxiservice_id` with the value set to 1. The data returned for this request from the server might look like the following example, which is written in PHP:

```php
<?php
//Return response as JavaScript
header('Content-Type: application/javascript');
echo '{
    "cars" : [
        {
            "id" : 1,
            "brand" : "BMW",
            "taxiservice_id" : 1
        },
        {
            "id" : 2,
            "brand" : "Mercedes",
            "taxiservice_id" : 1
        }
    ]
```

```
}';
?>
```

The FindACab app will not display the different brands of cars, which is why you won't implement any model associations. That is because you will use the Yelp API to provide data about taxi businesses. It will not supply information about car brands like the previous examples did.

 If you want to read more about associations, check out Rob Boerman's great tutorial (*http://bit.ly/boerman*) and MiamiCoder's tutorial (*http://bit.ly/miamicoder*) with PHP server-side code.

Summary

The Sencha data package contains the three key classes `Ext.data.Model`, `Ext.data.Record`, and `Ext.data.Store`. The model is the structure of the data; it needs data fields and they can be set to certain types. Optionally, you can set validations and associations (relationships with other models).

In this chapter, you have seen examples of how you can implement validations and associations into a model. Also, even though we didn't implement real server-side code, I've discussed how you can set up your models to save data to a server. When you follow the FindACab app examples in this chapter, you will have `validations` implemented in your model. You will need this when coding the form view and logic later in this book.

Models are registered via the `Ext.data.ModelManager`, and are used by stores, which are in turn used by many of the data-bound components in Sencha. Before we can discuss stores, however, you need to have data in your FindACab app. The FindACab app will retrieve taxi data from the Yelp.com web service. Data from an (external) web service loads via a so-called server proxy. So let's get our hands dirty!

## CHAPTER 8

Remote Connections (Server Proxies)

Models and stores can load and save data via a so-called *proxy*. Sencha Touch has two main types of proxies: client proxies and server proxies. Client proxies save and load their data locally. Server proxies interact with a remote server. You can read more about client proxies and saving data offline (with techniques such as Local Storage, Session Storage, Web SQL, and AppCache) in Chapter 10. In this chapter, I will talk about the different kinds of server proxies.

A server proxy communicates by sending requests to some remote server. There are four types of server proxies you can use out of the box:

Ext.data.proxy.Ajax

> Sends a request to the server on the same domain by using—you guessed it—AJAX.

Ext.data.proxy.JsonP

> Sends a request to a server on a different domain by using JSON with padding (JSONP).

Ext.data.proxy.Rest

> A kind of AJAX proxy that automatically maps to four readable actions, the RESTful HTTP verbs: create, read, update, and destroy.

Ext.data.proxy.Direct

> Uses the Ext.Direct technology (originally created for Ext JS) to remote server-side methods to the client side. Ext.Direct allows communication between the client side of a Sencha app and all popular server platforms.

Let's implement the two most used server proxies for receiving data: the AJAX proxy and the JSONP proxy. We'll also discuss how to communicate with a server without using a proxy, by making AJAX and JSONP requests.

For the FindACab app, you will implement a JSONP proxy to retrieve TaxiServices data for a certain location from an external web server (Yelp.com).

In this chapter, you'll learn about:

- Saving or retrieving data from the same domain with AJAX
  - How to implement AJAX proxies
  - How to implement an AJAX request
- Retrieving data from an external domain with JSONP
  - How to implement JSONP proxies
  - How to implement a JSONP request
- Saving or retrieving data from an external domain with AJAX
  - How to implement CORS

Saving or Retrieving Data from the Same Domain with AJAX

AJAX stands for Asynchronous JavaScript and XML. It is a common client-side remote scripting technique that operates through the browsers XMLHttpRequest (XHR) object. Despite the name, the use of XML is not required (it's more common to use JSON), and the requests do not need to be asynchronous per se—although the exchange of data asynchronously, between browser and server, avoids page refreshes. With AJAX, the data to be retrieved, or the script to post to, generally is on the same domain as where the (mobile) web application is running from.

Implementing AJAX Proxies

When you want to save or retrieve data in a store from the same domain as the app, you can connect to your server via the proxy in your data store or model.

At the top of your model or store class, you will require Ext.data.proxy.Ajax, so the Ext.Loader knows to load the AJAX proxy framework class first. Next, you will create a proxy object:

```
config: {
  //model or store configs here

  proxy: {
      type: 'ajax',
      url: 'data/data.json'
  }
}
```

The proxy object can be set into the config object from a store or a model. It contains a type that can be set to either a server-side proxy for requesting data from some source or a client-side proxy for storing data locally on your device. Beyond the `type` config, you will also have to set the `url` config. See Example 8-1.

Connect the Proxy to a Model or a Store?

In my Sencha Touch classrooms, I get this question regularly: which way is better—connect the proxy to a model or to a store? It depends. Originally, Sencha Touch first checks the store to try to find a proxy; if it doesn't find one there, then it will check the model. There are some cases where you want to implement the proxy on the model and others where you want to implement it on the store.

Picture this: you have two data stores, both representing the same data structure and sharing the same model. If the data comes from one place, you don't want to implement the proxy on both stores. That's double code and might also result in double requests. Implementing the proxy on the model would be a good solution. It could also be the other way around. Say you have two data stores that share the same data model and it can be retrieved via multiple URLs. In that case, you might want to add the proxy to the store.

Apart from that, you can create models without stores (e.g., the data pool is on the server, like an online database) or stores without models (by using the `fields` object instead of hooking up a `model`, which is technically an inline model). When you want to save a record with your server side—for example, to save your record in an online database—you need to provide the proxy on a model. In this chapter, we will talk about `re cord.save()`.

The URL can point to a web service URL, or it can just point to some file locally. In Example 8-1, an AJAX proxy was used to load the local file, */data/data.json*, which is in the same web folder as the *app* folder.

You can set a proxy object and it will load the data. To let the proxy understand (*read*) the data, you can set a `reader` object (`Ext.data.reader.Reader`).

Here's an example of a proxy with an `Ext.data.reader.Reader`:

```
proxy: {
    type: 'ajax',
    url: 'data/data.json',
    reader: {
        type: 'json',
        rootProperty: 'results'
    }
}
```

Note the steps to set up the reader object:

1. First, set up a type. There are two types of data responses that the reader can interpret: json and xml.
2. Define the rootProperty. It points to the root node of your data, from where it has to start reading the data.

There are more configs you can set in Ext.data.reader.Reader. The ones I use regularly are:

successProperty
> Should point to the response property with a *success attribute* (by default, it points to the property name success).

messageProperty
> Should point to the response property with a *response message* (this property is optional).

totalProperty
> Should point to the response property with a *total number of records* in the dataset. This is required only while paging, when the whole dataset is not passed in one go, but is being paged from the remote server (by default, it points to the property name total).

Let's take a look at the FindACab app in Example 8-1. Here I retrieve data from the same domain into the store by setting an AJAX proxy into the data store.

Example 8-1. Store with an AJAX proxy

```
Ext.define('FindACab.store.Cabs', {
    extend: 'Ext.data.Store',
    requires: ['Ext.data.proxy.Ajax'],
    config: {
        model: 'FindACab.model.Cab',
        autoLoad: true,
        proxy: {
                type: "ajax",
                url : "data/data.json",
                reader: {
                    type: "json",
                    rootProperty: "businesses"
                }
            },
    }
});
```

Do you need to make a simple mobile app for a customer that the customer can maintain but you don't want to set up a whole server-side architecture? Working with JSON files is the trick! "That's true, but my customer does not understand how to work with JSON files..." Why don't you set up a nice Microsoft Excel worksheet? Luckily, there are great tools online that can convert your Excel sheet (*.csv data) to a JSON object, such as Mr. Data Converter (*http://shancarter.com/data_converter/*).

As you can see in this example, I've declared a `requires` array that imports the `Ext.da ta.proxy.Ajax` class into the memory. The magic is in the `proxy` object. Notice the `type` that is set to `ajax`. The `URL` points to *data/data.json*; this file is in the root of your application folder and could look like:

```
{
    "message": {
        "text": "OK",
        "code": 0,
        "version": "1.1.1"
    },
    "businesses": [
        {
            "rating_img_url": "stars/v1/stars_5.png",
            "country_code": "NL",
            "city": "Amsterdam",
            "mobile_url": "http://m.yelp.nl/biz/taxi-klaas-amsterdam",
            "review_count": 2,
            "zip": "",
            "state": "Noord-Holland",
            "latitude": 52.3738007,
            "rating_img_url_small": "stars/v1/stars_small_5.png",
            "url": "http://www.yelp.nl/biz/taxi-klaas-amsterdam",
            "country": "Netherlands",
            "avg_rating": 5,
            "longitude": 4.8909347,
            "nearby_url": "http://www.yelp.nl/search",
        },
        {
            "rating_img_url": "stars/v1/stars_5.png",
            "country_code": "NL",
            "city": "Amsterdam",
            "mobile_url": "http://m.yelp.nl/biz/taxi-klaas-amsterdam",
            "review_count": 2,
            "zip": "",
            "state": "Noord-Holland",
            "latitude": 52.3738007,
            "rating_img_url_small": "stars/v1/stars_small_5.png",
            "url": "http://www.yelp.nl/biz/taxi-klaas-amsterdam",
            "country": "Netherlands",
```

```
        "avg_rating": 5,
        "longitude": 4.8909347,
        "nearby_url": "http://www.yelp.nl/search",
      }
    ]
}
```

 A great way to format your JSON response nicely is by using the jsonlint.com tool. Not only does it format your JSON, but it will also validate the JSON. If the JSON is invalid, the reader in your proxy can't interpret the JSON response. It's worth a shot to use this tool when you have strange proxy bugs.

The last step is to define the reader in the store proxy. The node that contains all the (child) items (the root property) is businesses, so it should be set in the reader object as a rootProperty. The type of the reader is json, which is actually also the default type for a reader, so you don't have to set it.

Sometimes when you want to retrieve data from an external server, the response data is just not what you expected. For example, you want to reorder, cache, or rename properties, or you just want to add more data or maybe you don't have control over the remote server to provide JSONP. In these cases, an AJAX proxy can be really handy. You can create an own "proxy" on the server side that connects to the external server and fetches the data. When it is retrieved on the server side, you modify the response. This custom proxy script is running on the same server as your app does, so you can hook it up with a Sencha Touch AJAX proxy back to the Sencha Touch data store. In PHP, such a scenario might look like this:

```php
<?php
  function URL_get_contents($URL) {
      if (!function_exists('cURL_init')){
          die('CURL is not installed!');
      }
      $ch = cURL_init();
      cURL_setopt($ch, CURLOPT_URL, $URL);
      cURL_setopt($ch, CURLOPT_RETURNTRANSFER, true);
      $output = cURL_exec($ch);
      $httpCode = cURL_getinfo($ch, CURLINFO_HTTP_CODE);
      //get the code of request
      cURL_close($ch);

      if($httpCode == 400) return 'Bummer';

      if($httpCode == 200) {
        $data = json_decode($output);

        // do some fancy stuff here
```

```
            $data = json_encode($data);

            header('Content-Type: application/json');
            echo $data;
        }
    }
?>
```

Retrieving data through AJAX proxies can be handy. The data is directly in your store, which is great for the data-bind components that connect to a store, such as the `Ext.List`. Sometimes you don't need to retrieve data through a proxy. Maybe you don't want to display the data results into a data-aware component, or you just don't need a model or a store. Other times, the proxy is already in use by a client proxy (you can set just one proxy per model or store). Although in such a scenario you could also switch proxies with `setProxy` on the model or store, you can also choose to make plain AJAX requests. I will discuss this option next.

Implementing an AJAX Request

In the previous section, we retrieved data in a store via an AJAX proxy. Sometimes you don't need to save or retrieve data in a store, maybe because you are not displaying the data in a data-aware component, such a as an XTemplate. In that case, a simple `Ext.Ajax` request, with parameters to pass in, might be an easier solution for saving and retrieving data on the same domain than hooking up an AJAX proxy to a store.

At the top of your class you will require `Ext.Ajax`, so the `Ext.Loader` knows to load the AJAX framework class first. Next you will create the request:

```
Ext.Ajax.request({
    URL: 'somescript.php',
    params: {
        location: 'Amsterdam NL'
    },
    success: function(response){
        try {
            var text = response.responseText;
            var results = Ext.JSON.decode(text);

            //process server response here
        } catch (e) {
            //you can never assume that data is the way you want.
            console.error(e);
        }
    },
    failure: function(response){
      //fail scenario
    }
});
```

Ext.Ajax is a singleton instance of an Ext.data.Connection, which is the class that is used to communicate with server-side code. Assuming that your app is on *http://domain-x.com*, the previous code sends a GET request to *http://domain-x/script.php*. Because AJAX calls are asynchronous, a callback function is called with the response argument as soon as the response comes back in a callback, success, or failure function.

It's possible to change the method in an Ext.Ajax request. You can set it to GET, POST, PUT, or DELETE. By default, the GET method is used for sending headers, though the previous code has the POST method as well. Why is that? Well, the method will change to POST as soon as you send parameters with the request. See the configuration object we pass into Ext.Ajax.request() in Example 8-2.

Example 8-2. Ajax request

```
Ext.Ajax.request({
    URL: 'somescript.php',
    method: 'POST'
});
```

When you want to send parameters as a GET request instead, you should specify the method again (to method: 'GET', in which case your params are automatically escaped and appended to the URL *http://domain-x.com/script.php?dc=1421443375411&location=Amsterdam%20NL*. Note that the dc parameter you see in the request URL is a *disable caching* timestamp to make sure none of the data sent back from the server is cached.

There are more handy configs you can set on the Ext.Ajax method—for example, the timeout config. By default, the timeout threshold is half a minute (30,000 ms). In Example 8-3, the timeout is set to a minute.

Example 8-3. Setting the Ajax headers

```
Ext.Ajax.request({
    URL: 'somescript.php',
    timeout: 60000,
    headers: {
        "Content-Type": "application/json"
    }
});
```

Another config for customizing the request is headers config, which enables you to send a custom header to your server—for example, the Content-Type entity header: "Content-Type": "application/json". This field indicates the media type of the entity body sent to the recipient, which is handy when the web server returns different content based on these headers. For example, if your web server returns JSON or XML based on the header that is passed, you can request JSON like in Example 8-3.

You can inspect requests in the Chrome Developer Tools. You can see that the Content-Type header has been set to *application/json* or *text/html*. See Figure 8-1.

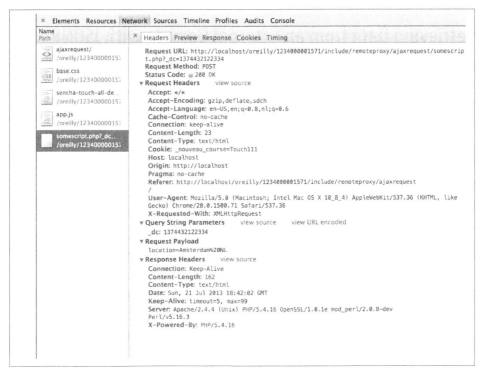

Figure 8-1. Check the Network → Headers tab in the Chrome Developer Tools to inspect the headers

XHR2, New in Sencha Touch 2.3

A new config setting, released in Sencha Touch 2.3, is to set up your AJAX request through the XHR2 (AJAX2) object. You will just need to enable the boolean property xhr2:true in the request object. XMLHttpRequest Level 2 is like XHR but with a huge makeover that allows you to do things like uploading progress events (Sencha Touch 2.3 also has a new progressbar component, Ext.ProgressIndicator!) and support for uploading/downloading binary data.

Check out "New Tricks in XMLHttpRequest2" (*http://bit.ly/xmlhttprequest2*) and "XHR2 Uploads and Downloads" (*http://bit.ly/xhr2-guide*) to get more information about XHR2.

Sometimes you don't have access to the source—for example, because the script is hosted on an external website. In the case of the FindACab app, we want it to receive data from Yelp.com. The next part discusses the tricks to retrieve data from an external domain.

Retrieving Data from an External Domain with JSONP

While AJAX in general cannot send and retrieve data from an external domain because of the cross-domain policy, JSONP *can* send and retrieve data from an external domain. It only uses HTTP GET and therefore *cannot use HTTP POST to post (large) data* to an external domain. In other words, you can send data, but it's sent in the query string rather than the request body. This limits the amount of data that can be stuffed into the request line (URL), and the limit is browser specific. It's safest to use less than 2KB of parameters, although some servers can handle up to 64KB. Also, sending data through GET is less secure than over POST because the data that will be sent is part of the URL. So it's visible in the browser history or in server logfiles.

As mentioned earlier, JSONP stands for "JSON with Padding." It allows cross-domain requests. Let's take a look at Figure 8-2 so we can compare both techniques. In general, AJAX asks (or sends) data from a service or script that is on the same domain as where your app is running from. It is impossible to request or send data to external domains because of the *same-origin policy*; the browser ignores any connection, assuming nobody else is allowed. JSONP works differently; it's a little like a magic trick—one that is well known.

Under the hood, it works as follows (again, see Figure 8-2):

1. In the background, JSONP (proxy) injects a script tag into the DOM, when a request is made. The src attribute of the <script> tag points to the URL of the server you want to retrieve data from, with a callback function as a GET parameter. For example: <script src="http://domain-x.com/script.php?callback=some Callback"></script>.

2. When the server supports JSONP, it responds with the JSON object, wrapped in the name of the callback function with brackets—for example, someCallback(). The JSON data that's requested is passed as an argument.

3. The browser thinks it's just loading an external JavaScript file. But as soon as the file is loaded, it sees the brackets and thinks it's a function, so let's execute it!

4. When you have this callback function with the same name in your code base, the browser will run it and pass in the JSON data as function parameter. That's how you will receive the data.

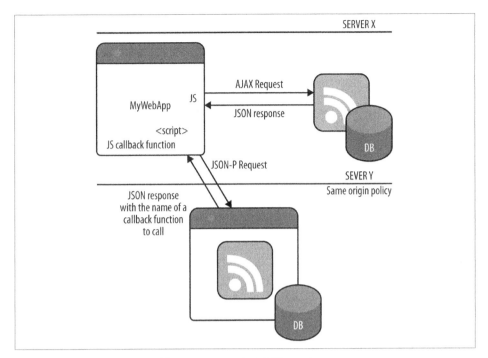

Figure 8-2. A comparison of how AJAX and JSONP work

Implementing JSONP Proxies

It looks like a major challenge to retrieve data in the store from an external domain. But you don't need to worry about it: Sencha Touch arranges this all on your behalf. For you, it's just another proxy to configure. Still, it's handy to understand what is going on. Because of this trick, the JSONP proxy works only when the server supports JSONP or when you have control over the server. Also, this trick can only send and retrieve data via GET requests.

The setup of a JSONP proxy is almost the same as setting up an AJAX proxy. The only difference is the type property, which should be set to jsonp. Flip back to the AJAX proxy examples if you are not familiar with proxies in general.

At the top of your model or store class you will require Ext.data.proxy.JsonP, so the Ext.Loader knows to load the JSONP proxy framework class first. Next you will create a proxy object:

```
proxy: {
    type: 'jsonp',
    URL : 'http://externaldomain.com/users',
    reader: {
        type: 'json',
        rootProperty: 'results'
    }
}
```

Implementing the JSONP Proxy for the FindACab App

For the FindACab app, I have created a JSONP proxy on the Cabs store, shown in
Example 8-5. All the different taxi services are retrieved via Yelp (*http://
www.yelp.com/*), an American company that offers a directory service for ratings and
reviews.

To retrieve data from Yelp, you have to create a request to the *business_review_search*
API and therefore it needs three parameters: ywid, the developers' API key; term, which
will be the search term to query for (in this case, "Taxi"); and a location, which we'll
set to "Amsterdam NL."

To obtain the Yelp API key, register for a free developer's account (*http://www.yelp.com/
developers*). Once you get the key, you can enter the URL in your browser; a correct
request should return a JSON response with all the businesses in the businesses root
property. If not, then you might have an error in your request. Are all the three parameters correct? Test it with the following URL in your browser: *http://api.yelp.com/busi-
ness_review_search?ywsid=yelp-key-here&term=Taxi&location=Amsterdam%20NL*.

If the API call is successful, you should see the following:

```
{
  "message": {
      "text": "OK",
      "code": 0,
      "version": "1.1.1"
  },
  "businesses": [
  ..
  ]
}
```

Awesome, right? This is a great way to test if a web service or API call works. I do this
all the time. Before I start diving into my own code, I like to know if the request just
sends me a nice response back.

Did you notice that the fields of the business object in the previous JSON response
have the same names as the fields from the Sencha FindACab.model.Cab model? These
fields *map* to the model fields, so you can later use them in your code. What if the JSON
response has a slightly different name than the name that is defined in the model? You

can either change the model field name, or you can add a `mapping` property to the model field.

For example, when you have a complex data feed that looks like this (note the `car:brand:` notation):

```
{
results: [
  car:brand: [{
    name: "BMW",
    series: 7
  },{
    name: "BMW",
    series: 5
  }]
  ...
}
```

You can add a `mapping` attribute to the field. In this case, `brand` maps to `["car:brand"][0].name`:

```
Ext.define("MyApp.model.Car", {
    extend: "Ext.data.Model",
    config: {
      fields: [
        {
          name: "brand"
          mapping: "['car:brand'][0].name"
        }
    ]}
});
```

Now that we know that the request to the external content is valid, let's implement the proxy for the FindACab app to retrieve our data from Yelp. The Yelp information will be written in a new JavaScript class: `utils/Commons.js` (see Example 8-4). This class has a `statics` object with key/value pairs for the URL, search term, search location, and the API key. We can get access to these key/value pairs from everywhere in the application. (See Chapter 4.)

Example 8-4. utils/Commons.js

```
Ext.define('Utils.Commons', {
    statics: {
        YELP_API: 'http://api.yelp.com/business_review_search?',
        YELP_KEY: '<API-KEY-HERE>',
        YELP_TERM: 'Taxi',
        LOCATION: 'Amsterdam NL'
    }
});
```

Now let's implement a `jsonp` proxy in the Cabs store. The values for the `url` and the URL parameters `extraParams` : (`term`, `ywsid`, and `location`) come from the static `Utils.Commons` class:

```
proxy: {
    type: 'jsonp',
    url: Utils.Commons.YELP_API,
    extraParams: {
        term: Utils.Commons.YELP_TERM,
        ywsid: Utils.Commons.YELP_KEY,
        location: Utils.Commons.LOCATION
    },
    noCache: false,
}
```

I have set the property `noCache` to `false`, which means it will cache all the responses. I did this because I don't expect the data to change. By default, `noCache` is set to `true`, which will add a `dc` (disable caching) parameter into the request that contains a timestamp. You don't have to set this property if you don't want to cache responses. When you want to require "fresh data" to be pulled from the server, you shouldn't change the default setting (`true`).

The next step is to implement a `json reader`, with the `rootProperty` set to the root node—in this case, `businesses` because I want to save only businesses to the store:

```
reader: {
  type: 'json',
  rootProperty: 'businesses',
}
```

Using the `jsonp` proxy requires `Ext.data.proxy.JsonP`, so you will need to add this class to the `requires` array:

```
requires: ['Ext.data.proxy.JsonP'],
```

This store also has the property `autoLoad` set to `true`. As soon as the application loads the `Cabs.js` store, it will start loading the external data. You can see this in Figure 8-3: the store proxy fires a successful request and returns JSON as a response.

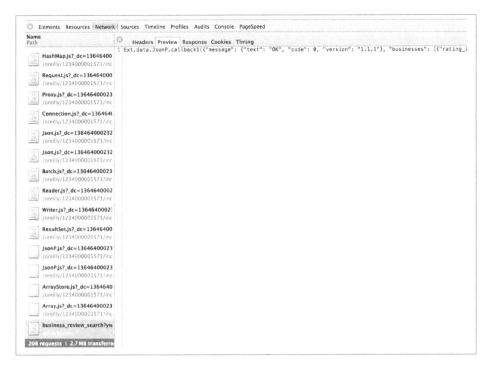

Figure 8-3. Successful load of a proxy

The reason why the store automatically loads is because the autoLoad config in the store is set to true. It's also possible to disable the store from automatically loading by setting autoLoad: false (e.g., because you programmatically want to change the request parameters and load the store manually with the store.load() method). Instead of using the proxy for a JSONP request, you can also use the Ext.data.JsonP method, which you will do in the next section.

Example 8-5 shows the complete code.

Example 8-5. store/Cabs.js

```
Ext.define('FindACab.store.Cabs', {
    extend: 'Ext.data.Store',
    requires: ['Ext.data.proxy.JsonP'],
    config: {
        model: 'FindACab.model.Cab',
        autoLoad: true,
                proxy: {
                type: 'jsonp',
                noCache: false,
                url: Utils.Commons.YELP_API,
                extraParams: {
                term: Utils.Commons.YELP_TERM,
```

```
            ywsid: Utils.Commons.YELP_KEY,
            location: Utils.Commons.LOCATION
    },
        reader: {
                type: 'json',
                rootProperty: 'businesses',
        }
    },
    }
});
```

Implementing a JSONP Request

View components—like lists, dataviews, or charts—are data-aware. You need to hook up a data store to preview the view with data. The previous section explained how to retrieve external data from Yelp in a data store. Later, this data will be displayed in an Ext.dataview.List view component. When retrieving external data, sometimes you don't need to retrieve data in a store—for example, when you're displaying data in an Ext.XTemplate (or another component that isn't data-aware)—because you want to have the control over the HTML and styling of the component. In that case, a simple Ext.JsonP request, with parameters to pass in, might be an easier solution for retrieving data from an external domain than retrieving it through a JSONP proxy.

At the top of your class, you will require Ext.data.JsonP, so the Ext.Loader knows to load the JSONP framework class first. Next, you will create the request:

```
Ext.data.JsonP.request({
    URL: 'somescript.php',
    callbackKey: 'callback',
    params: {
        location: "Amsterdam NL"
    },
    success: function(result, request) {
        // execute if the request succeeds.
    },
    failure: function(){
        //execute if the request fails.
    }
});
```

In the background, the Ext.data.JsonP.request() does the same thing as what the JSONP proxy does: it allows cross-domain (GET) requests by inserting a <script> tag in the head of your page. If you are not familiar with this concept, flip back to the examples about JSONP proxies.

Ext.data.JsonP is a singleton, so you can directly run the request() method on top of it. The request method takes one argument, the options object, with the properties listed in Table 8-1.

Table 8-1. JSONP options

Key	Value
url	String, the URL to the request.
params	Object (optional), an object containing a series of key/value pairs that will be sent along with the request.
timeout	Number (optional); sets the timeout for requests that are not completed within this time, in which case the failure callback will be fired. Defaults to 30ms.
callbackKey	String (optional); specifies the GET parameter that will be sent to the server containing the function name to be executed when the request completes. Defaults to be autogenerated: URL?call back=Ext.data.JsonP.callback1, URL?callback=Ext.data.JsonP.call back2...
callbackName	String (optional), see callbackKey.
disableCaching	Boolean (optional); adds a unique disable-caching timestamp parameter to the requests.
disableCaching Param	String (optional); changes the parameter that is sent when disabling caching. Defaults to _dc.
success	Function (optional); the function to execute if the request succeeds.
failure	Function (optional); the function to execute if the request fails.
callback	Function (optional); the function to execute when the request completes, whether it is a success or failure.
scope	Object (optional); the scope in which to execute the callbacks. Defaults to browser window object.

You need to set up your backend, or use a web service that responds with correct JSONP syntax. The following code shows an example of a JSONP response written in PHP:

```php
<?php
//Return response as JavaScript
header('Content-Type: application/javascript'); //❶

//Retrieve the callbackKey from Ext.data.JsonP.request()
$callbackkey = filter_input(INPUT_GET, 'callback', FILTER_SANITIZE_ENCODED); //❷

//Some array created for test purposes
$somearray = array(
  'fullname' => 'Lee Boonstra',
  'company' => 'Sencha'
);
//Encode php test array to json
$output = json_encode($somearray)

//Wrap it in the callback key
echo $callbackkey . '(' . $output . ');'; //❸
?>
```

❶   The trick is to set the headers to application/javascript.

❷   Capture the callback key.

❸   Wrap this as a function around the JSON output.

When you are using Google Chrome, try to install the JSONView extension. It formats your JSON response in a nice, readable way.

Saving or Retrieving Data from an External Domain with AJAX

Help! You want to post (or get) data from an external domain, but posting data is only possible with AJAX, not with JSONP. JSONP cannot send data with HTTP POST, and AJAX in general cannot retrieve and post data from external domains so you might run into a problem. What you actually want is an AJAX request to save and retrieve data to an external domain. Read on for the trick to this.

Implementing CORS

You will need to set up `Access-Control-Allow` HTTP headers on the web server to post (and retrieve) data with AJAX to an external URL.

Sencha Touch provides additional configuration. In an `Ext.Ajax.request` or AJAX proxy, you have to set the `withCredentials` boolean to `true` and set the `useDefaultXhr Header` boolean to `false` to not send the default `Xhr` header with every request.

The `Ext.Ajax()` method (and also the `model.save()` and `form.submit()` methods) transmit through the `XMLHttpRequest()` object, and therefore you can run into security restrictions—cross-domain restrictions—when posting to a different domain. However, there is a way to post data to another server with AJAX; you need to set up your server so it's possible to set up the HTTP headers (Access-Control-Allow headers) on the web server for that. This technique is called *cross-origin resource sharing* (CORS), and it enables you to override the default restrictions that prevent a web server from making AJAX requests to domains other than where the app is launched. CORS is supported by the modern browsers.

An example of such an HTTP header might look like:

```
Access-Control-Allow-Origin: *
```

Instead of the wildcard, you can also specify the URL of the allowed origin domain explicitly. When using the wildcard, you need to be aware that every domain can request this data when it has CORS set up, which can easily lead to CSRF (cross-side request forgery) attacks.

Sencha Touch provides support for CORS. Assuming your server is set up, the code for sending an AJAX request with CORS might look like this:

```
Ext.Ajax.request({
    URL: 'http://www.externaldomain.com/script.php',
    withCredentials: true,
    useDefaultXhrHeader: false
});
```

The magic is the useDefaultXhrHeader config, which should be set to false to not send the default Xhr header (X-Requested-With) with every request.

Set the withCredentials config to true to include cookies as part of the request. (Note that these cookies also deal with the *same-origin policies*, so your JavaScript code can't access the cookies with document.cookie or from the response headers. They can be controlled only by the remote domain.)

 Do you want to read more about CORS? Check out the Monsur Hossain's CORS tutorial (*http://bit.ly/usingCORS*) or see an overview of supported browsers (*http://enable-cors.org/client.html*).

Summary

By now, you know everything you need to know about retrieving data. We discussed how to retrieve data from a resource on the same domain as the application with AJAX. We looked into AJAX proxies and the Ext.Ajax request. We discussed how to retrieve data from a resource on a different domain than where the app is hosted, JSONP proxies, and how to make a JSONP request. Last but not least, we looked into a relatively new technique, CORS, and how to retrieve data from a different domain by creating an Ext.Ajax request that bypasses the cross-domain restrictions.

The FindACab app has a JSONP proxy set; it loads data from Yelp into the data store. In the next chapter, you'll find more in-depth information about stores.

## CHAPTER 9

Data Stores

A data store is a mechanism to cache your data and is part of the `Ext.data` package. It is like a bucket full of data records. You can pick (select) a record out of this bucket (the data store) and add or remove records. Stores also provide functions for sorting, filtering, and grouping the model instances. You'll need to give a model structure to the store with data. You can do this inline by setting the `fields` and `data` arrays (hardcoded), but a better MVC approach is to bind a model to the data store.

Sencha Touch has data-aware components—such as lists, dataviews, and charts—that need to be hooked up to a store in order to display data. I will discuss those in Chapter 11.

In this chapter, you'll learn:

- How to load data in a store
- How to sort a data store locally
- How to sort data on a server
- How to group a data store
- How to filter a data store locally
- How to filter a data store on a server
- How to save/sync data in a store

Loading Data in a Store

For the FindACab app to be able to display the data, the data needs to be contained in the store. By default, when you create a store (and the data is not hardcoded), you will have to *load* the model data into your store.

When autoLoad is not enabled, you have to manually load the store from your code, or from your developer's console:

```
Ext.getStore('MyStore').load(this, records, successful, operation, eOpts);
```

Ext.getStore("MyStore") is a lookup method; it finds a store (if the store is registered in the Ext.application() or controller) based on the store instance name or storeId through the StoreManager. Really, it's a short alias for Ext.data.StoreManager.lookup("myStore");.

We want the FindACab app to retrieve a list of cabs in the area. We already hooked up a proxy to the store, so we can load the data. When you run the Ext.getStore("Cabs").load() event in the console, it will look up the Cabs store through the StoreManager and return a store object with a data array that contains 20 items.

Instead of just loading the store, you can also handle a callback:

```
Ext.getStore('Cabs').load({
    callback: function(records, success, operation) {
        //callback function here
        console.log(records);
    },
    scope: this
});
```

The store has a callback function, which in this case logs all records after the store is loaded. You can also set a scope. In this case, when you log console.log(this) in your callback, it won't log the scope within the callback, but rather the scope of the class where the store load() event is called.

There are more events you can listen for in the store; for example, addrecords, beforeload, beforesync, refresh, removerecords, updaterecords, and write. Check the API docs for more details about the different store events.

Let's go back to the FindACab app and modify the Utils.Commons class (which we created in Chapter 4) so the Yelp API and API key are saved in a central place:

```
statics: {
    YELP_API: 'http://api.yelp.com/business_review_search?',
    YELP_KEY: 'yelp-key-here',
    YELP_TERM: 'Taxi'
}
```

Now you will modify the store proxy config. Instead of entering a full proxy URL, you will retrieve the URL, the YELP_API key, and the YELP_TERM from the Utils.Commons static file, so it's better organized. You can send parameters with the request by using the extraParams object, and you can modify these parameters from elsewhere in your code, as shown in Example 9-1.

Example 9-1. store/Cabs.js

```
Ext.define('FindACab.store.Cabs', {
    extend: 'Ext.data.Store',
    requires: ['Ext.data.proxy.JsonP'],
    config: {
        model: 'FindACab.model.Cab',
        autoLoad: false,
        proxy: {
                type: 'jsonp',
                url: Utils.Commons.YELP_API,
            noCache: false,
                extraParams: {
                term: Utils.Commons.YELP_TERM,
                ywsid: Utils.Commons.YELP_KEY,
                location: Utils.Commons.LOCATION
            },
                reader: {
                        type: 'json',
                        rootProperty: 'businesses',
                }
            },
        }
    }
});
```

In order to maintain the store callback in the controller, you will create a system event listener to listen to the store load event. For now, this code will only log the results, and show and hide a loading indicator. Example 9-2 shows the new FindACab.control ler.CabController.

Example 9-2. controller/CabController.js

```
Ext.define('FindACab.controller.CabController', {
    extend: 'Ext.app.Controller',
    config: {
        models: ['Cab'],
        stores: ['Cabs']
    },
    init: function() {

        Ext.Viewport.mask({
            xtype: 'loadmask',
            message: 'loading...'
        });
```

```
        Ext.getStore('Cabs').load();
        Ext.getStore('Cabs').addListener('load',
            this.onCabsStoreLoad,
            this);
    },

    onCabsStoreLoad: function(records, success, operation) {
        console.log(records.getData());
        Ext.Viewport.unmask();
    }
});
```

After initializing the controller, this code will load the Cabs store, and add a *load* listener to listen to the load system event of the store. It will also add a loading animation to the application viewport, Ext.Viewport.mask(), that spins a loading animation. When a load() event callback comes in, it will run the function onCabsStoreLoad(). This will print the received data object into your debugging console and hide the loading application by setting Ext.Viewport.unmask().

So far, so good: you have all the data in your app. There are nice ways to manipulate your store results collections. For example, you can sort, filter, or group a store, as we'll discuss in the next section.

Sorting a Data Store Locally

After you retrieve data in your store, you might notice that the store is not sorted. It is possible to sort the records in a data store on the client side. You will use the Ext.data.Store.sort(sorters, [defaultDirection], [where]) method, and you can pass in sorters_ object, which specifies the fieldname to sort and the direction, either ASC (ascending, A–Z) and DESC (descending, Z-A).

Here I construct a sorters array to sort the fieldname property by ASC:

```
sorters: [{
    property: "fieldname",
    direction: "ASC"
}]
```

The sorters array or the sort() method on the store sorts the data collection inside the store by one or more of its properties.

To programmatically sort a store from elsewhere in your code, you can pass in a single argument, the fieldname to sort. This will toggle between ascending and descending:

```
Ext.getStore("Cabs").sort("name");
```

Or you can pass in the full `sorters` configuration:

```
Ext.getStore("Cabs").sort({
    property: "fieldname",
    direction: "ASC"
});
```

Or just the string `fieldname` and strings "ASC" or "DESC":

```
Ext.getStore("Cabs").sort("name", "DESC");
```

In the FindACab app, you will sort the `Cabs` list on the cab service name in alphabetical order. Therefore, the default sorter will be set to `name`:

```
sorters: [{
    property: "name",
    direction: "ASC"
}],
```

It is possible to add sorters on top of each other. For example, first sort on the field *name* and afterward filter on the field *distance*. You do so by passing an array:

```
store.sort([
    {
        property : 'name',
        direction: 'ASC'
    },
    {
        property : 'distance',
        direction: 'DESC'
    }
]);
```

When the `sort()` method is called again with a new sorter object, any existing sorters will be removed. When the `sort()` method is called without any arguments, the existing sorters will be reapplied. To keep existing sorters and add new ones, you will need to run the `add()` method on the `sorters` object. Here is how you can add sorters to a store:

```
store.sorters.add(new Ext.util.Sorter({
    property : 'phone',
    direction: 'ASC'
}));
store.sort();
```

The previous examples make sense when you want to sort on local stores. However, it's also possible to sort remotely on the server side. Let's take a look at that in the next examples.

Sorting Data on a Server

The data that you retrieve from the server side might be very large. It could be faster to sort it on the server side instead of locally. Luckily, Sencha Touch provides a way to implement server-side paging, called *remote sorting*. You will use the Ext.da ta.Store.remoteSort boolean, and you will use the sorters object directly in the store or run the Ext.data.Store.sort(sorters, [defaultDirection], [where]) method where you can pass in a sorters object. (See the previous section on how to sort a store.)

If you want to enable remote sorting, set the following settings in the store class definition:

- A pageSize to define the number of records that constitutes a "page." (Note that the default page size is set to 25.)
- The boolean remoteSort config in the store class definition to true. (Note that remote sorting is false by default.)
- The sorters object, as described in the previous section:

```
pageSize: 30,
remoteSort: true,
sorters: [{
    property: "fieldname",
    direction: "ASC"
}]
```

Unfortunately, because we do not have control over the Yelp server side, we won't implement a remote sorter for the FindACab app. However, I do want to share a running example of a remote sorter. In this demo, there is another data store with Car objects that sorts cars by brand in ascending order:

```
Ext.define('RemoteTest.store.Cars', {
    extend: 'Ext.data.Store',
    requires: ['Ext.data.proxy.JsonP'],
    config: {
        model: 'RemoteTest.model.Car',
        autoLoad: true,

        remoteSort: true, //❶
        sorters: [{ //❷
            property: "brand",
            direction: "ASC"
        }],
        pageSize: 20, //❸

        proxy: { //❹
            type: 'jsonp',
            url: 'http://someurl.com/test.php',
```

```
                  reader: { //❺
                      rootProperty: 'results',
                      totalProperty: 'total',
                      successProperty: 'success'
                  }
              },
          }
      });
```

❶   Enable remote sorting.

❷   Sort the cars by brand, in ascending order.

❸   By setting the `pageSize` to 20, you are requesting 20 records per page from the server.

❹   A JSONP proxy, to retrieve `Car` objects from *http://<someurl>.com/test.php*.

❺   The proxy reader, which can read `result`, `total`, and `success` properties from the server response.

> The previous store has an `autoLoad` property. This makes sense for demo purposes, but in a real application, you would probably want to programmatically sort and load the store.

Currently, this `Car` store doesn't do much. That's because there is no server side implemented. This is OK, because the server-side code can be a black box for us. However, let's assume that *http://<someurl>.com/test.php* is a working web service that sends `Car` objects back.

In the Google Developer network tab, you can see a request is made, which sends the following `GET` request to your server:

```
http://someurl.com/test.php?_dc=1386924081041&page=1&start=0&limit=20
&sort=%5B%7B%22property%22%3A%22brand%22%2C%22direction%22%3A%22ASC%22%7D%5D
&callback=Ext.data.JsonP.callback1
```

Let's format the query string parameters:

```
page:1
start:0
limit:20
sort:[{"property":"name","direction":"ASC"}]
```

The `limit` parameter comes from the store `pageSize`. The `page` and `start` parameters are used for paging. On the server side, you can calculate which set of items you have to send back to the client-side code.

The *http://<someurl>.com/test.php* web service requires some logic to sort the data (e.g., in a database) and send the correct set of data back.

The server response for sending back `Car` objects (in PHP) could look like Example 9-3. The names of the `success`, `total`, and `results` properties should be set in the store's reader.

Example 9-3. A server response in PHP

```
{
  "success": true,
  "total": 500,
  "results": [{ "id": 1, "brand": "BMW", "type" : 7 },
    { "id": 2, "brand": "Mercedes", "type" : 5 }
    ... //20 results in total
  ]
}
```

Now that you know how to sort data, let's discuss how to group it.

Grouping a Data Store

Grouping a data store makes sense when you want to display data into an `Ext.List` component in Sencha Touch and you want to visually group data. For example, when you have a store with companies, you could, for example, group by "city." This will list every company per city.

To enable grouping in a store, implement the `groupField` and `groupDir` configurations directly in the store class definition. The `groupFields` sets the field to group and the `groupDir` sets the direction (ASC or DESC):

```
groupField: '<model-field-name>',
groupDir: 'ASC' //or DESC
```

To dynamically group a store, you can run the `setGrouper()` method on a store object:

```
Ext.getStore('Cabs').setGrouper({
    direction: 'ASC', //or DESC
    property: '<model-field-name>'
});
```

You will implement grouping on the `Cabs` store for the FindACab app list. This time, you will not group on city, because all the data that is in the `Cabs` store already shares the same city—for example, Amsterdam. Therefore, let's group on the first alphabetical character of a cab service name. (See Figure 9-1.) You would see a group "A" that lists all names that start with an A, a group "B" that lists all names that start with a B, and so on. It's the same behavior as when you open the contacts list on an iPhone. Names are grouped, and if you want, you can even display an index bar on the side to quickly browse to the corresponding character.

Figure 9-1. The Cabs store needs grouping to display taxi services in a grouped list

To achieve this, you will need the Ext.data.Store.grouper object, with a custom group function: groupFn(). You can set the grouper object directly in the store class definition, as shown in Example 9-4.

Example 9-4. app/store/Cabs.js

```
grouper: {
    groupFn: function(record) {
        return record.get('name')[0].toUpperCase();
    }
}
```

The groupFn function with the code return record.get("name")[0].toUpper Case(); will group the data in the store on the first (uppercase) character of the name field.

Filtering a Data Store Locally

A data store can also filter records. When a filter is applied, the data store will not remove records. The same records are still available in the store, but only the records that match the filter criteria are displayed.

Filters are added as arrays. Here's how to implement a filter array directly in the store class definition:

```
filters: [{
    property: "fieldname",
    value: "match"
}],
```

You can also filter programmatically. Just run the following method from a store instance:

```
Ext.data.Store.filter(filters, [value], [anyMatch], [caseSensitive]);
```

The `filters` array (or the `filter()` method on the store) filters the data collection by one or more of its filter properties, and returns only the data that matches the `value` of the filter.

It's possible to filter on the first characters of a field or from anywhere (argument: `anyMatch`), and it's also possible to filter for case sensitivity (argument: `caseSensitive`).

Custom Filter Functions

You can also create custom filter functions. To do so, you can set a `filterFn` in the array or use the `filterBy(fn)` method on the store.

Let's implement a custom filter for the FindACab app. By default, the FindACab app is filtered by a function that checks whether a phone number is specified. This filters the `Cabs` store on phone numbers that have at least one character (see Example 9-5).

Example 9-5. app/store/Cabs.js

```
filters: [{
    filterFn: function(item) {
        return item.get("phone").length > 0;
    }
}],
```

Stacking Filters

To add filters on top of each other—for example, to filter on a name with a value of `Taxi` *and* filter on a distance of 20 miles—you pass in an array. Here, I stack a couple of filters on top of each other:

```
store.filter([
    {property: "name", value: "Taxi"},
    {property: "distance", value: "20"}
]);
```

 Instead of passing an array with filter objects into the `filter()` method, I could call the `filter()` method again without the filter objects as arguments. Unlike sorters, filters won't reset if you call them again. When you want to renew the filter, you have to clear it first:

```
store.clearFilter();
```

Filtering Data on a Server

The data that you retrieve from the server side might be very large. It could be faster to filter it on the server side instead of locally. Luckily, Sencha Touch provides a way to implement server-side filtering.

You will use the `remoteFilter` boolean and the array with `filters`. Here's an example of the store class definition:

```
remoteFilter: true,
filters: [{
    property: "fieldname",
    value: "match"
}],
```

Here I set the boolean `remoteFilter` in the store to `true` to enable remote filtering (note, it is off by default).

Again, because we do not have server-side control over Yelp.com, we won't implement a remote filter for the FindACab app. I do want to share an example of a remote filter, however. In this demo, there is another data store with `Car` objects and with remote filtering enabled. It has a filter set that filters on car brand:

```
Ext.define('RemoteTest.store.Cars', {
    extend: 'Ext.data.Store',
    requires: ['Ext.data.proxy.JsonP'],
    config: {
        model: 'RemoteTest.model.Car',
        autoLoad: true,
        pageSize: 20,

        remoteFilter : true,
        filters: [{
            property: "brand",
            value: "BMW"
        }],

        proxy: {
                type: 'jsonp',
            url: 'http://someurl.com/test.php',
                reader: {
                rootProperty: 'results',
                totalProperty: 'total',
                successProperty: 'success'
            }
            },
    }
});
```

Again, this store has an autoLoad property. This makes sense for demo purposes, but in a real application, you would probably want to programmatically filter and load the store.

When the remoteFilter configuration has been set to true, you will have to manually call the load method after every filter you set to retrieve the filtered data from the server.

Let's assume that *http://<someurl>.com/test.php* is a working web service that sends Car objects back. We'll filter on a car brand of BMW, 20 per time (page).

In the Google Developer Network tab, you can see a request is made that sends the following GET request to your server:

```
http://someurl.com/test.php?_dc=1387182737587&page=1&start=0&limit=20
&filter=%5B%7B%22property%22%3A%22brand%22%2C%22value%22%3A%22BMW%22%7D%5D
&callback=Ext.data.JsonP.callback1
```

Let's format the query string parameters:

```
page:1
start:0
limit:20
filter:[{"property":"brand","value":"BMW"}]
```

As you might have noticed, the implementation and server requests of a remote filter are similar to the implementation and server requests of a remote sorter. The limit parameter comes from the store pageSize. The page and start parameters are used for paging. On the server side, you can calculate which set of items you have to send back to the client-side code.

The *http://<someurl>.com/test.php* requires some logic to filter their data (e.g., in a database), and send the correct set of data back.

The server response for sending back Car objects (in PHP) could look like Example 9-6. The names of the success, total, and results properties should be set in the store's reader.

Example 9-6. A server response in PHP

```
{
  "success": true,
  "total": 500,
  "results": [{ "id": 1, "brand": "BMW", "type" : 7 },
    { "id": 2, "brand": "BMW", "type" : 5 }
    ...
    ]
}
```

Syncing Data in a Store

To save/synchronize records in a data store with the server, you will have to run the `sync()` method on the store. It's also possible to automatically sync the store with the server side. That way, the remote server keeps in close sync with your Sencha Touch app. You can enable this by setting the `autoSync` property to `true`. Although that setting is very easy, it also uses a lot of bandwidth and it's not possible to batch updates.

More likely, you will use the `Ext.data.Store.sync()` method to synchronize the store with its proxy programmatically:

```
store.sync(options);
```

Before the sync process, Sencha Touch will fire a `beforesync` system event. When you run the `sync()` method, all inserts, updates, and deletes are sent as three separate requests, and if you want, you can declare the order in which the three operations should occur. After the sync process, an object is returned with the child objects `added`, `updated`, and `removed`.

For the FindACab app, let's start by creating a simple store. In Example 9-7, the store has a reference to the `Setting` model, which has the corresponding fields and a proxy to save the data in the browsers' Local Storage.

Example 9-7. store/Settings.js

```
Ext.define('FindACab.store.Settings', {
    extend: 'Ext.data.Store',
    config: {
        model: 'FindACab.model.Setting',
        autoLoad: true
    }
});
```

You will also need a `SettingsController` that's hooked up to the *app.js* file, which you accomplish by adding `SettingsController` to the controllers array. The controller will look like Example 9-8—again, nothing fancy.

Example 9-8. controller/SettingsController.js

```
Ext.define('FindACab.controller.SettingsController', {
    extend: 'Ext.app.Controller',
    config: {
        models: ['Setting'],
        stores: ['Settings']
    }
});
```

Now when you run the FindACab app, the Settings store (which is empty) should be loaded and created. Here's how I add and sync data to a store. You will manually start to add records to the store.

First, create a reference to the store (you can run this line from the browser dev console):

```
var store = Ext.getStore('Settings');
```

The next step is to create some data, a model object that contains the corresponding fields:

```
var model = Ext.create('FindACab.model.Setting', {
    city: 'Amsterdam',
    country: 'The Netherlands'
});
```

Add the data to the store:

```
store.add(model);
```

Now comes the magic, the store.sync(). The store and Sencha Touch will make sure the data will persist and get saved to the browsers, Local Storage, through the model:

```
store.sync()
```

The preceding line will return an object, with these three arrays:

added
> An array with new records added to the store

removed
> An array with removed records from the store

updated
> An array with edited records in the store

In our case, this code just added one record to the client-side store (see Figure 9-2). We didn't implement a client-side proxy to save data offline yet, so the data will be gone as soon as you refresh the browser.

Example 9-9 shows the completed code.

Example 9-9. How to add and sync data to a store

```
var store = Ext.getStore('Settings');
var model = Ext.create('FindACab.model.Setting', {
    city: 'Amsterdam',
    country: 'The Netherlands'
});

store.add(model);
store.sync();
```

Figure 9-2. The result in your browser dev console after adding and syncing a record to the store

You can add records one by one, as you can see in the third step of the previous example. You could also add an array of model objects to the store and then sync it. Whether you add it one by one or add an array with model data, the data looping happens before the sync() call to save performance.

Sometimes you want to get a success response after syncing the store. For example, later in the FindACab app, you will sync a form with user input with the application, and when it's successful you will reset the markers on a Google Map. As of Sencha Touch version 2.3, it is possible to retrieve a callback after syncing a store. It works very well; you can pass in an options object that makes use of the proxy's batch method (Ext.data.Batch):

```
store.sync({
    callback: function(batch, options){
        console.log(batch);
    },
    success: function(batch, options){
        console.log("succes", batch, options);
    },
    failure: function(batch){
        console.log("error", batch, options);
    }
});
```

Retrieving the created, updated, or deleted records is not so straightforward, because you will work with three different batches:

create
> This batch will run after adding new records to the store.

update
> This batch will run after editing records in the store.

destroy
> This batch will run after deleting records in the store.

If you want, you could request these records via the batches, but what is most important are the success and failure callbacks. We will use these callbacks in our FindACab app later.

Summary

This chapter explained how to load data in a store, how to group a data store, and how to sort and filter data on the client as if on a remote server. At the end of the chapter, I showed you how you can sync a data store with a remote (or client) proxy.

For the FindACab app you have everything set—a configured store and proxy and a model that can be validated. It is just a bit heavy, however: every time I run the FindACab app, it downloads external content from the Internet. When the data doesn't change often, it's better to store the data in the app. The app doesn't need to be connected to the Internet and it loads much faster, because it doesn't need to download. In the next chapter, then, we will discuss how to save and load data offline.

## CHAPTER 10

Offline Storage (Client Proxies)

We discussed how to save and load remote data via the server proxy in Chapter 8. Proxies can also save and load data from the client side via the client proxy. This comes in handy when you want to load or save data offline. When working with external APIs, you might want to think about offline storage. For example, for the FindACab app, you are using the Yelp web service, so every time you load the app you retrieve data from the API. But suddenly your console throws an error message. Bummer: you've reached the daily API request limit. There's nothing you can do anymore, but there is a way to prevent this scenario from happening in the first place: storing your data results in the app itself. So what are the options, and how can you save all your data?

Although mobile devices are portable, this doesn't necessarily mean that users are always online. They could have a bad WiFi signal, they may be on the subway, or they might have a limited data plan, for example.

This is why offline storage is so important. HTML5 offers a powerful way to achieve this with Local Storage, Session Storage, Web SQL, and Application Cache.

HTML5 Local Storage
> HTML5 Local Storage saves its data with no expiration date. You use it to save key/value pairs. The Sencha framework uses it internally to save persisted JavaScript (Sencha) classes. When you open a Sencha Touch app while you are offline, the Sencha Touch app itself can run because all the assets are stored offline in the Local Storage. The FindACab app makes use of Local Storage by saving the user settings offline.

HTML5 Session Storage
> This method saves its data in a session. The session will be over after the browser is closed. This is the main difference from Local Storage, which won't lose its data at all. Usually, the HTML5 Session Storage is used for online shopping baskets. It

stores all the products in the session. After the products are purchased, the session can be cleared.

Web SQL Databases

This method, formerly known as "WebDB," provides a thin wrapper around a SQL database. In 2007, Google launched Google Gears, an open source cross-browser plug-in that included an embedded database based on SQLite. This early prototype later influenced the creation of the HTML5 Web SQL Database specification.

Application Cache

This can make your application available offline, and can cache files and assets into the browser. You will need to set up an AppCache manifest file.

 There is a SQL client proxy available in Sencha Touch 2.3. However, unfortunately, on November 18, 2010, the W3C announced (*http://www.w3.org/TR/webdatabase/*) that Web SQL database is a deprecated specification. This means that web developers should no longer use the technology, as the spec will receive no further updates, and browser vendors aren't encouraged to support this technology. You can still use Web SQL databases in Google Chrome and in Safari browsers, but at your own risk. That said, it works very well with Sencha Touch, and there is no officially supported alternative.

You might want to check out IndexDB instead. See Grgur Grisogono's Sencha IndexDB Proxy (*http://bit.ly/indexDB-proxy*).

The Sencha Touch client proxy saves and loads the data locally on its device or in its memory. Sencha Touch's client proxy has four important subclasses:

- `Ext.data.proxy.Memory`
- `Ext.data.proxy.LocalStorage`
- `Ext.data.proxy.SessionStorage`
- `Ext.data.proxy.Sql`

The `MemoryProxy` uses a local variable for data storage and retrieval, but the contents are lost on every page refresh. For that reason, I will not discuss it in this chapter.

This is not the case with the `LocalStorage` proxy, the `SessionStorage` proxy, and the SQL proxy. When the browser provides support for these, it will save the model data as a key/value data store into the browser, so it will remain after the browser is closed and reopened. If the HTML5 Storage API is not supported by the browser, the constructor will throw an error.

Because the data is saved as key/value pairs, where the key needs to be unique, you cannot save complex objects like JSON—unless you convert these JSON objects to strings with `Ext.JSON.encode()`. `LocalStorageProxy` automatically serializes and deserializes data when saving and retrieving it.

Here is an example showing how to implement a client proxy to your model or store class:

```
proxy: {
    type: "<client-proxy>"
}
```

The `type` can be set to `memory` (the default), `localstorage`, `sessionstorage`, or `sql`.

In this chapter, you'll learn:

- How to save data into Local Storage
- How to save data into Session Storage
- How to save data into a Web SQL database
- How to save assets locally by using the Application Cache

Saving Data into Local Storage

When you want to save data locally so that it can always be accessed offline, you should use Local Storage.

Local Storage is like a super-cookie. You use it to save key/value pairs, like a cookie does, but you can save much more data than that. A cookie can save up to 4KB, whereas Local Storage has space for 5MB. (When that amount is exceeded, the user will get a QUO TA_EXCEEDED_ERR exception.) Also, Local Storage is much faster and more secure than cookies. Cookies are included with every HTTP request, and thereby send data unencrypted over the Internet (unless your entire web application is served over SSL), while the Local Storage data will always be available.

To save data in the Local Storage with Sencha Touch, you will have to implement a client proxy to your model or store with the type `localstorage`.

When this proxy is used in a browser where Local Storage is not supported, the constructor will throw an error.

You will require `Ext.data.proxy.LocalStorage` at the top of your model or store class, so the `Ext.Loader` knows to load the `LocalStorage` framework class first.

Every key/value pair in the Local Storage should have a unique key, to refer to its model data. Sencha Touch can generate a unique record id for you; you will only need to set an id on the proxy, which will be prefixed to the unique record id to make the Local Storage key.

In the FindACab app, you will use the LocalStorage proxy for saving user settings locally on the device. The Settings model in the FindACab app will contain a proxy like this:

```
proxy: {
    type: 'localstorage',
    id: "Setting"
}
```

Later, you will create a user form for the app, so users can save their settings to the device. You will only need to save the model (MyModel.save) or sync the store (MyStore.sync()). to make sure the data will be saved offline.

Note that the key/value pairs in the client proxies are strings! When you retrieve this data later from a store—by using, for example, the command Ext.getStore("MyS tore").getAt(0)—it will decode this string to a JavaScript object for you. In other words, it serializes and deserializes data automatically when saving or retrieving it. Awesome!

An example Local Storage key/value pair for the FindACab app could look like this:

```
"Setting-51726e64-ae85-4fe8-9bea-aa085f499da6" : "{
    "id":"51726e64-ae85-4fe8-9bea-aa085f499da6",
    "gps":null,
    "city":"Amsterdam",
    "country":"NL"
}"
```

To generate an id with Sencha Touch, you need to implement an id strategy. There are three strategies you can use:

- Ext.data.identifier.Sequential is a sequential id generator. It generates ids in sequential order (1, 2, 3, etc.).

- Ext.data.identifier.Simple is the default id generator in Sencha Touch. It generates ids in sequential order, prefixed with a prefix parameter. When no pre fix parameter is set, it prefixes ids by default with ext-record- (e.g., ext-record-1, ext-record-2, ext-record-3, etc.).

- Ext.data.identifier.Uuid is a UUID (Universally Unique IDentifier, also known as GUIDs (Globally Unique IDentifier generator). A UUID is a 128-bits id that can guarantee uniqueness across space and time. UUIDs were originally used in the Apollo Network Computing System and later in the Open Software Foundation's

(OSF) Distributed Computing Environment (DCE), and then in Microsoft Windows platforms.

To set an id strategy, you have to require one of the identifiers at the top of your model; for example: `requires: ["Ext.data.identifier.Uuid]`. The model should also have the `idProperty` set to the model field that can be used as an `id`, which defaults to the `fieldname: id`. (Make sure the field type matches!) In addition, the model should contain the `identifier` property. In this case, it can be set to `uuid`, which is why you are requiring this class at the top of the file.

Let's take a look at the full code for the `Settings` model of the FindACab app, `FindACab.model.Setting`:

```
Ext.define('FindACab.model.Setting', {
    extend: 'Ext.data.Model',
    requires: ['Ext.data.identifier.Uuid'],
    config: {
        idProperty: 'id',
        identifier: 'uuid',
        fields: [
            { name: 'id', type: 'auto' },
            { name: 'gps', type: 'boolean' },
            { name: 'city', type: 'string' },
            { name: 'country', type: 'string' }
        ],
        validations: [{
            type: 'presence',
            field: 'city',
            message: "Please provide a city."
        },
        {
            type: 'presence',
            field: 'country',
            message: "Please provide a country."
        }],
        proxy: {
            type: 'localstorage',
            id: "Setting"
        }
    }
});
```

As you can see, there is an `identifier` and an `idProperty` set. The type of the id field is set to `int`.

The model also contains a client `proxy` object with the type set to `localstorage` and the `id` name (prefix) set to the word `"Setting"`. Let's see if this works. Open the FindACab app in your browser and open Google Developer Tools.

Open the browser's console and enter the following line of code to create a `Settings` model:

```
var m = Ext.create('FindACab.model.Setting', {
    city: "Amsterdam",
    country:"NL"
});
```

This line saves some data into a variable called m. From now on, you can log the data that is saved in the m variable with the line `console.log(m)`, because it is saved in the browser's memory. However, it is not saved into the Local Storage yet. For that, you will need to save the model instance. You can do this with the command `m.save()`. Now you can see the data entry that is saved into the browser's Local Storage. Open the Resources tab and select Local Storage. You should see two settings, a key/value pair. One contains the `id`, and the other contains the data. See Figure 10-1.

Figure 10-1. Chrome Developer Tools, Resources → Local Storage

Find more information about HTML5 storage in the article "The Past, Present, and Future of Local Storage for Web Applications." (*http://diveintohtml5.info/storage.html*)

Saving Data into Session Storage

When you want to save data locally so that it can be accessed offline temporarily as long the session exists, you might want to use Session Storage. A use case for this could be when you have a mobile web shop and you want to save the products a user has selected in a shopping cart. The data is present as long as the session exists, but as soon as the user closes the mobile browser, the data is gone.

Implementing a `SessionStorageProxy` works exactly the same as the `LocalStorage` proxy. If you want to read more about implementing Session Storage, flip back to the examples about Local Storage.

You will require `Ext.data.proxy.SessionStorage` at the top of your model or store class, so the `Ext.Loader` knows to load the `SessionStorage` framework class first.

Then create a proxy. Instead of setting the `type` to `localstorage`, you will set it to `sessionstorage` (see Figure 10-2):

```
proxy: {
    type: "sessionstorage",
    id: "session-id-prefix"
}
```

Figure 10-2. Chrome Developer Tools, Resources → Session Storage

Saving Data into a Web SQL Database

Sencha Touch provides a solution to save data in a Web SQL database. You might want to choose a local database instead of Local Storage when your app needs to save a lot of data offline.

The Web SQL local database can save many megabytes and has good performance. The storage limit is by default set to 5MB for most browsers but you can scale up, although it differs per browser and device. For example, Safari desktop supports 500MB of database storage and Safari mobile supports 50MB of database storage. Safari prompts you if you try to create a database over the size of the default database size, 5MB. It will ask you whether you want to grant the database permission to scale up to the next size of database: 5, 10, 50, and so on. Refusing the permission will throw a security error exception. If the Web SQL quota is an issue for you and you want to create a hybrid app, you could look into Adobe PhoneGap or Apache Cordova (*http://bit.ly/storage-opts*), which provide a database wrapper via a plug-in, and pass the native class data that it will then store on the device.

 At the time of writing, there is a bug in iOS 7, when you're using Web SQL in mobile Safari that can cause big problems if you're trying to create a database bigger than 5MB. You will still see the permission dialog, but even if you grant permission, the quota stays at 5MB and you will get a `DOMException`.

To save data in the Web SQL database with Sencha Touch, you will have to implement a client proxy to your model or store with the type `sql` and specify the `database` and `table` names.

At the top of your model or store class, you will require `Ext.data.proxy.Sql`, so the `Ext.Loader` knows to load the `Sql` framework class first. Next you will create a `proxy` object:

```
proxy: {
    type: "sql",
    database: "MyDbName",
    table: "MyTableName"
}
```

Once you have the proxy connected to your model or store, you will still need to have some content for the SQL proxy. When you want to save user input into your database, it will work as designed. You would just save your model, and the input is saved. The next time you want to request some data, you can request it from the store. For example, `Ext.getStore("Users").getById(1)` would get from a `Users` store the record whose `id` equals 1. But what if you want to request some data from some external source and save this to your Web SQL database? You can create just one proxy per store. There are a few ways of doing this:

- You set the proxy to `sql`, create an `Ext.data.JSONP` call, and then in the callback save the data to the store with `Ext.getStore("MyStore").sync()`, which will save it to the local database.

- You set the proxy to `sql`, and when no data is available, switch the proxy to `jsonp`. You load the data through the model or store and in the callback, switch the proxy back to `sql`. Now you can sync the store with `Ext.getStore("MyStore").sync()` and it will save the data to the local Web SQL database.

- You create a second store, which has a proxy that is set to `sql`; the other store's proxy is set to `jsonp`. On the callback of the data load, you save the data to the offline store. While this solution works, you have to maintain two stores, so it might not be ideal.

 Find more information about HTML5 Web SQL databases at "Introducing Web SQL Databases." (*http://bit.ly/intro-web-db*) Read more about IndexDB at "A Simple TODO list using HTML5 IndexedDB." (*http://bit.ly/indexed-todo*)

Saving Data into a Web SQL Database for the FindACab App

Let's take a look at your FindACab app `Cabs` store, Example 10-1. It will take the second approach; see Figure 10-3 for the full flow.

Example 10-1. store/Cabs.js

```
Ext.define('FindACab.store.Cabs', {
    extend: 'Ext.data.Store',
    requires: [
        'Ext.data.proxy.JsonP',
        'Ext.data.proxy.Sql'
    ],
    config: {
        model: 'FindACab.model.Cab',
        autoLoad: false,

        //sort on Taxi name
        sorters: [{
            property: "name",
            direction: "ASC"
        }],

        //group on the first character of Taxi name
        grouper: {
            groupFn: function(record) {
                return record.get('name')[0].toUpperCase();
            }
        },
        //groupField: 'name',
        //groupDir: 'DESC',

        //only display Taxi services that contain a phone number
        filters: [{
            filterFn: function(item) {
                return item.get("phone").length > 0;
            }
        }],

        proxy: {
            type: 'sql',
            database: "FindACab",
            table: "Cabs"
        }
    }
});
```

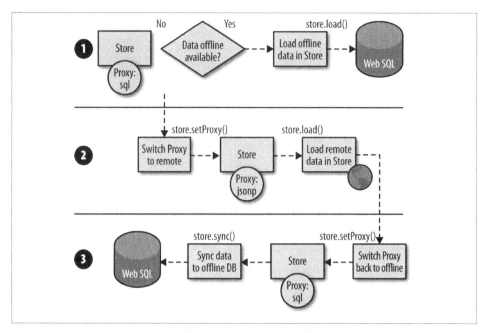

Figure 10-3. The FindACab app flow for saving data offline

Now you want to make sure that the FindACab app saves taxi addresses offline so that users can order taxis without the Internet.

I have defined a store class definition and some `sorters`, `groupers`, and `filters` are set. You don't need to worry about this now, but if you want to find out more, see Chapter 9. What is important in this store is the client proxy. I have created a proxy with the type `sql`. It has the `database` name `FindACab`, and the database `table` is called `Cabs`.

There is not much magic in the store file, apart from the proxy. The real coding fun comes from the `FindACab.controller.CabController` class:

```
Ext.define('FindACab.controller.CabController', {
    extend: 'Ext.app.Controller',

    config: {
        models: ['Cab'],
        stores: ['Cabs']
    },
```

OK, here you go. I moved from the *app.js* file the `models` and `stores` array because the functionality of the `Cab` model and the `Cabs` store belongs to the `CabController`. Why would I do this? If the FindACab app ever becomes bigger and gets more functionality, it will be easier to maintain.

If I ever decide to remove this functionality from my application, I don't need to browse through all my models and stores—I could simply disconnect the CabController from the *app.js* controllers array:

```
launch: function() {
    Ext.Viewport.setMasked({
        xtype: 'loadmask',
        indicator: true,
        message: 'Fetching Data...'
    });

    this.loadLocal();
},
```

As soon as the controller is ready and launched, it will show a loading mask (Ext.View port.mask()) to indicate to the user that it is loading some data. Then it runs the controller function loadLocal():

```
loadLocal: function() {
    var me = this;
    Ext.getStore('Cabs').load(function(item) {
        var count = Ext.getStore('Cabs').getCount();
        if (count < 1) {
            me.downloadData();
        } else {
            Ext.Viewport.unmask();
        }
    });
},
```

It will load the data from the offline Web SQL database and it checks whether the database has records. If it has records, then later you will code a Google Map to center to a lat/long position. For now, the loading mask just hides, but when it has *no* records it should download the data from an external source. In that case, it will run the down loadData() function from the controller scope:

```
downloadData: function(location) {
    var me = this;
    location = Utils.Commons.LOCATION;
```

Let's hardcode the location to the value written in the static member Utils.Com mons.LOCATION. (this way, the rest of the function won't fail):

```
if (!location) {
    Ext.getStore('Settings').load(function() {
        try {
            var data = Ext.getStore('Settings').getAt(0);
            var loc = data.get('city') + " " + data.get('country');
            me.downloadData(loc);
        } catch (e) {
            Ext.Viewport.unmask();
```

```
                    Ext.Msg.confirm(
                        "No location saved",
                        "Please prefill your location,
                        to detect nearby Taxiservices.",
                        function(buttonId) {
                            if (buttonId === 'yes') {

        me.getApplication
        ().getController
        ('SettingsController')
        .toggleSettings();

                            }
                        }
                    );
                }
            });

        }
```

Later in this book, the hardcoded value will be replaced for a settings form that can pass in a location entered by the user.

The downloadData() method has one argument: location. When no location is passed, the FindACab app will show a messagebox with a warning. When the user clicks OK, it will pop up a settings form where the user can enter the location. After posting the form, it should come back to the downloadData() function, now with a valid location:

```
        else {
            ❶
            var store = Ext.getStore('Cabs');
            store.setProxy({
                type: 'jsonp',
                url: Utils.Commons.YELP_API,
                extraParams: {
                    term: Utils.Commons.YELP_TERM,
                    ywsid: Utils.Commons.YELP_KEY,
                    location: location
                },
                ❷
                reader: {
                    type: 'json',
                    rootProperty: 'businesses',
                }
            });

            ❸
            store.load(function(records) {
                me.syncRecords(records, location);
            });
```

```
    }
}, //end downloadData
```

❶ When a location is passed in, the downloadData() function switches the proxy of the Cabs store, which is by default set to the sql proxy, to a jsonp proxy. It will set the url to the Yelp *business_review_search* web service URL. This one is set in the Utils.Commons static member. It will also set some extraParams in the jsonp server proxy, like the search term for Taxi, the ywsid that has my personal Yelp key, and the location, which is still hardcoded to Amsterdam NL but later can be set to be prefilled by a form.

❷ The proxy reader is set to json and the rootProperty is set to businesses because the Yelp web service will send a JSON response back and then can start looping through the business nodes.

❸ After the store proxy is switched, the store needs to load. In the load callback, it will run the syncRecords() controller method and pass in the records and a location.

Here's the code for the syncRecords() function:

```
syncRecords: function(records, userinput) {
    /*
     * Loop through all the items that are downloaded
     * and add these to the items array.
     */
    var items = [],
        me = this,
        total = records.length,
        i = 0,
        store = Ext.getStore('Cabs');

    for(i;i<total;i++) {
        var item = records[i];
        items.push({
            'name': item.get('name'),
            'latitude': item.get('latitude'),
            'longitude': item.get('longitude'),
            'address1': item.get('address1'),
            'phone': item.get('phone'),
            'state_code': item.get('state_code'),
            'zip': item.get('zip'),
            'city': item.get('city'),
            'country_code': item.get('country_code'),
            'avg_rating': item.get('avg_rating'),
            'distance': item.get('distance'),
            'userinput': userinput
        });

    };
```

The syncRecords() method creates an items array and loops through all the downloaded items. It pushes every item nicely to the items array, so it will save only the item fields that are declared in the Cab model, and it will be saved in one batch:

```
store.setProxy({
    type: 'sql',
    database: "FindACab",
    table: 'Cabs'
});
```

After that, it will do the same trick—switch back to the original client sql proxy:

```
store.removeAll();
store.sync({
    success: function(batch){
        /*
         * Add the downloaded items array to the Cabs Store
         * and sync() the store to start saving the
         * records locally.
         * When it is done, we can remove the Loading mask.
         */
        store.add(items);
        store.sync({
            success: function(batch){
                me.setTitleCount(store.getCount());
                store.load();
                Ext.Viewport.unmask();
            }
        });
    }
});

    }
});
```

At last, remove the items from the offline database store, sync() it, and when the sync succeeds, start adding the complete items array to the offline database store and sync() again. In the callback, set the Cab counter and remove the loading mask because the data is present. You will load the store again, to make sure it sorts the offline database store. In Chapter 11, you will code a loadMarkers() method, which will be invoked from here.

You can test the FindACab app by opening the Chrome Developer Tools → Resources → Web SQL tab. It will show the FindACab database and the Cabs table with all the records. See Figure 10-4.

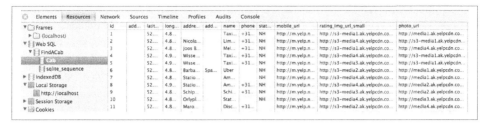

	id	add...	latit...	long...	addre...	add...	name	phone	stat...	mobile_url	rating_img_url_small	photo_url
▼ ☐ Frames												
▶ ☐ (localhost)	1		52...	4.8..			Taxi...	+31...	NH	http://m.yelp.n...	http://s3-media1.ak.yelpcdn.co...	http://media1.ak.yelpcdn.co...
▼ ☐ Web SQL	2		52...	4.8..	Nicola...		Lim...	+31...	NH	http://m.yelp.n...	http://s3-media4.ak.yelpcdn.co...	http://s3-media4.ak.yelpcdn.co...
▼ ☐ FindACab	3		52...	4.8..	Joos B...		Mel...	+31...	NH	http://m.yelp.n...	http://s3-media4.ak.yelpcdn.co...	http://s3-media4.ak.yelpcdn.co...
☐ Cab	4		52...	4.9..	Wisse...		Taxi...	+31...	NH	http://m.yelp.n...	http://s3-media4.ak.yelpcdn.co...	http://s3-media1.ak.yelpcdn...
☐ sqlite_sequence	5		52...	4.9..	Wisse...		Taxi...	+31...	NH	http://m.yelp.n...	http://s3-media3.ak.yelpcdn.co...	http://s3-media1.ak.yelpcdn...
	6		52...	4.8..	Barba...	Spa...	Uber		NH	http://m.yelp.n...	http://s3-media2.ak.yelpcdn.co...	http://media1.ak.yelpcdn.co...
▶ ☐ IndexedDB	7		52...	4.8..	Statio...		Am...		NH	http://m.yelp.n...	http://s3-media4.ak.yelpcdn.co...	http://media2.ak.yelpcdn.co...
▼ ☐ Local Storage	8		52...	4.9..	Statio...		Am...	+31...	NH	http://m.yelp.n...	http://s3-media4.ak.yelpcdn.co...	http://media2.ak.yelpcdn.co...
☐ http://localhost	9		52...	4.8..	Schip...		Schi...	+31...	NH	http://m.yelp.n...	http://s3-media3.ak.yelpcdn.co...	http://media3.ak.yelpcdn.co...
▶ ☐ Session Storage	10		52...	4.8..	Orlypl...		Stat...		NH	http://m.yelp.n...	http://s3-media4.ak.yelpcdn.co...	http://media3.ak.yelpcdn.co...
▼ ☐ Cookies	11		52...	4.8..	Maro...		Disc...	+31...		http://m.yelp.n...	http://s3-media2.ak.yelpcdn.co...	http://media4.ak.yelpcdn.co...

Figure 10-4. Chrome Developer Tools → Resources → Web SQL

The next time I load the app, you will notice that there is no request to Yelp made. This is because the database has records!

Do you want to test the downloading process again? In the Chrome Developer Tools → Console, enter the following command: **Ext.getStore("Cabs").removeAll();**. This removes all the items from the store. But you do need to sync the store to see the changes: Ext.getStore("Cabs").sync(). Now refresh the application and notice that the data will download again.

Argh, isn't it annoying that you cannot delete a Web SQL database directly with the Google Chrome Dev Tools? Well, there is a solution to remove a database (and its tables). Just open the following URL in your Google Chrome browser: *chrome://settings/cookies*. Here you can search for any particular site or remove all locally stored data. In my case, I just search for *localhost*, and I get an exact overview of all my cookies, Local Storage, and Web SQL databases. I can double-click a database, and I'll be prompted to remove the database. I click the Remove button, and it is gone!

Saving Assets Locally by Using the Application Cache

The last technique in this chapter I would like to discuss is not a client proxy. However, it is a technique for making your application available offline, without downloading the stylesheets, images, Sencha Touch framework, and custom classes. It will create a cached version of your mobile app by setting up a HTML5 cache manifest file, better known as the HTML5 AppCache.

AppCache is extremely handy for users who want to bookmark their mobile apps to their phone home screen. This is nice because the browser address bar will be gone, so it will give you a more native experience.

Whereas Web Storage saves key/value pairs in the browser's Local or Session Storage, AppCache has the HTML5 ability to save (*cache*) a whole web app (the *index.html* file and all its assets, such as stylesheets, JavaScript, images, icons, fonts, etc.) in the browser's cache to make it available, even if the client has no Internet connection at all.

The Application Cache manifest file is a simple text file that lists the resources that the browser should cache for offline access. Another reason for using AppCache is speed (because it caches and therefore loads faster) and performance (it reduces server load).

 Read the W3C spec about AppCache (*http://bit.ly/apps-offline*). Also, take a look at Jake Archibald's blog post (*http://bit.ly/appcache-db*) at A List Apart about troubleshooting AppCache.

Now how can you implement this? You don't have to do much to make Application Cache work. First, you will have to edit the *app.json* file; it should define the `appCache` object. Let's take a look:

```
"appCache": {
    "cache": [
        "index.html",
        "resources/css/app.css"
    ],
```

The `cache` section lists all the items that need to be cached. Make sure that these files exist, or else the caching will fail (and if it fails, you will not be happy):

```
"network": [
    "*"
],
```

The `network` section is basically used for (white) listing files that require an online connection. All requests to these resources bypass the cache, even if the browser is offline. Note you can also set this to a wildcard, `*`. This might be handy when the files from the cache section are cached but some assets are not listed and therefore missing. It will make sure that those unlisted assets will still be downloaded, no matter what. If I didn't create a network section that points to the wildcard, then the application would miss these files:

```
"fallback": [
    //fall back items
]
}//end appCache
```

The `fallback` section in the app cache file will let us list fallback solutions for when a request fails. See, for example, the line `resources/images/resources/images/place holder.gif`. If any image in the *resources/images* folder fails, it will display the *place-holder.png* file.

Then build the application with Sencha Cmd:

```
sencha app build
```

Be aware that the Application Cache can be a pain sometimes for the following reasons:

- You cannot specify an expiration date/time for files in the cache. But you can expire the cache by making a change to the manifest file—for example, by adding a comment. Any change to the file causes all files to be recached. This is what Sencha does: it changes the Application Cache manifest by adding comments that represent generated unique keys.

- If any of the files listed on the manifest are not found, no caching will occur.

- While waiting for the manifest file, the browser will load the site from the cache. Therefore, changes to your cache manifest are acted upon only after a *second* refresh from when the file was modified.

- Manually clearing the browser cache from the Google Chrome Dev Tools does not force all files to be recached.

Let's see how the Application Cache manifest for a Sencha production build will look after we build the application. Sencha generated the *cache.appcache* manifest file shown in Example 10-2.

Example 10-2. build/FindACab/production/cache.appcache

```
CACHE MANIFEST
# 012e27c4c1189aa484c92bd7bf3740cb89395da7
index.html


FALLBACK:


NETWORK:
*
```

The Sencha production build of the app makes sure that the manifest file is loaded by adding the following attribute into the <html> tag of the *index.html* file: `manifest="cache.appcache"`. The manifest file will be present in the project root.

 A manifest file must be served with the MIME-type `text/cache-manifest`. You may need to add this custom file type to your web server or to a *.htaccess* file: `AddType text/cache-manifest .appcache`.

It might be handy to get an overview to see which files are cached by the browser. When using the Google Chrome Developer Tools (or Safari Dev Tools), you can inspect the files in your AppCache under the Resources → Application Cache heading. See Figure 10-5.

Figure 10-5. Resources → Application Cache

How do you clean *app.cache* files? Browse with Google Chrome to *chrome://appcache-internals/*, and click the Remove link for the corresponding website or app.

So actually that is all there is to it. Creating a production build will do the trick; you just have to maintain the list of the files to cache.

Summary

This chapter explained all the possible ways to save application data offline. You can use one of the client proxies, which allows you to sync the data store with the browser memory (default), HTML5 Local Storage, HTML5 Session Storage (saved in the session), or a Web SQL database. When you want to make the full application available for offline usage, you can set up the HTML5 AppCache manifest file, which will cache a version of your app automatically.

If you have followed the tutorials in this book, you will now have the base of the FindACab app ready: a configured `Cabs` store that loads data from the Yelp web service and saves it offline with a client Web SQL proxy. Also, you created a `Settings` model that can be validated and eventually can save the data to the Local Storage with a `localstorage` client proxy.

But the FindACab app doesn't display anything yet. That's because we still haven't talked about views and UI (user interface) components. So now is the time to do that—let's create some good-looking applications!

View Components

This chapter is all about view components. I will discuss how to implement message-boxes, lists, panels, toolbars, charts, and maps. Of course, there are many other components included in Sencha Touch, such as tabpanels, carousels, dataviews, progress-bars, and touch grids.

Whatever view component you choose, the implementation for all components is more or less the same because components all extend from `Ext.Component`. To display views on your screen, you will either nest them via the `xtype` property (the object literal way), or you create an instance via `Ext.create()`. You can also define your own blueprint of a view component by extending from an existing Sencha Touch view component.

Nobody knows all the component class properties off the top of her head, and the thing is, you don't need to. This is where the API docs come into play. Just open the docs (*http://docs.sencha.com/touch/2.3.1*), search for the view component (e.g., `Ext.List`) and browse through all its configs and methods.

The FindACab app does not have a face yet. We need to start creating views. This chapter will show you a couple of techniques for creating view component instances used for the FindACab app. Knowing these, you can easily master all the view components in general. Let's start with the very early basics, such as implementing a messagebox.

In this chapter, you'll learn how to implement:

- A messagebox
- Toolbars and title bars
- Buttons
- Lists
- A Google Map

- Overlays
- Charts

Implementing a Messagebox

Unlike the standard JavaScript `alert` method, a messagebox in Sencha Touch is asynchronous. In standard JavaScript, the browser pauses execution until you press OK. In Sencha Touch, showing a messagebox will not cause the code to stop. For this reason, if you have code that should run only after some user feedback from the messagebox, you should use a callback function.

When you want to implement a messagebox, you will have to require `Ext.Message Box` at the top of your view class. You don't need to instantiate a messagebox (although you could); `Ext.Msg` is a global shared singleton instance of the `Ext.MessageBox` class that you can use in most cases:

```
Ext.Msg.alert('Title', 'The quick brown fox jumped over the lazy dog.',
    function(){
    //callback
    console.log(arguments);
});
```

The previous code describes the `alert()` method, which you can visually compare with the standard `alert` messagebox in JavaScript. See Figure 11-1.

Figure 11-1. An alert messagebox in Sencha Touch

It displays a small window, with a title, a message, and an OK button. In addition to the `alert`, there are these types of messageboxes:

- `prompt()`, shown in Figure 11-2, which is a messagebox with a title, message, a textfield, and Cancel and OK buttons
- `confirm()`, shown in Figure 11-3, which is a messagebox with a title, a message, and No and Yes buttons
- `show()`, which provides even more options.

Here's an example of the `prompt()` messagebox; the callback contains the button `id` and the entered value. The button `id` can be Yes, No, or Cancel (Cancel means close the messagebox without pressing the Yes and No buttons):

```
Ext.Msg.prompt('Welcome', 'Please enter your name', function(btn, val){
    //callback
    console.log(btn, val);
});
```

Figure 11-2. A prompt() messagebox in Sencha Touch

Here's an example of the `confirm()` messagebox; the callback contains the button `id`, which can be Yes, No, or Cancel (Cancel means close the messagebox without pressing the Yes and No buttons):

```
Ext.Msg.confirm('Reload', 'Do you want to reload the page?', function(btn){
    //callback
    console.log(btn);
});
```

Figure 11-3. A confirm() messagebox in Sencha Touch

There is one more messagebox method that is worth mentioning: `show()`. As you can see, the `alert()`, `prompt()`, and `confirm()` methods are pretty basic. The `show()` method will give you many more options; you can pass in a `config` object. Here I set up a customized `prompt()` messagebox. It has a `width` of 500 pixels, it accepts multiline input, it has an info icon, and I want to specify my own set of buttons. Also, I will define a callback function:

```
var myPromptBox = Ext.Msg.show({
    title: 'Address',
    message: 'Please enter your address:',
    width: 500,
    buttons: Ext.MessageBox.YESNOCANCEL,
    iconCls: Ext.MessageBox.QUESTION,
    multiLine: true,
    prompt : { maxlength : 180, autocapitalize : true },
    fn: function(buttonId) {
        alert('You pressed the "' + buttonId + '" button.');
    }
});
```

The `iconCls` can set an icon CSS class on the messagebox to showcase an icon. You can maintain this in your theme, but out of the box Sencha Touch ships with the following messagebox icons:

- `Ext.MessageBox.ERROR` (a round error sign)
- `Ext.MessageBox.INFO` (a round info sign)
- `Ext.MessageBox.QUESTION` (a question mark)
- `Ext.MessageBox.WARNING` (a warning sign)

The following sets of `buttons` are available in Sencha Touch:

- `Ext.MessageBox.OK` (OK button with `action` UI skin)
- `Ext.MessageBox.YES` (Yes button with `action` UI skin)
- `Ext.MessageBox.NO` (No button)
- `Ext.MessageBox.CANCEL` (Cancel button)
- `Ext.MessageBox.YESNOCANCEL` (Cancel button, No button, and Yes button with `action` UI skin)
- `Ext.MessageBox.OKCANCEL` (Cancel button, and OK button with `action` UI skin)
- `Ext.MessageBox.YESNO` (No button, and Yes button with `action` UI skin)

 You can test these button sets in the Sencha API docs, which contain an iframe with live preview and code example (JS Duck). It allows you to directly test and preview view components.

If these button sets are in the wrong order, or you would like to specify your own button text and UI skins, you can pass in an array with `Ext.Buttons` into the `buttons` config, as you can see in Figure 11-4:

```
var pirateBox = Ext.Msg.show({
    title: 'Ahoy!',
    message: 'Stop pirate, would ye like t\' proceed?',
    iconCls: Ext.MessageBox.ERROR,
    width: 200,
    buttons: [
        {text: 'Aye', itemId: 'yes', ui: 'action'},
        {text: 'Avast',  itemId: 'no', ui: 'decline'}
    ],
    fn: function(buttonId) {
        alert('You pressed the "' + buttonId + '" button.');
    }
});
```

Figure 11-4. A customized messagebox, with custom icon and buttons

To hide the previous messagebox, just run the `hide()` method on the `pirateBox`.

The FindACab app also uses an `Ext.MessageBox`. Take a look at *app.js*; this autogenerated code has a confirmation messagebox. If there is a newer version of your app available online, the Sencha Touch app will automatically update the dependencies (saved in the *deltas* folder after a production build). After updating the code, the confirmation messagebox will ask you to reload the page:

```
Ext.Msg.confirm(
    "Application Update",
    "This application has just successfully been" +
      " updated to the latest version. Reload now?",
    function(buttonId) {
        if (buttonId === 'yes') {
            window.location.reload();
        }
    }
);
```

The confirm method takes three arguments: a title, a message, and a callback function that reloads the page if the user pressed the Yes button. This is nice, but knowing how to code a messagebox still won't give our FindACab app a face. So let's discuss how to implement toolbars next.

Implementing Toolbars and Title Bars

When you want to implement a toolbar (or title bar) view component (Figure 11-5), you will have to add the Ext.Toolbar (or Ext.TitleBar) to the requires at the top of your view class. After that, you can instantiate the component by using the Ext.cre ate("Ext.Toolbar", {}) syntax, or by lazy instantiating (nesting the xtype called toolbar). Using the xtype is the best practice for coding real-world MVC applications.

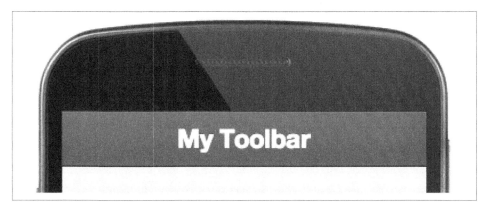

Figure 11-5. A preview of a toolbar in Sencha Touch

Either way, you will use the object literal notation for specifying the configs, such as title for setting the title or docked for making the toolbar dock to the top, bottom, left, or right:

```
{
    xtype: 'toolbar', //or 'title bar'
    docked: 'top',
    title: 'Text',
```

```
    items: [{
        text: 'Button'
    }]
}
```

There are many additional configs you can set for Ext.Toolbar, so check the API docs for more in-depth information.

Implementing a title bar works exactly the same. The only difference is that the class from which you implement the instance is called Ext.TitleBar and the xtype is called titlebar. Although the title bar does not extend from Ext.Toolbar, they have a very similar appearance and setup, as you can see in Figure 11-6. The main difference between a Ext.TitleBar and a Ext.Toolbar is that the title config is always centered horizontally in a title bar, between any items aligned left or right. By default, any item in a title bar or toolbar is a button, so you do not need to explicitly set it. Items in a title bar, such as buttons, can be docked to the left or right side of the bar, via the align config.

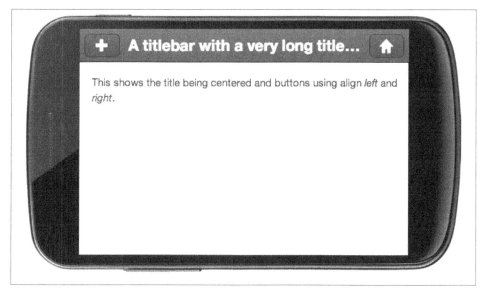

Figure 11-6. A preview of a title bar in Sencha Touch

When you create a tool or title bar, your view immediately looks *mobile*. Let's take a look again at the FindACab app. I have created three new views (or actually two, because *app/view/Main.js* was already generated, but I have changed the contents): FindA Cab.view.Main, FindACab.view.Overview, and FindACab.view.DetailView.

The *Main* view is nothing more than an `Ext.Container` with the layout set to `hbox` to horizontally align the two new views, `overview` and `detailview`. Take a look at *view/Main.js* and also notice the `requires`:

```
Ext.define('FindACab.view.Main', {
    extend: 'Ext.Container',
    requires: [
        'FindACab.view.Overview',
        'FindACab.view.DetailView'
    ],
    config: {
        layout: 'hbox',
        items: [{
                xtype: 'overview',
                flex: 1,
                store: 'Cabs'
        }, {
                xtype: 'detailview',
                flex: 3
        }]
    }
});
```

We created an empty `overview` component. Later you will build an `Ext.List` view there.

What else? You can set a `flex` property. *Flexing* means that you divide the available area based on the `flex` value of each child component (i.e., sizes are a ratio). For more information about flexing and layouts, flip back to Chapter 5.

Next, let's code the *view/Overview.js* view:

```
Ext.define('FindACab.view.Overview', {
    extend: 'Ext.Container',
    xtype: 'overview',
    requires: [
        'Ext.TitleBar',
    ],
    config: {
        items: [{
                xtype: 'titlebar',
                docked: 'top',
                title: 'Overview'
        }],

        html: 'list here'
    }
});
```

The `overview` component is just a simple container. It has an `html` config to stub out the view. The fancy stuff is the `titlebar` in the `items` array.

The code for *view/DetailView.js* will be almost the same, only this time you'll use the titlebar. It contains one child item with the xtype set to titlebar. (Make sure that the requires array requires Ext.TitleBar so the class loader loads the correct class.) Dock the toolbar to the top by setting docked: 'top', use a lighter variant of the UI by setting ui: 'light', and pass the title FindACab.

```
{
  xtype: 'titlebar',
  ui: 'light',
  docked: 'top',
  title: 'FindACab',
},
```

That's not all. The title bar should have a settings button aligned to the right of the title bar. This button should display a gear icon. Take a look at the items array, which has one child item (by default, a button) with the following configs: iconCls for choosing the icon CSS class (the settings icon CSS class points to the gear icon that ships with the framework), align for setting the alignment, and ui for changing the skin of the button:

```
items: [{
    iconCls: 'settings',
    ui: 'plain',
    align: 'right'
}]
```

By now, you should see two toolbars, and a stubbed-out overview and detail view (see Figure 11-7). Here is the complete code for *view/DetailView.js*:

```
Ext.define('FindACab.view.DetailView', {
    extend: 'Ext.Container',
    xtype: 'detailview',
    requires: [
        'Ext.TitleBar',
        'Ext.Button'
    ],
    config: {
        items: [{
            xtype: 'titlebar',
            ui: 'light',
            docked: 'top',
            title: 'FindACab',
            items: [{
                iconCls: 'settings',
                ui: 'plain',
                align: 'right'
            }]
        }],
        html: 'detail view'
    }
});
```

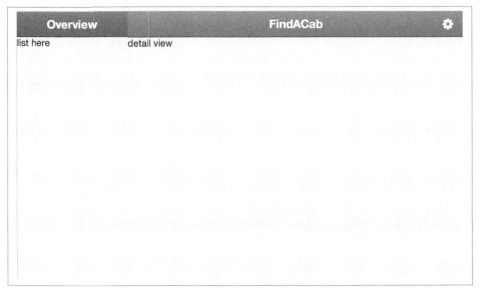

Figure 11-7. Your FindACab app should look like this after you implement the title bars

Implementing Buttons

When you are implementing buttons, it makes the most sense to create a new instance from the Ext.Button class by nesting the xtype called button. You will use the object literal notation for specifying the configs, such as text to set the button text:

```
{
    xtype: 'button',
    handler: function(){
        //Do something
    },
    iconCls: 'compose',
    text: 'Compose',
    ui: 'confirm'
}
```

Again, make sure you have added the Ext.Button to the requires array at the top of your view class so the Ext.Loader can load the framework class.

Buttons have events. When talking about buttons, you think about events. You can *click* on it. When it's a Touch application you can't really click on it, you *tap* it. Mobile browsers that support touch event bindings (e.g., WebKit) also have to support click bindings on the components; otherwise, you couldn't use the app on desktop environments. So for every tap in an app, a click is fired right along with it.

The `tap` event fires when the button is tapped. It takes the following arguments `tap(this, e, eOpts)`, where `this` is the button component `Ext.Button`, `e` is the event object `Ext.EventObject`, and `eOpts` is the options object that is passed the `Ext.util.Ob servable.addListener` method.

The `release` event fires when the button is released. It takes the arguments as the `tap` event. Both event actions are preventable. When any of the listeners returns `false`, the action is cancelled, to prevent execution.

Some devices are both a laptop and a touch device. They support tap, pinch, and swipe gestures as well as keyboard/mouse events. Think about the Microsoft Surface Pro or Chromebook Pixel. With the release of Sencha Touch 2.2, both mouse and touch events are allowed at the same time. You don't need to code anything special! Want to read more about creating apps for the Chromebook Pixel? Check out this great blog post on DailyJS (*http://bit.ly/dailyjs-pixel*).

Buttons can also contain an icon. Out of the box, Sencha Touch ships with a nice set of icons. All of these icons are from an *icon font*, a font built from scalable vector icons. This is pretty awesome. A font is small and fast to download, plus it's easy to scale and style these vector icons with CSS code—which means they look beautiful on retina displays. Sencha Touch is using the Pictos (*http://pictos.cc/font/*) icon font, but if you want, you can add or create your own custom icon fonts as well.

Check Chapter 13 for more information about implementing (icon) fonts. The icons implemented in the Pictos font by Sencha Touch are mapped to readable text strings. You can use these mapping names as `iconCls` values. See Figure 11-8 for a complete overview of all the icons shipped with Sencha Touch. Not all of these mappings work out of the box; some need to be enabled in the Sass stylesheet.

There are different button *skins* (see Figure 11-9). In Sencha terminology this is called a *UI*. Some components in Sencha Touch can have a different skin, a different look than the default design. Under the hood, these UIs are Sass mixins (we will discuss mixins in Chapter 13). The mixin for Sencha Touch buttons is called `$sencha-button-ui`.

You can create your own skins for buttons in the Sass stylesheet (as described in Chapter 13). You can set the UI with the `ui` config.

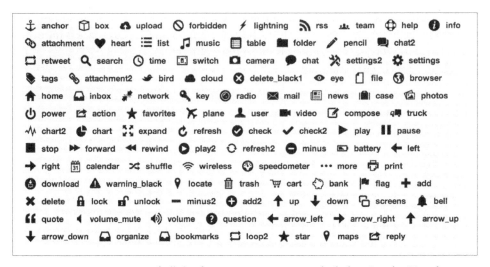

Figure 11-8. An overview of all the font icon mappings included in Sencha Touch

Out of the box, buttons can apply the following UIs:

- normal (a basic gray button)
- back (a back button in the shape of an arrow to the left)
- forward (a forward button in the shape of an arrow to the right)
- small (a small button)
- round (a round button)

The following UIs are like the normal button UI but with a different color, which can be handy for visualizing an action:

- action (dark blue by default; use $active-color in the Sass stylesheet to change the color)
- decline (red by default; use $alert-color in the Sass stylesheet to change the color)
- confirm (green by default; use $confirm-color in the Sass stylesheet to change the color)

You can also append -round or -small to each of the last three colored UIs to give it a round or small shape:

- action-round
- decline-round
- confirm-round

- action-small
- decline-small
- confirm-small

Figure 11-9. An overview of all button UIs in Sencha Touch

There are many different kinds of buttons—confirmation buttons, decline buttons, round buttons—and they all show up in different places, such as toolbars, title bars, or forms. In fact, Sencha tabpanels also consist of buttons! Every tab extends from the Ext.Button class, so you can use the same properties and methods on tabs. So an Ext.TabPanel (Figure 11-10) is nothing more then a collection of containers stacked on top of each other (with a card layout, Ext.layout.Card) and a set of buttons docked on the top or bottom of the tabpanel.

Figure 11-10. A preview of a tabpanel in Sencha Touch

Buttons may also have a badge (see Figure 11-11). When you hear the word *badges*, you might think about some emblem or token to showcase some achievement. This is exactly what a button badge is in Sencha Touch. It's a little bullet that displays information about something that's been achieved. For example, in iOS when you receive a new email, you will see a red badge with a counter on top of the app icon. Sencha Touch badges are just like that. You can set or get a badge text string badgeText—getBadgeText() and set BadgeText()—or add a CSS class with the badgeCls config.

Figure 11-11. A preview of button badges in Sencha Touch

There is another type of button that might be interesting: the segmented button (shown in Figure 11-12). The Ext.SegmentedButton is a container for a group of buttons. It looks like a big pill and by default you can press just one "segment" (like the behavior of HTML radio buttons), although you can allow for pressing multiple segments with the allowMultiple config. The segmentedbutton has a toggle event that takes the arguments toggle(this, button, isPressed, eOpts), where this is the full segmen tedbutton, button is the button that is toggled, and isPressed is a boolean that indi- cates whether the button is pressed in or out. Generally, a segmented button would be a child of a Ext.Toolbar and would be used to switch between different views.

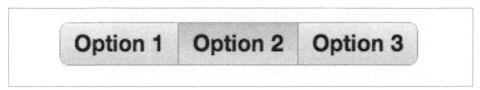

Figure 11-12. A preview of the segmented button in Sencha Touch

There are a lot more configs you can set for Ext.Button, so check the API docs for more in-depth information.

Implementing Lists

Let's talk about one of the Sencha Touch components that Sencha Touch is most famous for: the list component (list scroller). Sencha Touch has a list scroller that gives you the total native experience—not only in the way it looks but also in its performance.

A list is a data-aware component. You will need to hook up a data store to the list (with a fields model) to display any items. Following is an example of an Ext.List. First you must make sure you add the Ext.List to the requires array at the top of your view class so the Ext.Loader can load the framework class. Afterward you will use the object literal notation to create a Sencha Touch list:

```
{
    xtype: 'list',
    store: {
        fields: ['name'],
        data: [
            {name: 'Leonardo'},
            {name: 'Donatello'},
            {name: 'Michelangelo'},
            {name: 'Raphael'}
        ]
    },
    itemTpl: '{name}'
}
```

A Sencha Touch Ext.List extends from Ext.dataview.DataView. The dataview renders all the items of a store into the component. What makes a list a Sencha Touch list is the custom styling (it looks just like a native list), which allows mechanisms for grouping, indexing, or filtering data with an optional index bar or pinned headers, and optional disclosure icons and labels on each item.

Because stores are attached to a dataview or list, any changes to the store are immediately reflected on the screen. For example, if you add a new record to the store it will be rendered into the list immediately. The list component will use the tpl config for rendering the data (model fields) in curly bracket placeholders.

You can also attach listeners to events on the list. The following events are available:

- refresh(list)
- select(list, record)
- deselect(list, record)

These all have the same signature of (`list, index, target, record, event`):

- itemtap
- itemdoubletap
- itemtaphold
- itemsingletap
- itemswipe
- itemtouchstart
- itemtouchend
- itemtouchmove

Events can be implemented via the `listeners` object:

```
listeners: {
    select: function(view, record) {
        Ext.Msg.alert('Selected!', 'You selected ' + record.get('name'));
    }
}
```

When you want to dock items to the bottom or top of a list, use the `scrollDock` configuration on child `items` in the list. Here is an example of a toolbar docked under the list:

```
items: [{
    xtype: 'toolbar',
    scrollDock: 'bottom', //magic!
    docked: 'bottom',
    title: 'people'
}]
```

Sencha Touch lists are optimized for the best performance. Figure 11-13 shows how this works. Previously, in Sencha Touch 1.x, you would render all your store items in the DOM. This would be inefficient on a mobile phone with less processing power. It becomes an even larger issue when every list item has CSS3 shadows, gradients, and so on. Luckily, this is changed. As you can see in Figure 11-13, list items are being reused. This makes it much faster to repopulate a list item as soon it is out of the screen, rather than having all items already in the DOM.

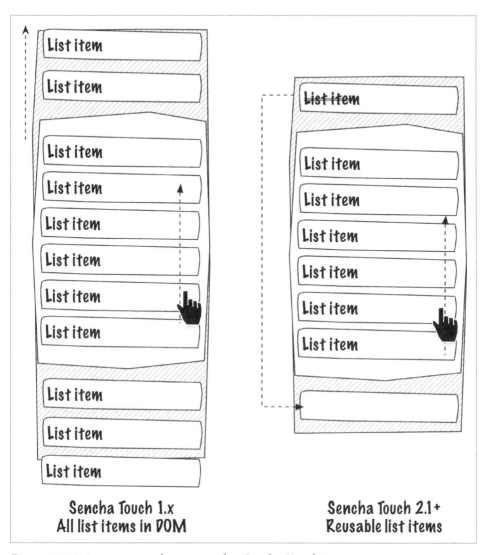

Figure 11-13. *List items are being reused in Sencha Touch 2*

Implementing a List for the FindACab App

Let's take a look at the FindACab app. You will finalize the previously stubbed-out custom Overview class. First, you will extend from Ext.List. This list has an emptyText config set to the string "No data", which will be displayed when there are no items in the store. Remember, the store was set in the FindACab.view.Main class. You can set the *Cabs* store while defining the overview xtype in the *Main.js* view. This way, you can reuse the overview list for other stores too:

```
Ext.define('FindACab.view.Overview', {
    extend: 'Ext.List',
    xtype: 'overview',
    requires: [
        'Ext.TitleBar',
    ],
    config: {
        emptyText: 'No data',
    }
});
```

You can enable grouping with the grouped config. The groupers themselves are set in the Cabs store. You can also enable the disclosure icon with the onItemDisclosure config. This is an icon next to the item text. You do need to build logic for displaying the detail page after tapping this disclose icon, but we will implement this later:

```
grouped: true,
onItemDisclosure: true,
```

You will also set the itemTpl to display the distance in 2 digits and the name in 16 characters:

```
itemTpl: "<span class="distance">{[values.distance.toFixed(2)]}
    </span> {name:ellipsis(16, true)} "+.
```

You will pass in true in the ellipsis formatter function to find a common word break:

```
itemTpl: '<span class="distance"> {[values.distance.toFixed(2)]}' +
    ' </span> {name:ellipsis(16, true)} ',
```

Next, we will add an extra toolbar to the bottom of the list. Define in the items array another docked toolbar and dock it to the bottom:

```
items: [{
    xtype: 'titlebar',
    docked: 'top',
    title: 'Overview'
},{
    xtype: 'toolbar',
    layout: {
        type: 'hbox',
        pack: 'center'
    },
    docked: 'bottom',
    ui: 'light',
}
```

This toolbar will contain two buttons to filter the list. You will nest another items array into this toolbar component. One small button will filter on the TaxiService name and one button will filter on the TaxiService distance. You don't need to specify the xtype as button, because a toolbar and title bar have buttons as items by default.

When a filter button is tapped (handler), it will fire a custom event to CabController. This button will listen to it and filter the overview list:

```
items: [{
    handler: function(){
        this.fireEvent('filtername');
    },
    ui: 'small',
    text: 'name'
},{
    handler: function(){
        this.fireEvent('filterdistance');
    },
    ui: 'small',
    text: 'distance'
}],
```

Here is the complete code for *view/Overview.js*:

```
Ext.define('FindACab.view.Overview', {
    extend: 'Ext.List',
    xtype: 'overview',
    requires: [
        'Ext.TitleBar',
    ],
    config: {
        emptyText: 'No data',
        grouped: true,
        onItemDisclosure: true,

        itemTpl: '<span class="distance">' +
            '{[values.distance.toFixed(2)]}' +
                '</span> {name:ellipsis(16, true)} ',


        items: [{
            xtype: 'titlebar',
            docked: 'top',
            title: 'Overview'
        },{
            xtype: 'toolbar',
            layout: {
                type: 'hbox',
                pack: 'center'
            },
            docked: 'bottom',
            ui: 'light',

            items: [{
                handler: function(){
                    this.fireEvent('filtername');
                },
                ui: 'small',
```

```
                    text: 'name'
            },{
                handler: function(){
                    this.fireEvent('filterdistance');
                },
                ui: 'small',
                text: 'distance'
            }],
        }]
    }
});
```

The two filter buttons have no logic yet. Filtering the list (actually, the store) shouldn't be so hard. See the following code: first you will reference the overview titlebar and the overview list in *controller/CabController.js*, and you will use the refs object so you can refer to the list and the list title bar:

```
refs: {
    'titlebar' : 'overview titlebar',
    'overview': 'overview'
},
```

Next, you will listen to the two custom events, filtername and filterdistance (defined in the *view/Overview.js* button handlers), using the control object:

```
control: {
    'overview toolbar button' : {
        filtername: 'setFilterName',
        filterdistance: 'setFilterDistance'
    }
}
```

When these events occur, you will invoke one of the two new methods in *controller/ CabController.js*: setFilterName and the setFilterDistance. The bodies of setFil terName and setFilterDistance functions run a sort() function. In this example, they also need a store load() function because the data comes from the local Web SQL database and needs to be loaded. If the data had already been in the store, then this step would not be necessary:

```
setFilterName: function() {
    Ext.getStore('Cabs').sort('name');
    Ext.getStore('Cabs').load();
},
setFilterDistance: function() {
    Ext.getStore('Cabs').sort('distance');
    Ext.getStore('Cabs').load();
}
```

That's it. Now that you have finalized the list overview of the FindACab app (see Figure 11-14), let's see how to implement a Google Map. Check out the next technique.

Figure 11-14. Your FindACab app should look like this after you implement the list component

Implementing a Google Map

Sencha Touch uses Google Maps to display geographical data on mobile devices. The `Ext.Map` component wraps a Google Map in an `Ext.Component` using the Google Maps API.

You do need to have a remote connection, which loads the Google API into memory before creating the Sencha Google Map wrapper. Therefore, you can add the URL to the Google Maps API into the *app.json* file's `js` array:

```
"js": [
{
  "path" : "http://maps.google.com/maps/api/js?sensor=true",
  "remote" : "true"
},
..
]
```

You have to specify the remote (true) property to make sure the Google Maps script will download (even when all the other nonremote scripts are loaded from the cache). When the device is offline, you can't download scripts that are specified as "remote": "true".

Implementing the map in your Sencha Touch layout works the same way as implementing any other view component. You will nest the xtype: "map" into the items array of the parent component, and you have to add the Ext.Map to the requires array at the top of your view class:

```
{
    xtype: 'map',
    mapOptions: {
        zoom : 12,
        mapTypeId : google.maps.MapTypeId.ROADMAP,
        //more google maps options here
    },
    useCurrentLocation: false
}
```

The Google Map has a couple of additional properties, mapOptions and useCurrentLocation, that you will use as follows:

- useCurrentLocation is a boolean setting that defaults to false. When set to true, it will center the map based on the geolocation coordinates of the device. It's also possible to specify a Geolocation object instead to have more control over the geolocation used. The Ext.util.Geolocation class provides a cross-browser solution for retrieving location information.

- The mapOptions object specifies the Google API-specific properties. It's possible to specify the key/value pairs as written in the Google Maps API documentation (*http://bit.ly/googlemaps-v3*), such as enabling panControl or scaleControl. However, the zoom level (in integers) needs to be set and the map needs to have a default location to center to.

Take a look at the *view/DetailView.js* code to see how the map for the FindACab app is configured:

First, add two more classes into the requires array to load the Ext.layout.Card and Ext.Map in the memory:

```
requires: [
    'Ext.TitleBar',
    'Ext.Button',
    'Ext.layout.Card', //add the layout class
    'Ext.Map' //add the map class
],
```

To create a stack of cards (panels) on top of each other, set the layout to card; you can add this to the config object. With the card layout, you can navigate through the different cards by setting an active card (see Chapter 5):

```
config: {
  layout: 'card',

  //below is the code (items array) for the toolbar with settings button...
```

Add to the items array the Ext.Map view component. This map will have a Google API mapOptions object to disable most of the interface controls of the Google Map, like pan, rotate, map type, street view, and overview control. Also disable geolocation (via use CurrentLocation):

```
{
  xtype: 'map',
  mapOptions: {
    overviewMapControl: false,
    panControl: false,
    rotateControl: false,
    streetViewControl: false,
    mapTypeControl: false,
    zoom : 12,
    mapTypeId : google.maps.MapTypeId.ROADMAP
  },
  useCurrentLocation: false
},
```

Add another item to the items array to create a second panel in the card layout deck. This will be the detail panel, which contains an Ext.XTemplate with placeholders that can be populated with the data of the selected record. Also, specify padding and a CSS class for future styling:

```
{
  padding: '20',
  cls: 'taxitpl',
  tpl: Ext.create('Ext.XTemplate', '<h1>{name}</h1>' +
    '<address>{address1}<br/>' +
    '{zip} {city} {state_code} {country_code}' +
    '</address>' +
    '<a href="tel:{phone}" class="x-button callnow">' +
    'Call now: {phone} </a><p>Distance: {distance}</p>'),
}
```

Now, the last step: create an items array in the detail panel card, with a button docked to the right side of the details panel. This button fires a custom close event. The Cab Controller can listen to this custom event and switch back to the map view:

```
items: [{
  docked: 'right',
  xtype: 'button',
```

```
            action: 'close',
            cls: 'closebtn',
            iconCls: 'delete',
            padding: 20,
            height: 50,
            handler: function() {
                this.fireEvent('close');
            },
            ui: 'plain'
    }],
```

Here's the complete *view/DetailView.js* code:

```
Ext.define('FindACab.view.DetailView', {
    extend: 'Ext.Container',
    xtype: 'detailview',
    requires: [
        'Ext.TitleBar',
        'Ext.Button',
        'Ext.layout.Card',
        'Ext.Map'
    ],
    config: {
        layout: 'card',
        items: [{
                xtype: 'titlebar',
                ui: 'light',
                docked: 'top',
                title: 'FindACab',
                items: [{
                    iconCls: 'settings',
                    itemId: 'settingsbtn',
                    ui: 'plain',
                    align: 'right'
                }]
            },

            {
                xtype: 'map',
                mapOptions: {
                    overviewMapControl: false,
                    panControl: false,
                    rotateControl: false,
                    streetViewControl: false,
                    mapTypeControl: false,
                    zoom : 12,
                    mapTypeId : google.maps.MapTypeId.ROADMAP
                },
                useCurrentLocation: false
            }, {
                padding: '20',
                cls: 'taxitpl',
                tpl: Ext.create('Ext.XTemplate','<h1>{name}</h1>' +
```

```
                    '<address>{address1}<br/>' +
                    '{zip} {city} {state_code} {country_code}' +
                    '</address>' +
                    '<a href="tel:{phone}" class="x-button callnow">' +
                    'Call now: {phone} </a><p>Distance: {distance}</p>'),

            items: [{
                docked: 'right',
                xtype: 'button',
                action: 'close',
                cls: 'closebtn',
                iconCls: 'delete',
                padding: 20,
                height: 50,
                handler: function() {
                    this.fireEvent('close');
                },
                ui: 'plain'
            }],
        }
    ]
  }
});
```

The Google Maps view might be finished for the FindACab app, but there is still no logic implemented for this app. What this app needs are markers plotted on the Google Map for each taxi company. Once you tap a marker or a taxi company from the overview list, it should open the detail panel and display the TaxiService information. When you press the close button, it should close the detail panel and navigate back to the Google Map.

Sit back and read it carefully; the *controller/CabController.js* is going to be quite long, but we have discussed most of the script already, so I will skip those parts.

First, define a markers array in the config (line 1). This will automatically create a magic getter function. The getter function makes it possible to retrieve the markers array. Later, when markers need to be removed from the map, this array is required to loop through all the markers. After this, add a reference to the detailview (line 2):

```
markers: [], //1

refs: {
    'titlebar': 'overview titlebar',
    'overview': 'overview',
    'detailView': 'detailview' //2
},
```

The next step is to add three more event listeners to the control object. You will listen to the maprender event (line 3). As soon as the map is rendered, it should invoke the loadMarkers() function. You will also listen to the select event on the overview list (line 4). As soon as a taxi company is selected, it should invoke the `prefillDetail()` function. When the close button is tapped, it will fire a custom `close` event. The controller will listen to the `close` event (line 5). As soon as this event is fired, it should invoke the `onDetailClose()` function:

```
control: {
    'overview toolbar button': {
        filtername: 'setFilterName',
        filterdistance: 'setFilterDistance'
    },
    'map': {
        maprender: 'loadMarkers' //3
    },
    'overview': {
        select: 'prefillDetail' //4
    },
    'detailview button[action=close]': {
        close: 'onDetailClose' //5
    },
}
```

In order to display, the map requires a point to center on. When there is data available (the `else` in the `loadLocal()` check), let's center the map on the lat/long position of the first item (line 6). Then load the markers in the map with the `loadMarkers()` function and pass in the reference to the `Ext.Map` wrapper and the reference to the Google Map itself (line 7). Because you know the total of `TaxiService` items in the store, you can update the `list overview` title bar with the correct number (line 8). Remember, although you can request 20 items from the web service through the proxy, only 16 items will display because of the `filter` implemented in the store:

```
var lat = item[0].get('latitude');
var lng = item[0].get('longitude');
var position = new google.maps.LatLng(lat,lng);
var map = Ext.ComponentQuery.query('map')[0];
map.getMap().setCenter(position); //6

me.loadMarkers(map, map.getMap()); //7
me.setTitleCount(count); //8

Ext.Viewport.unmask();;
```

Every time the `Cabs` store is synced (the retrieval of new records), it should update the map with new markers. At the bottom of the `syncRecords()` class method, in the second `sync()` callback, invoke `loadMarkers()` and pass in the reference to the map:

```
me.loadMarkers(Ext.ComponentQuery.query('map')[0]);
```

Unfortunately, the Google API has no `remove-marker-from-map` method. The idea is to loop through all the markers and remove the connection from the marker to the map (line 10). You will write this `removeMarkers()` function:

```
removeMarkers: function() {
    var me = this,
        markers = me.getMarkers(),
        total = markers.length;

    for (var i = 0; i < total; i++) {
        markers[i].setMap(null); //10
    }
    markers.splice(0, total);
    me.setMarkers(markers);
},
```

This next big function, loadMarkers(), looks complicated, but this is what it does: first it gets references to the store, markers, overview list, and the map. Then it removes all the current markers from the map (line 11).

It will loop through every item in the data store and create from every model latitude and longitude floating-point numbers, a real Google Maps LatLng object (line 12). With this LatLng object, a marker can be created and plotted to the map.

Center the map based on the lat/long coordinates of the first item in the store (line 13).

Create Google Markers with the Google LatLng object, a reference to the map, and a marker image (line 14). After creation, add the marker to the class markers array, so later you can refer to it.

Add an event listener (line 15), which listens for a marker click, and bind a record to it. Every time a marker gets selected, select the matching record in the overview list. The overview list will handle the event listeners for every selection and invoke the prefill Detail() method.

At last, plot the marker on the Google Map (line 16).

```
loadMarkers: function(comp, map) {
    var me = this,
        store = Ext.getStore('Cabs'),
        markers = me.getMarkers(),
        gm = comp.getMap(),
        list = me.getOverview();

    //clear markers when stored
    if (markers.length > 0) me.removeMarkers(); //11

    store.each(function(item, index, length) {
        var latlng = new google.maps.LatLng(item.get('latitude'),
            item.get('longitude')); //12

        //center the map based on the latlng of the first item.
        if (index === 0) comp.setMapCenter(latlng); //13

        var marker = new google.maps.Marker({ //14
```

```
                map: gm,
                position: latlng,
                icon: 'resources/images/marker.png'
            });
            markers.push(marker);

            google.maps.event.addListener(marker, 'click', function() { //15
                var i = store.indexOf(item);
                list.select(i);
            });

            me.setMarkers(markers); //16
        });
    },
```

Every time an item in the list gets selected, navigate to the detail panel. The map and the detail panel are both in a card layout, so you can navigate by setting the detail panel card to active. (It's the second card in the [zero-based] card deck.) Finally, set the detail panel by setting the record data to the selected record (line 17):

```
    prefillDetail: function(list, record) { //17
        this.getDetailView().getLayout().setAnimation({
            type: 'slide',
            direction: 'up'
        });
        this.getDetailView().setActiveItem(1);
        this.getDetailView().getActiveItem().setData(record.getData());
    },
```

Every time the panel close button gets tapped, navigate back to the map. The map and the detail panel are both in a card layout, so you can navigate by setting the map card to active. (It's the first card in the [zero-based] card deck.) Finally, deselect the item from the overview list (line 18):

```
    onDetailClose: function() { //18
        this.getDetailView().getLayout().setAnimation({
            type: 'slide',
            direction: 'down'
        });
        this.getDetailView().setActiveItem(0);
        this.getOverview().deselectAll();
    }
```

Here's the complete *controller/CabController.js* code:

```
Ext.define('FindACab.controller.CabController', {
    extend: 'Ext.app.Controller',

    config: {
        models: ['Cab'],
        stores: ['Cabs'],
        markers: [], //1
```

```
    refs: {
        'titlebar': 'overview titlebar',
        'overview': 'overview',
        'detailView': 'detailview' //2
    },
    control: {
        'overview toolbar button': {
            filtername: 'setFilterName',
            filterdistance: 'setFilterDistance'
        },
        'map': {
            maprender: 'loadMarkers' //3
        },
        'overview': {
            select: 'prefillDetail' //4
        },
        'detailview button[action=close]': {
            close: 'onDetailClose' //5
        },
    }
},

launch: function() { },

loadLocal: function() {
    /*
     * Load the data from the local database and
     * check if database has some records.
     * if not, then download data else hide the loading mask.
     */
    var me = this;
    Ext.getStore('Cabs').load(function(item) {
        var count = Ext.getStore('Cabs').getCount();
        if (count < 1) {
            me.downloadData();
        } else {
            var lat = item[0].get('latitude');
            var lng = item[0].get('longitude');
            var position = new google.maps.LatLng(lat,lng);
            var map = Ext.ComponentQuery.query('map')[0];
            map.getMap().setCenter(position); //6

            me.loadMarkers(map, map.getMap()); //7
            me.setTitleCount(count); //8

            Ext.Viewport.unmask();;
        }
    });
},

downloadData: function(location) { },
```

```
syncRecords: function(records, userinput) {
    /*
     * Loop through all the items that are downloaded
     * and add these to the items array.
     */
    //...

    /*
     * Switch the Cabs store proxy back to the
     * SQL local proxy
     */
    //...

    /*
     * remove current items from the database.
     * and sync this first.
     */
    store.removeAll();
    store.sync({
        success: function(batch){
            /*
             * Add the downloaded items array to the Cabs store
             * and sync() the store to start saving the
             * records locally.
             * When it is done, we can remove the loading mask.
             */
            store.add(items);
            store.sync({
                success: function(batch){
                    // BEGIN COMPONENTS-CAB-CONTROLLER-4
                    me.loadMarkers(Ext.ComponentQuery.query('map')[0]);
                    // END COMPONENTS-CAB-CONTROLLER-4
                    me.setTitleCount(store.getCount());
                    store.load();
                    Ext.Viewport.unmask();
                }
            });
        }
    });

},

setFilterName: function() { },
setFilterDistance: function() { },
setTitleCount: function(count) { },

removeMarkers: function() {
    var me = this,
        markers = me.getMarkers(),
        total = markers.length;

    for (var i = 0; i < total; i++) {
```

```
            markers[i].setMap(null); //10
        }
        markers.splice(0, total);
        me.setMarkers(markers);
    },

    loadMarkers: function(comp, map) {
        var me = this,
            store = Ext.getStore('Cabs'),
            markers = me.getMarkers(),
            gm = comp.getMap(),
            list = me.getOverview();

        //clear markers when stored
        if (markers.length > 0) me.removeMarkers(); //11

        store.each(function(item, index, length) {
            var latlng = new google.maps.LatLng(item.get('latitude'),
                item.get('longitude')); //12

            //center the map based on the latlng of the first item.
            if (index === 0) comp.setMapCenter(latlng); //13

            var marker = new google.maps.Marker({ //14
                map: gm,
                position: latlng,
                icon: 'resources/images/marker.png'
            });
            markers.push(marker);

            google.maps.event.addListener(marker, 'click', function() { //15
                var i = store.indexOf(item);
                list.select(i);
            });

            me.setMarkers(markers); //16
        });
    },

    prefillDetail: function(list, record) { //17
        this.getDetailView().getLayout().setAnimation({
            type: 'slide',
            direction: 'up'
        });
        this.getDetailView().setActiveItem(1);
        this.getDetailView().getActiveItem().setData(record.getData());
    },
    onDetailClose: function() { //18
        this.getDetailView().getLayout().setAnimation({
            type: 'slide',
            direction: 'down'
        });
```

```
            this.getDetailView().setActiveItem(0);
            this.getOverview().deselectAll();
    }

});
```

Now that the Google Map for the FindACab app is implemented (Figure 11-15), let's prepare a form view so the user can enter a proper location. The next technique will discuss how to invoke a pop-up overlay that will later display a form.

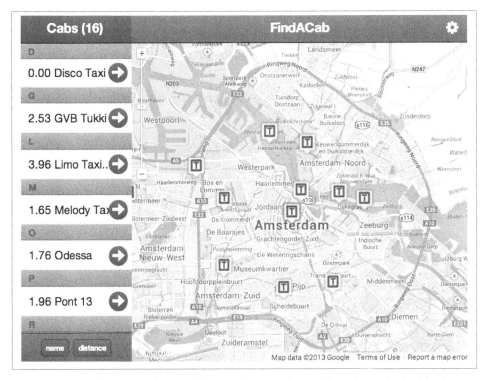

Figure 11-15. After we implement the Google Map, the FindACab app looks like this

Implementing Overlays

Panels extend from Ext.Container. When you don't touch the configurations, they can even look like containers. What's the difference between panels and containers? Panels can float as an overlay on top of your app, as shown in Figure 11-16. They can contain extra styling like a rounded black border with a shade, or they might contain an arrow pointing to a referring component so it will look like a speech bubble or tool tip.

Figure 11-16. A tip overlay shown by a button

If you don't need all these capabilities, you should use `Ext.Container` instead; it will create less overhead in the DOM code. This is different than in Sencha Ext JS. In Ext JS, the panel also subclasses the container, but it's not used for overlays; instead it's used to display a title header and to visually define a block with borders. The closest comparable component to Sencha Touch panel overlays is the Ext JS `Ext.window.Window` class.

To show an overlay centered in the screen, you could add the panel to the viewport. (There is just one viewport, the highest parent container that is generated in the DOM and resizes based on device screen size.) See the following code:

```
Ext.Viewport.add({
    xtype: 'panel',
    centered: true,
    modal: true
});
```

Make sure you add `Ext.Panel` into the `requires` array in the top of your view class. Often, when I create overlays I add those once, hidden to the viewport:

```
if(!this.overlay){
  this.overlay = Ext.Viewport.add({
    xtype: 'panel',
```

```
        itemId: 'settingsview',
        modal: true,
        hideOnMaskTap: true,
        centered: true,
        width: 320,
        height: 380,
        hidden: true,
        html: 'Content here',
        showAnimation: {
            type: 'popIn',
            duration: 250,
            easing: 'ease-out'
        },
        hideAnimation: {
            type: 'popOut',
            duration: 150,
            easing: 'ease-out'
        }
    });
}
```

As soon as I want to invoke them, I inject the data and show() the panel:

```
Ext.ComponentQuery.query('#settingsview')[0].show();
```

While closing the panel I just hide() the overlay again. This way, I am 100% sure that I created the overlay just once in the DOM:

```
Ext.ComponentQuery.query('#settingsview')[0].hide();
```

You can center overlays on the screen by setting the boolean centered to true. Instead of showing the overlay in the center, it's also possible to show the overlay as a tool tip or speech bubble by pointing to some referring component. Instead of the show() method, you will use the showBy(component) method. For an argument you can pass in the referring component (e.g., a button) that invoked the overlay:

```
var button = Ext.ComponentQuery.query('settingsbutton')[0];
Ext.ComponentQuery.query('#settingsview')[0].showBy(button);
```

To gray out the background underneath the overlay, and to block the user from interacting with the underlying components, you can create a mask that covers those components by setting modal to true. With the (boolean) setting hideOnMaskTap, you can dismiss the modal mask and overlay by tapping on the modal mask. If you don't use this functionality, you will need to programmatically hide the overlay:

```
this.overlay = Ext.Viewport.add({
    xtype: 'panel',
    modal: true,
    hideOnMaskTap: true,
    //more settings
});
```

showAnimation and hideAnimation do what their names say: they create an animation
for showing and hiding overlays. In both objects you can set an animation type, such
as fadeIn, fadeOut, popIn, popOut, flip (flip over the panel), slideIn (slide in from
the right), and slideOut (slide out to the left). You can set a duration in milliseconds
and the easing property to either ease-in or ease-out, which are aliases for
Ext.fx.easing.EaseIn and Ext.fx.easing.EaseOut. *Easing* is an animation technique that gives a different interaction by varying the rate at which animations move and
whether the animation begins, ends, or transitions at different speeds:

```
this.overlay = Ext.Viewport.add({
    xtype: 'panel',
    showAnimation: {
        type: 'popIn',
        duration: 250,
        easing: 'ease-out'
    },
    hideAnimation: {
        type: 'popOut',
        duration: 150,
        easing: 'ease-out'
    }
    //more settings
});
```

Let's build the overlay for the FindACab app. You will stub out the settingsform, a
floating panel that contains a title bar with a close button. Later, in Chapter 12, you will
implement a nice form that listens to the user input in *view/SettingsView.js*:

```
Ext.define('FindACab.view.SettingsView', {
    extend: 'Ext.Panel',
    xtype: 'settingsview',
    requires: [
        'Ext.TitleBar'
    ],
    config: {
        items: [{
                xtype: 'titlebar',
                ui: 'light',
                docked: 'top',
                title: 'Settings',
                items: [{
                iconCls: 'delete',
                itemId: 'close',
                ui: 'decline',
                align: 'right'
                }]
        },
        {
            padding: '20',
            html: 'Forms here'
        }]
```

```
    }
});
```

This `settingsform` view is a view that extends from `Panel` (which is a container). Containers need a `layout` to position items. This settings panel will have a `fit` layout, to display one single item. It also has an `Ext.TitleBar` docked to the top of the panel, with a close button. This close button contains an `itemId: "close"`, which sets an `id` in the scope of the `settingsform`. For the rest, just stub out an `html` string.

The previous code does not let the panel float. You will create the overlay in the *controller/SettingsController.js*. Currently, your *controller/SettingsController* will look like this:

```
Ext.define('FindACab.controller.SettingsController', {
    extend: 'Ext.app.Controller',
    config: {
        models: ['Setting'],
        stores: ['Settings']
    }
});
```

Most importantly, you must add `settingsform` to the `requires` array, so the `settings form` will be in the memory and you can add the `xtype` to the viewport:

```
requires: ['FindACab.view.SettingsView'],
```

In the `config` object, create a reference to the `settingsview` and listen to the close and settings buttons. You can get a reference to the close button via the `#close itemId` in the `settingsview`, and the settings button via the `itemId #settingsbtn` in the `detail` view. When any of these buttons are tapped, invoke the `toggleSettings()` function:

```
refs: {
    'settingsView': 'settingsview'
},
control: {
    'detailview #settingsbtn': {
        tap: 'toggleSettings'
    },
    'settingsview #close': {
        tap: 'toggleSettings'
    }
}
```

This `toggleSettings` function just toggles the visibility. When the overlay is shown, hide it. When the overlay is hidden, show it. You will use the `settingsView` reference for this, defined in the `refs` object. It will autocreate a `getSettingsView()` getter method that points to the `settingsview` xtype. Here's the code for the `toggleSettings` function; you can define it below the `config` object:

```
toggleSettings: function(){
    if(this.getSettingsView().getHidden()) {
```

```
        this.getSettingsView().show();
    } else {
        this.getSettingsView().hide();
    }
}
```

Now let's check to see if there is an overlay already added to the viewport. You can code this while initializing the controller:

```
init: function(){
  if (!this.overlay) {
    //create overlay here
  }
}
```

If there is no overlay, proceed to add a new overlay to the viewport. This overlay contains the settingsform xtype, which subclasses a panel and therefore can float. It has a couple of settings: a modal mask (modal), to gray out the background and to hide the overlay when you click on it (hideOnMaskTap). The panel also has a fixed height and a dynamic 50% width, and it will be centered to the absolute center of the screen. In addition, the overlay will stay hidden on the page until the toggleSettings() function invokes it to show:

```
this.overlay = Ext.Viewport.add({
  xtype: 'settingsview',
  modal: true,
  hideOnMaskTap: true,
  centered: true,
  width: 320,
  height: 380,
  hidden: true,
});
```

The last step is to create some animations while hiding and showing the overlay. Add to the overlay the following two objects: showAnimation and hideAnimation. showAnimation pops the overlay in, in 250 milliseconds. The animation starts fast and ends more smoothly because of the ease-out setting. hideAnimation pops the overlay away, in 250 milliseconds. The animation starts fast and ends more smoothly because of the ease-out setting:

```
showAnimation: {
    type: 'popIn',
    duration: 250,
    easing: 'ease-out'
},
hideAnimation: {
    type: 'popOut',
    duration: 250,
    easing: 'ease-out'
}
```

When you're done coding, the overlay should look like Figure 11-17. Here's the complete code for *controller/SettingsController.js*:

```
Ext.define('FindACab.controller.SettingsController', {
    extend: 'Ext.app.Controller',
    requires: ['FindACab.view.SettingsView'],
    config: {
        models:['Setting'],
        stores: ['Settings'],

        refs: {
            'settingsView': 'settingsview'
        },
        control: {
            'detailview #settingsbtn': {
                tap: 'toggleSettings'
            },
            'settingsview #close': {
                tap: 'toggleSettings'
            }
        }
    },

    init: function(){

        if (!this.overlay) {
            this.overlay = Ext.Viewport.add({
                xtype: 'settingsview',
                modal: true,
                hideOnMaskTap: true,
                centered: true,
                width: 320,
                height: 380,
                hidden: true,
                showAnimation: {
                    type: 'popIn',
                    duration: 250,
                    easing: 'ease-out'
                },
                hideAnimation: {
                    type: 'popOut',
                    duration: 250,
                    easing: 'ease-out'
                }
            });
        }
    },

    toggleSettings: function(){
        if(this.getSettingsView().getHidden()) {
            this.getSettingsView().show();
        } else {
```

```
                this.getSettingsView().hide();
            }
        }

    });
```

Figure 11-17. The FindACab app overlay

This stubbed-out overlay panel is all for now. Before we discuss forms, let's take a look
at another data-aware component: charts. Charts are a nice way to display data.

Implementing Charts

Charts are an effective way to visualize data. A chart is a data-aware component, so you'll
have to hook up a store to it. Every chart needs one or more `series` objects. This object
describes the type of chart you wish to use and how you want to visualize your data. See
Table 11-1 for an overview of all the different series.

Table 11-1. The different series types

Type	Base chart	Description
pie	Ext.chart.PolarChart	Displays quantitative information for different categories.
pie3d	Ext.chart.PolarChart	Displays quantitative information for different categories, but in 3D.
radar	Ext.chart.PolarChart	Compares different quantitative values for a constrained number of categories.
bar	Ext.chart.CartesianChart	Compares among categories. One axis of the chart shows the specific categories being compared, and the other axis represents a discrete value.
line	Ext.chart.CartesianChart	Displays quantitative information for different categories or other real values that can show some progression (or regression).
area	Ext.chart.CartesianChart	Displays graphically quantitive data. It is based on the line chart. The area between axis and line is commonly emphasized with colors. Commonly used to compare multiple quantities.
candle stick	Ext.chart.CartesianChart	Similar to a bar chart but mostly used to describe price movements of a security, derivative, or currency over time.
scatter	Ext.chart.CartesianChart	Displays more than two data variables in the same visualization.
gauge	Ext.chart.SpaceFilling Chart	Displays a value from 0 to 100%. The value is displayed as a gauge. Typically used for dashboards.

Charts are classified in the following base charts:

Cartesian charts

A Cartesian chart (Figure 11-18) has two directions, the x- and y-axes. Series are coordinated along these axes. Examples are bar and line charts.

Polar charts

These charts have polar coordinates. Examples are pie or radar charts.

Space-filling charts

This is a more unique chart. It fills the entire area with the chart. An example is the gauge chart.

Take a look at the following code. Basically every chart extends from one of its base charts, as described in Table 11-1. Almost every chart requires a store (except the gauge chart). Every chart needs to have a `series` object that describes the type and the data, and possibly visual styling. All Cartesian charts (and also the radar chart) need to have an `axes` array, with `axis` objects. An axis could have a `title`, a `position`, and record `fields` that map along the axis:

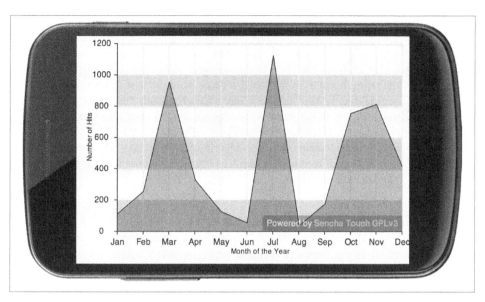

Figure 11-18. Example of a Cartesian chart, a line chart with a fill

```
var chart = Ext.create('Ext.chart.CartesianChart', {
    renderTo: Ext.getBody(),
    store: [],
    axes: [{
        type: 'numeric',
        position: 'left',
        title: 'Y Title',
        fields: 'data'
    }, {
        type: 'category',
        position: 'bottom',
        title: 'X Title'
        fields: 'categoryname'
    }],
    series: [{
        type: 'bar',
        xField: 'categoryname',
        yField: 'data'
    }]
});

Ext.Viewport.setLayout('fit');
Ext.Viewport.add(chart);
```

Ext JS includes both a bar chart and a column chart. The difference between these two Cartesian charts is that a column chart has the category plotted on the x-axis and the numeric value plotted on the y-axis, while the bar chart has the category plotted on the y-axis and the numeric value plotted on the x-axis. So how does this work for Sencha Touch? How do you create a bar chart with the category on the y-axis and the numeric values on the x? Just extend from `Ext.chart.CartesianChart` and pass a `flipXY:true` boolean value as a config. Of course you also need to specify the axes. The category axis should have a `position:'left'` and the numeric axis should have a `position:'bottom'`.

Sencha Touch charts use the Sencha Touch drawing package. On the desktop, Ext JS 4 charts use either VML or SVG as the underlying browser drawing API. In the mobile space, VML is obviously not present (because it's IE-specific) and SVG is inconsistently available (Android didn't provide SVG capability until 3.x). So in order to get a high performance native feel, the drawing package in Sencha Touch uses the HTML5 canvas. That has some great benefits (e.g., leveraging drop-shadow capabilities that are hardware accelerated on many browsers). By utilizing HTML5 Canvas on mobile devices, Sencha Touch Charts draws faster and more efficiently than its desktop counterparts.

Another great reason why I like Sencha Touch charts more then Ext JS charts is because of the animations and interactions based on gestures. On any chart, you can change or modify the kinds of interactions you want to use by adding an `interactions` array to the chart config. For example, you can enable a pie chart to spin with a drag or a pinch. On a bar graph you can let your users pinch to zoom, drag to pan, and so on.

The Sencha Touch charts are available as part of the Sencha Touch GPL framework, and as part of the Sencha Touch/Complete bundles.

Let's visualize the `avg_rating` from Yelp in the FindACab app. You will use the gauge chart for the review score of every `TaxiService`. See Figure 11-19. You will even make it look like a taxi meter.

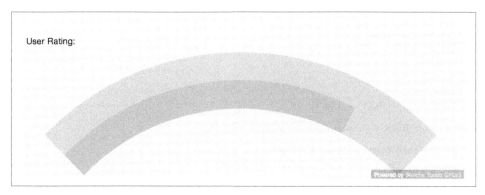

Figure 11-19. The FindACab app rating gauge chart

Create the file *view/RatingChart.js*. The gauge chart extends from an `Ext.chart.Space FillingChart` base class and will get the `xtype` `ratingchart` as an alias name:

```
Ext.define('FindACab.view.RatingChart', {
  extend: 'Ext.chart.SpaceFillingChart',
  xtype: 'ratingchart',

});
```

To display it properly, you need to load some extra classes into memory: `Ext.chart.ser ies.Gauge` for the gauge series, which makes use of `Ext.chart.series.sprite.Pie Slice`:

```
requires: [
  'Ext.chart.series.Gauge',
  'Ext.chart.series.sprite.PieSlice',
],
```

Next you will create a `series` object into the `config` and set the `series` `type` to `gauge`, to display a gauge chart:

```
config: {
    series: [{
      type: 'gauge',
      //chart configuration here
    }]
}
```

Now you will configure the gauge chart. Assign the `avg_rating` data model field to this chart. It points to the data of the `Cab` model (i.e., the data from the Yelp web service). The remaining configurations are simply visual: a default `value` of 0, a `minimum` and `maximum` value, a value to set the radius of the inner (half) circle (`donut`) of the gauge chart, and an array with chart `colors`:

```
field: 'avg_rating',
labelField: 'Rating',
value: 0,
minimum: 0,
maximum: 5,
donut: 80,
colors: ["#ffb13a", "lightgrey"]
```

Here's the complete code for *.view/RatingChart.js*:

```
Ext.define('FindACab.view.RatingChart', {
        extend: 'Ext.chart.SpaceFillingChart',
        xtype: 'ratingchart',
        requires: [
                'Ext.chart.series.Gauge',
                'Ext.chart.series.sprite.PieSlice',
        ],
        config: {
                series: [{
                        type: 'gauge',
                        field: 'avg_rating',
                        labelField: 'Rating',
                        value: 0,
                        minimum: 0,
                        maximum: 5,
                        donut: 80,
                        colors: ["#ffb13a", "lightgrey"]
                }]
        }
});
```

Implement the `ratingchart` into the `items` array of the `DetailView` class. Make sure you also include it into the `requires` array, to load the `FindACab.view.RatingChart` class into the memory:

```
{
    docked: 'bottom',
    xtype: 'ratingchart',
    height: '30%'
}, {
    docked: 'bottom',
    xtype: 'component',
    html: '<h1>User Rating:</h1>',
    padding: '0 20'
}
```

The chart needs a layout, like a `height` or `padding` in order to be displayed. You will set the `height` on the `DetailView` class so the `RatingChart` can be reused for other purposes. In addition to the chart, which will be docked to the bottom, you will also dock a header, which is just an `Ext.Component` with an `html` string.

Finally, in the `CabController` `prefillDetail()` method, add the following line to update the `RatingChart` with the current record:

```
Ext.ComponentQuery.query('ratingchart')[0].getSeries()[0].setValue(
                                              record.get('avg_rating')
                                              );
```

Summary

You're almost done with the logic of the FindACab app. The only thing that is left is entering and listening to user input. How else could the app display taxi data? This is a topic I will discuss in the next chapter, which covers everything you want to know about Sencha Touch forms! T

## CHAPTER 12

Forms

I have a love/hate relationship with forms. I love them, because they look so great. Some components feel really nice on a touch device. Thanks to HTML5, some fields are recognized by (mobile) browsers and therefore present a correct device keyboard. But I hate them too because I don't want to enter a lot of data—especially not when I am traveling and need to look things up quickly. In general, people don't like to write whole books on a mobile phone. The screen is too small and therefore hard to read. The keyboards on touch devices are often too small for your fingers, and the feedback for pressing the keys is often too poor. It's just not like a physical keyboard, like on your desktop or laptop computer. That's why I always try to limit textarea fields on mobile applications.

However, Sencha Touch does a really good job with form fields (see Figures 12-1 and 12-2). Some form fields really feel good on a touch device. Now it is up to you to choose the best form fields for your user input. Every form field in Sencha Touch extends from `Ext.field.Field`.

`Ext.field.Field` is the base class for all form fields used in Sencha Touch. It's an input field and a label all in one key/value pair. Every form field should have a unique name (the key) and can have a value (the user input). It provides a lot of shared functionality to all field subclasses (simple validation, clearing, and tab index management), but is rarely used directly. See Table 12-1 for an overview of all form fields used by Sencha Touch.

Figure 12-1. The email keyboard that is shown when you are using an Email field in Sencha Touch

Figure 12-2. The number keyboard that will be shown when you are using a number field in Sencha Touch

Table 12-1. Sencha Touch form fields

Name	xtype	Description
Ext.field.Text	textfield	Most basic field. Just a normal text input: `<input type="text">`.
Ext.field.Number	numberfield	Creates an HTML5 number input. Most (mobile) browsers will show a specialized virtual numeric keyboard for this field.
Ext.field.Spinner	spinner field	Like the numberfield but contains two little plus and minus buttons to increase steps.
Ext.field.Email	emailfield	Creates an HTML5 email input. Most (mobile) browsers will show a specialized virtual keyboard for this field.
Ext.field.Url	urlfield	Creates an HTML5 URL input. Most (mobile) browsers will show a specialized virtual keyboard for this field.

Name	xtype	Description
Ext.field.Search	searchfield	Creates an HTML5 search input. The visual styling of this input is slightly different from normal text input controls (the corners are rounded).
Ext.field.Password	password field	Masks all the input. Under the hood, it's an HTML password field too: `<input type="password">`.
Ext.field.File	filefield	A file upload field. Under the hood, it's an HTML file upload field too: `<input type="file">`.
Ext.field.Checkbox	checkbox field	A checkbox; multiple boxes can be selected from a group. Under the hood, it's an HTML checkbox too: `<input type="checkbox">`.
Ext.field.Radio	radiofield	A radiobox; only one radio item can be selected from a group. Under the hood, it's an HTML radio too: `<input type="radio">`. Note, radio field extends from checkboxfield.
Ext.field.Datepicker	datapicker	A field specified for entering dates. Instead of a calendar widget, it has roller fields that pop up from the bottom of the screen on phones and float on tablets.
Ext.field.Hidden	hiddenfield	Invisible in a form but will be sent while data is submitting.
Ext.field.TextArea	textarea field	A field for entering multiple lines of text. Under the hood, it's an HTML textarea too: `<textarea>`.
Ext.field.Select	selectfield	A drop down/combo box from which to select a value. Under the hood, it is *not* a select `<select>` tag.
Ext.field.Slider	sliderfield	Allows the user to select a value from a given numerical range. You might use it for choosing a percentage or combine two of them to get min and max values.

In this chapter, you'll learn how to:

- Implement a form
- Validate a form
- Submit a form
- Implement form handling

Implementing a Form

People used to think that creating a form in Sencha Touch simply meant adding a set of form fields into a container. Although you could take that approach, it might be better to add form fields to a formpanel (`Ext.form.Panel`).

I used to say that a formpanel is actually like an HTML `<form>` tag. Only, it is really not. No, in fact, under the hood, it's just a `<div>` tag. What makes it behave more like a `<form>` tag is that a formpanel can contain a url—the action to post to when submitting a formpanel. And, yes, a formpanel is submittable.

You can generate forms from the command line with Sencha Cmd. You will have to specify a form name, which will be used as a view class name. This view class will extend from `Ext.form.Panel`. As a second argument, you can specify one string of form field names; when you use the colon character, you can even specify the field type. Be aware that you don't enter any spaces; doing so will break the form because everything after the space will be seen as a third argument and thus ignored:

```
sencha generate form -name MyForm -fields field,field2:textfield
```

Implementing the FindACab App Form

Let's start with generating the formpanel for the FindACab app from the CLI, with two new fields, `city` and `country`, both of which are text fields:

```
sencha generate form -name SettingsView -fields city:textfield,country:textfield
```

Yikes! Looks like you've got a merge error:

```
[ERR] MERGE CONFLICT - ../app/view/SettingsView.js
[ERR] Please resolve manually
```

If you followed all the steps of this book, you might see the previous error. Why is that? Remember when you created the `SettingsView` at the end of Chapter 11? You've got a conflict because you already have a copy of a `SettingsView` class in the *view* folder. So now what? Well, let's resolve it manually, and merge both classes into one. This looks harder than it is. Open *SettingsView.js* , and you will see that it tried to merge your old file with the newly generated form class. Just remove the old version (the duplicate code and the strange >>> characters), and you're good to go.

Apart from that, notice the `items` array with the nested textfields, and the `extend`, which is set to `Ext.form.Panel`. It's really awesome that you don't have to write the form view class by yourself.

Implementing a Fieldset

The previous Sencha Cmd command generated a basic formpanel with both fields and a button, but that is not totally what we want. We also want to add some user instructions. What you need is a `fieldset`, which groups the form fields and adds instructions (see Figure 12-3).

A `fieldset` in Sencha Touch is not the same as the HTML `<fieldset>` tag. Yes, a Sencha `fieldset` can visually separate form fields, but under the hood it's just a set of `<div>` tags. Also, `fieldset`s in Sencha Touch can contain a title and an `instructions` help text underneath the `fieldset`.

Figure 12-3. A fieldset with two form fields and a title

Let's implement a `fieldset` for the FindACab app. You will wrap a `fieldset` around the two `textfields`. Also don't forget to add the `Ext.form.FieldSet` to the `requires` array to add the `fieldset` class into the memory:

```
{
    xtype: 'fieldset',
    title: 'Your location',
    instructions: "Please enter your city and country.
    (For US addresses please provide city + statecode and country,
    for example: Naperville IL, USA)",
    items: [
        //code with the two textfields here
    ]
}
```

Let's also modify the Submit button. Give it an `action:'submit'` so later you can refer to it, and a `margin:10` to make it look nicer:

```
{
    xtype: 'button',
    text: 'Submit',
    action: 'submit',
    margin: 10,
    ui: 'confirm'
}
```

When everything is done, you can confirm that the code for *view/SettingsView.js* looks like this:

```
Ext.define('FindACab.view.SettingsView', {
    extend: 'Ext.form.Panel',
    xtype: 'settingsview',
    requires: [
            'Ext.TitleBar',
            'Ext.form.FieldSet'
    ],
    config: {
        title: 'SettingsView',
        items: [{
                xtype: 'titlebar',
                ui: 'light',
                docked: 'top',
                title: 'Settings',
                items: [{
                        iconCls: 'delete',
                        itemId: 'close',
                        ui: 'decline',
                        align: 'right'
                    }
                ]
            }, {
            xtype: 'fieldset',
            title: 'Your location',
            instructions: "Please enter your city and country.
                            (For US addresses please provide city + statecode
                            and country, for example: Naperville IL, USA)",
            items: [{
                    name: 'city',
                    xtype: 'textfield',
                    label: 'City'
                }, {
                    name: 'country',
                    xtype: 'textfield',
                    label: 'Country'
                }
            ]
        },
        {
            xtype: 'button',
            text: 'Submit',
            action: 'submit',
            margin: 10,
            ui: 'confirm'
        }
        ]
    }
});
```

The implementation for the FindACab app form is finished (see Figure 12-4). However, this form doesn't do anything. Eventually, you will want to validate or post this form. First things first: let's talk about validating a Sencha Touch form!

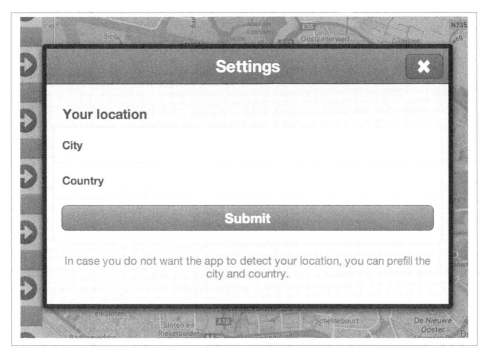

Figure 12-4. Your FindACab app form should look like this, after you've implemented the fieldset and button

Validating a Form

Form validation in Sencha Touch is pretty basic when you compare it to form validation with its big brother Ext JS. Whereas in Ext JS you have built-in form validation on every form field by default, in Sencha Touch you'll have to build in the validation yourself.

All data that comes in your app, whether it's user input or data from an external web service, comes in via the proxy through the model and store. We learned in Chapter 7 that models can be validated. When you want to validate a form, you will have to use the model instead.

Take a look at the following code snippet, which shows the flow of validation. First you will create a model instance, update it with the data that is in your form, and then validate the model:

```
var model = Ext.create("MyApp.model.MyModel");
myForm.updateRecord(model);

var validationObj = model.validate();

if (!validationObj.isValid()) {
```

```
    validationObj.each(function(errorObj) {
        //loop through all errors
    }
} else {
    //form is valid, now do something!
}
```

The idea is to update your model with the user input that is written in the form. That's possible with the `updateRecord(model)` method, which you can call from a `Ext.form.Panel`. It persists the values in the form into the passed-in `Ext.data.Model` object (a record). Once the new data is in your model, you can run the `validate()` method on the model.

This will return an `Ext.data.Errors` object. The name is somewhat misleading, because you will also retrieve this object if there are no errors. That's why I prefer to call it a *validation* object. When you run the `isValid()` method on it, it will return `true` if the form does not contain any errors, and `false` if the form is not valid. If that is the case, on the validation object you can loop through the collection of errors. It stores the model `field` name that contains the error, and the validation message (that's set in the model). You can show these validation messages directly in form fields on the screen or in an `Ext.MessageBox`.

Do you want to highlight the form field in red when an error occurs? You have to implement this yourself, but it's not that hard. First, implement an `error` style in the (Sass or CSS) stylesheet, */resources/css/app.css*:

```
.error input {
    border: 3px solid red;
}
```

Note that a form field in Sencha Touch is the label and the actual input. Under the hood, it's wrapped by a `<div>` tag. This `<div>` element will get the `error` CSS class, and therefore if you want to add a red border around the input field, you'll have to specify this in the stylesheet.

Then add the `error` CSS class to the form field that contains the error. For example:

```
Ext.ComponentQuery.query
("textfield[name=\'\+errorObj.getField()\+\']")[0]
.addCls("error");
```

Validating a Form in the FindACab App

The FindACab app should have the code for validating a form in the *controller/Settings-Controller.js* file. Let's review it together.

Start with defining an event listener in the control object of the Settings Controller. You will listen to the tap event of the Submit button. This will dispatch you to the onSubmitTap function:

```
'button[action=submit]': {
    tap: 'onSubmitTap'
}
```

Next, create the onSubmitTap() function and loop through all textfields. While looping, remove every possible error CSS class. This is to reset the error states. If a form was invalid before and you fixed it, it at least should be shown as a valid field:

```
onSubmitTap: function() {
    var t = Ext.ComponentQuery.query('textfield').length;
    var i = 0;
    for(i;i<t;i++){
        Ext.ComponentQuery.query('textfield')[i].removeCls('error');
    }

    //TODO logics
}
```

You will implement more logic. Let's throw a loading indicator on the viewport. This can take some time while saving valid data, so let the user know this. Of course, when it's done, clear the loading indicator from the viewport:

```
Ext.Viewport.setMasked({
    xtype: 'loadmask',
    indicator: true,
    message: 'Save Settings...'
});

//TODO validation logics

Ext.Viewport.unmask();
```

Now, prepare the form validation. Because form validation in Sencha Touch goes through the data model, make a reference to the Settings model. Also, create an empty errorstring, which you will use to display error messages:

```
var errorstring = "";
var model = Ext.create("FindACab.model.Setting", {});
```

You will run the updateRecord() method on the formpanel, which will make the connection between the settingsform and a data model (FindACab.model.Setting). As soon as you enter user input and press the Submit button, it will run the onSubmitTap function, which will update the FindACab.model.Setting model with the user input:

```
this.getSettingsView().updateRecord(model);
```

The next part is where the magic happens. Validate the data model (which is hooked up to the form):

```
var validationObj = model.validate();
```

Is the validation object not valid? Does the model contain any errors? When the validation object is not valid, let's loop through every error and save the error messages to the errorstring, which you will display in an alert messagebox later. You also need to add the error CSS class to every form textfield that contains a validation error. If the form is valid, you can hide the settingsform.

Later in this book, you will implement some code that saves the user input to Local Storage and start running the application logic for displaying Cab information:

```
if (!validationObj.isValid()) {
    validationObj.each(function(errorObj) {
        errorstring += errorObj.getMessage() + "<br />";
        Ext.ComponentQuery.query
        ('textfield[name='+errorObj.getField()+']')[0]
        .addCls('error');
    });

    Ext.Msg.alert("Oops", errorstring);
} else {
    //TODO save settings

    this.getSettingsView().hide();
}
```

The complete code for the onSubmitTap() function looks like this (see Figure 12-5):

```
onSubmitTap: function() {
    //reset cls
    var t = Ext.ComponentQuery.query('textfield').length;
    var i = 0;
    for(i;i<t;i++){
        Ext.ComponentQuery.query('textfield')[i].removeCls('error');
    }

    Ext.Viewport.setMasked({
        xtype: 'loadmask',
        indicator: true,
        message: 'Save Settings...'
    });

    var errorstring = "";
    var model = Ext.create("FindACab.model.Setting", {});
    this.getSettingsView().updateRecord(model);

    //start validating
    var validationObj = model.validate();

    if (!validationObj.isValid()) {
        validationObj.each(function(errorObj) {
            errorstring += errorObj.getMessage() + "<br />";
```

```
        var field = Ext.ComponentQuery.query
        ('textfield[name='+errorObj.getField()+']')[0];
        field.addCls('error');
    });

        Ext.Msg.alert("Oops", errorstring);
    } else {
        //TODO save settings

        this.getSettingsView().hide();
    }

    Ext.Viewport.unmask();
}
```

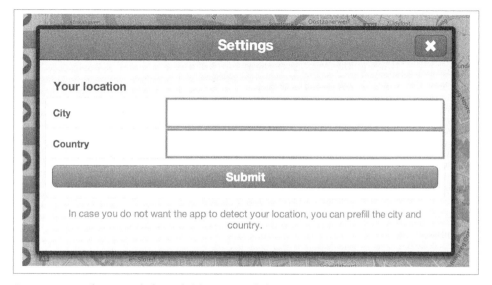

Figure 12-5. Oh no! Both form fields are invalid

Now that you know how to validate your form input (or actually the model), the FindACab app needs some logic for saving the data. You can save data in a form either with the form submit() method, or through the model or store. The next sections will show you both ways.

Submitting a Form

In the previous technique, you learned how to validate the model, to check if the user input in the form is valid. When it is valid, you might want to post it to a server:

```
myForm.submit();
```

`form.submit()` is the traditional way of sending data to a server. You might be familiar with this in HTML, where you can submit an HTML `form`.

Although in Sencha Touch a formpanel under the hood is not an HTML `<form>` tag, but rather just a plain old `<div>` tag, it behaves like a `<form>` tag. It will submit the form on AJAX-based key/value pairs (on the same domain) because every form field should have a name (the key) and a value (the user input).

It's possible to pass in some settings for the form submit with the `Ext.data.Connec tion` object. See Table 12-2 for all the options to set.

Table 12-2. The Ext.data.Connection options for a form submit

Key	Description
url	The URL for the action
method	For example, POST (or GET)
params	Arguments you want to send with (use Ext.urlEncode)
headers	The request headers to set for the action
autoAbort	true to abort pending AJAX request
submitDisabled	true to submit all fields regardless of disabled state
waitMsg	If specified, you will see a loading mask (indicator) with a message
success	The callback when the submit succeeds
failure	The callback when the submit fails
scope	The scope from which to call the callback

Here's an advanced example of the form submit that passes in the `Ext.data.Connec tion` object:

```
myForm.submit({
    url: 'data.php',
    method: 'post',
    submitDisabled: true,
    waitMsg: {
        xtype: 'loadmask', message: 'Submitting Data...'
    },
    success: function (objForm,objResult) {
        //success code
        myForm.reset();
    },
    failure: function(objForm,objResult) {
        Ext.Msg.alert('Oops',result.responseText);
    }
})
```

The form submit will return either a `success` or `failure` callback. However, note that if there is some server-side failure—like the database doesn't accept the data, or any other problem—then it won't return a `failure` callback. A failure is when an HTTP error code occurred—for example, 404 for a Not Found Error or 500 for an Internal Server Error.

To determine whether everything went well on the server side, you can send a JSON message back. When you have a server in PHP, your response message could look like this:

```php
<?php
header('Content-Type: application/json');
echo '{"success":true, "msg":'.json_encode('Thanks!').'}';
?>
```

Always be aware of having your client-side and server-side validations in sync. You can end up with really crazy situations, when on the client side it accepts a `max-length` of 5 and on the server a `min-length` of 6. This may seem unlikely, but trust me, unfortunately I have seen implementations like this.

Because you cannot be sure what the server will send back to you, it's not advisable to immediately sync your store locally after a model validation returns no errors. It could be that it passes all your client-side checks and the server has some database error. In that case, your app would be out of sync; there can be data on your device that's not available on a server. In those cases, always let the server send a response, such as the previously shown PHP example.

The form `submit` method can be handy for posting AJAX data to a server (on the same domain). Instead of the form submit, you could also use the `Ext.Ajax.request()` call for posting data to a server. Typically, you would use the `jsonData` (or `xmlData`) objects for posting the key/value pairs. (Note that only the `POST` method will work.) Here is an example of how to post data through an AJAX call:

```
Ext.Ajax.request({
    url: 'data.php',
    jsonData : {city : "Amsterdam", country : "Netherlands"},
    success: function(response) {
        //success code
        myForm.reset();
    },
    failure: function(response) {
        Ext.Msg.alert('Oops',result.responseText);ſϛ¿
    }
});
```

There are more ways for posting (or syncing) data to a server. This could be through a model or a store. You would also use this technique when you want to sync your data with a client proxy, like saving into Local Storage. Interested? Check out the next technique.

Implementing Form Handling

You have a valid form, and you want to sync it either with a server-side script or an offline storage. For syncing user input to a server, you can use an AJAX request or a formpanel submit, but you can also choose to save your model or sync your store. The latter is also the option you would choose for syncing your data offline. So what do you need? A store with a proxy (and/or a model with a proxy). How does it work? By calling `Model.save()` or `Store.sync()`. `Model.save()` you can save data to a server. No store is required. The `Store.sync()` synchronizes the store with its proxy. This will ask the proxy to batch together any new, updated, and deleted records in the data store and update the store's internal representation of the records as each operation completes. It is also possible to sync a store by adding `autoSync` to the store's config. In that case, it will automatically sync every operation immediately on the fly. That's easy, but it's also a heavy performance hit because of multiple syncs.

Does this sound familiar? Yes, see Chapter 7's coverage of the `save()` technique and Chapter 9's discussion of the `sync()` method for more information about both concepts.

However, first I want to show you how to finalize the FindACab app. Now that you know everything about forms and syncing stores, it will probably also make much more sense. So the FindACab app will save all the user settings into the Local Storage, by setting a client proxy on the model of the `Settings` store.

Let's take a look at the code of the *controller/SettingsController.js*. It shows the code solution for saving the user input to your Local Storage when the form is valid. First, try to get a reference to the previous saved user input (the `city` and the `country` fields) from the store:

```
} else {
    var me = this;
    var settingsStore = Ext.getStore('Settings');
    try{
        var oldLocation = Ext.getStore('Settings').getAt(0).get('city')
            + ' ' + Ext.getStore('Settings').getAt(0).get('country');
    } catch(e){
        var oldLocation = "";
    }

    //TODO logics here

});
```

Then, clear the user settings store and add the new user input data model into it. On a successful sync of the settings in the Local Storage, create a callback function as follows:

```
settingsStore.removeAll();
settingsStore.add(model.getData());
settingsStore.sync({
    success: function(){
        //
    }
});
```

In this callback function, you will need to run the logic for clearing the Web SQL database. Therefore, you will code a `removeOldData()` function later. You will pass in two arguments, the old user input (to decide what to remove from the database) and a callback that will invoke the logic for removing old markers from the Google Map (the `removeMarkers()` function in the `CabController`) and to load new `Cab` data into the store (the `loadLocal()` function in the *CabController*):

```
this.getApplication().getController('CabController')
    .removeOldData(oldLocation, function(){
    me.getApplication().getController('CabController').removeMarkers();
    me.getApplication().getController('CabController').loadLocal();
    me.getSettingsView().hide();
});
```

Here is the complete solution that belongs in the `else` of the `SettingsController`:

```
var me = this;
//remove all current Settings and save new
var settingsStore = Ext.getStore('Settings');
try{
    var oldLocation = Ext.getStore('Settings').getAt(0).get('city') + ' ' +
    Ext.getStore('Settings').getAt(0).get('country');
} catch(e){
    var oldLocation = "";
}
settingsStore.removeAll();
settingsStore.add(model.getData());
settingsStore.sync({
    success: function(){
        //remove all Cabs from store and database
        me.getApplication().getController('CabController').removeOldData
          (oldLocation, function(){
            //remove all Markers from the map
            me.getApplication().getController('CabController').removeMarkers();
            //load new data
            me.getApplication().getController('CabController').loadLocal();
            //hide loading mask
            me.getSettingsView().hide();
        });
    }
});

}
```

```
Ext.Viewport.unmask();
```

Are we there yet? Well, almost. The removeOldData() function needs to be coded into the CabController. This is one more function that removes old data when there is already data in the local Web SQL database. It takes the old user input as a first argument. It gets a reference to the Cabs store, clears previous filters, and filters on the userinput model field that should match with the old user data. Then we'll loop through all the matches and remove it from the store.

When you are done, you can remove the filter again and pass in the callback to the sync store method, to sync the removed items first and then run the callback to to load the new data into the store and add the new Google Map markers.

When there is no old user input saved in the Local Storage, we can assume the app is running for the first time. In that case, continue downloading data.

```
removeOldData: function(loc, callback){
    if(loc == ""){
        //this is the very first time you load data
        //there is nothing to remove, just download
        callback();
    } else {
        var store = Ext.getStore('Cabs');
        store.clearFilter();
        store.filter("userinput", loc);
        store.load(function(records){

            var i = 0,
                t = records.length;

            for(i; i<t; i++){
                store.remove(records[i]);
            }

            store.clearFilter();
            store.sync({
                failure: function(){
                    console.error(arguments);
                },
                success: function(batch){
                    callback();
                }
            });
        });
    }
},
```

One more thing! You need to remember to remove the hardcoded `LOCATION` settings written in the `downloadData()` function in your `CabController: location = Utils.Commons.LOCATION;`. After uncommenting out or removing this line, you can start testing your FindACab app in your desktop browser.

 If you want to test the FindACab app with a U.S. address, enter the name of the city and the U.S. state code (e.g., "Naperville IL") in the city field and as a country enter "USA."

Summary

Awesome, the FindACab app is finally finished! See Figure 12-6. There are just some minor things left for us to do. For example, we want to make it look better, and finally, we want to create a production build. You'll learn how to do that in the last couple of chapters.

Figure 12-6. Hooray! The code for the FindACab app is finished!

## CHAPTER 13

Themes and Styles

I once had a Sencha Touch 1 app in the Apple App Store and somebody gave me a very bad review. "This is a weird-looking iOS app." What happened? Well, I just modified the default Sencha Touch stylesheet and gave all of the toolbars the same colors as native iOS components. The result was that the components *almost* looked like native, but they were just a little off. The users didn't know that it was a mobile web application that was ported to native, so they expected the same experience as a native app, but it was just not the same. I learned from this that mobile web applications should either look and behave *exactly the same* as native apps, or they shouldn't look like native at all. When the design is totally customized, people will get used to its design experience.

Sencha Touch Stylesheets

Times have changed. In Sencha Touch version 2.3, the framework ships with stylesheets that mimic native designs and experiences of all modern major devices (see Table 13-1). In addition to supporting iOS and Android, Sencha even works closely with the mobile device and browser makers like BlackBerry and Microsoft. Ahead of phone releases, Sencha gets access to test devices and style guides to make sure the Sencha Touch stylesheets look the same as native apps. When you create a production build of your app and you want to host it on the Web, it's even possible to make use of the Sencha platform switcher. This switcher can make sure that the correct stylesheet will be shown for each platform. For example, the BB10 theme will be used when the platform is BlackBerry and show the Windows theme when the app is being viewed on Internet Explorer 10.

Table 13-1. Stylesheets that are shipped with Sencha Touch out of the box

Name	Filename	Description
Base	*base.css*	This is the Base theme, so you wouldn't directly use it. Under the hood, it is used to define all Sencha Touch variables and mixins. The Base theme is inherited by all out-of-the-box stylesheets. See Figure 13-9.
Default	*senchatouch.css*	This is the default blue Sencha Touch stylesheet.
BlackBerry	*bb10.css*	This is the that mimics the BlackBerry 10 experience. See Figure 13-3.
Windows	*wp.css*	This is the Windows theme that mimics Windows Phone and Surface experience. See Figure 13-6.
Cupertino	*cupertino.css*	This is the that mimics the Apple iOS 7 experience. See Figures 13-1 and 13-8.
Cupertino Classic	*cupertino-classic.css*	This is the Cupertino theme that mimics the classic Apple iOS 6 experience. See Figures 13-2 and 13-7.
MountainView	*mountainview.css*	This is the that mimics the Android experience. See Figure 13-5.
Tizen	*tizen.css*	This is the Tizen theme that mimics the Tizen 2.1 Nectarine device; it has two tones, dark and light. See Figure 13-4.

Figure 13-1. The Cupertino theme is named for the city in California where the Apple headquarters are located

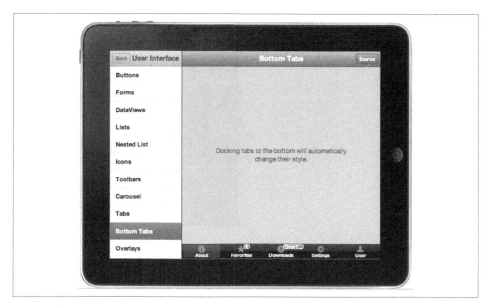

Figure 13-2. The Cupertino Classic theme

Figure 13-3. The BlackBerry theme

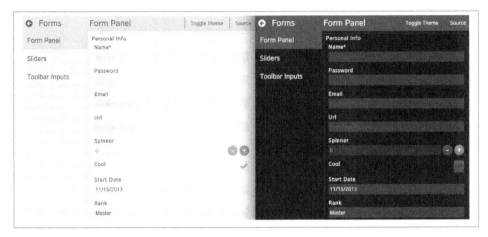

Figure 13-4. The Tizen theme

Using Sass

Maybe you are building an application for a company, or you just want to create an awesome theme designed all by yourself. I can tell you that not only is this possible, but it's even fairly easy. You don't have to overrule the CSS (cascading style sheet) with nasty !importants. You can make use of the Sencha Sass themes, which provide a dynamic way of coding stylesheets.

Sass stands for "syntactically awesome style sheets," a powerful CSS extension. And yes, it is *awesome*! I describe it as CSS infused with a lot of coffee and Red Bull, because it overcomes many of the shortcomings of CSS.

Sass is a preprocessor, which means that Sass files should be compiled to (*minified*) CSS files. A CSS file is the stylesheet your browser uses to display Sencha Touch components. (And that's also the file that goes into your production build or server.) Therefore, Sass needs a compiler. You can compile Sencha Sass themes with Sass and Compass installed on top of Ruby (see Appendix A), but if you are not really into design, you can also use just the Sencha Cmd build process. A Sencha app build can compile Sass files too, but it just takes a little bit longer.

Sass has two syntaxes. The most commonly used syntax is known as *SCSS* (which stands for *Sassy CSS*), and is a superset of CSS3's syntax. This means that every valid CSS3 stylesheet is valid SCSS as well. SCSS files use the extension *.scss*.

The second, older syntax is known as the indented syntax (or just *.sass*). Instead of brackets and semicolons, it uses line indentation to specify blocks. Files in the indented syntax use the extension *.sass*.

The Sencha themes are Sassy CSS files. You can combine CSS3 syntax with the amazing features of Sass. These features include nesting, defining variables (to set values and make math or color calculations), and creating mixins (little blocks of style rules to add Sass scripting like if/else or loop directives). If you are interested in learning Sass or Compass, my advice is to check out the official Sass website (*http://sass-lang.com/*), The Sass Way (*http://thesassway.com/*), and Compass (*http://compass-style.org/*). They are really interesting, and Sencha uses some of these ideas to create its own themes. For example, Sencha ships with Global CSS variables and a handful of Sencha UI mixins. You will be amazed at how easy it is to create your own customized themes in just a few minutes.

In the next couple of sections, I will discuss how to use the out-of-the-box themes and how to create your own custom theme, with custom fonts and custom icons.

In this chapter, you'll learn how to:

- Use platform-specific out-of-the-box themes
- Create your own custom theme
- Incorporate custom fonts
- Incorporate custom icons
- Optimize your stylesheet for best performance

Using Platform-Specific, Out-of-the-Box Themes

When you generate a Sencha Touch app with Sencha Cmd, it will create an *app.json* file in the project root. This file contains all references to external JavaScript files, AppCache information, and references to used stylesheets.

By default, this file is linked to the *app.css* CSS file in your *resources/css/* folder. It is a custom stylesheet that you can easily change with Sass, but by default it just extends from the Sencha Touch default theme. So, you will see only the default blue colors:

```
"css": [{
    "path": "resources/css/app.css",
    "update": "delta"
}],
```

The update property can be set to "delta" or "full". By default, the stylesheet will be cached in your Local Storage. When you make changes in your stylesheet while the app is already online, you can let the app autoupdate only the changes (deltas) or the full stylesheet.

You can let Sencha Touch detect the platform, and based on the platform, show matching resources. You can set it to use all out-of-the-box (platform-like) stylesheets, such as the

BlackBerry 10 theme or the iOS- and Android-like themes, or you can set it up to utilize custom stylesheets:

```
"css": [{
        "path": "touch/resources/css/sencha-touch.css",
        "platform": ["desktop", "firefox"],
        "theme": "Default",
        "update": "delta"
    },
    {
        "path": "touch/resources/css/wp.css",
        "platform": ["ie10"],
        "theme": "Windows",
        "update": "delta"
    },
    {
        "path": "touch/resources/css/bb10.css",
        "platform": ["blackberry"],
        "theme": "Blackberry",
        "update": "delta"
    },
    {
        "path": "touch/resources/css/cupertino.css",
        "platform": ["ios"],
        "theme": "Cupertino",
        "update": "delta"
    },
    {
        "path": "touch/resources/css/mountainview.css",
        "platform": ["android"],
        "theme": "MountainView",
        "update": "delta"
    },
    {
        "path": "touch/resources/css/tizen.css",
        "platform": ["tizen"],
        "theme": "Tizen",
        "update": "delta"
    }
],
```

To enable themes with the platform switcher, you will have to open the *app.json* file. In the css array, you can specify theme objects. These consist of a path to the available CSS, the platform to detect (see the list below), the name of the theme, and the update to specify either delta or full. You can test each of these platforms by appending the platform parameter to your URL when running your app—for example, *http://localhost/findacab/?platform=ie10*.

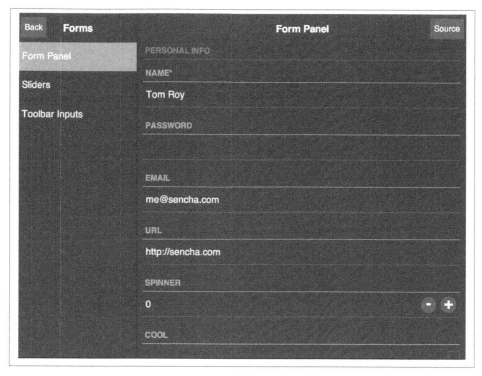

Figure 13-5. The MountainView theme is named for a city in California where the Google headquarters are located

The available platforms are:

- androidj
- blackberry
- chrome
- desktop
- firefox
- ie10
- ios
- ios-classic
- phone
- safari

- tablet

- tizen

The platform detection not only works for stylesheets, but also for JavaScript resources. See the js array in *app.json*. When you want to include platform detection in your Sencha Touch scripts, you can use `platformConfig`.

Figure 13-6. The Windows theme

I have discussed how to implement an out-of-the-box (platform-specific) theme for your app. For a general app that would need to work on multiple devices, it's good to rely on Sencha's out-of-the-box themes. However, you may need to make your own custom theme. Creating a custom theme is ideal for when you want to showcase your own branding.

Figure 13-7. How the FindACab app looks on an iOS 6 iPad

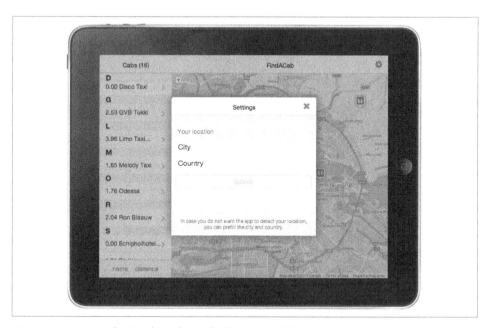

Figure 13-8. How the FindACab app looks on an iOS 7 iPad

Creating Your Own Custom Theme

When you generate a Sencha Touch application with Sencha Cmd, it will also generate an *empty* theme for you. It is called the *app.scss* (Sass) file, and it can be found in the *resources/sass* folder. Aside from the *app.scss*, it will also contain a *resources/fonts* folder with a Pictos icon font and a *config.rb* Ruby file that sets the paths to the framework mixins and variables (see Example 13-1).

Example 13-1. config.rb

```
# Get the directory that this configuration file exists in
dir = File.dirname(__FILE__)

# Load the sencha-touch framework automatically.
load File.join(dir, '..', '..', '../../touch', 'resources', 'themes')

# Compass configurations
sass_path = dir
css_path = File.join(dir, "..", "css")

# Require any additional compass plug-ins here.
images_dir = File.join(dir, "..", "images")
output_style = :compressed
environment = :production
```

This empty custom theme extends from the Sencha Touch *default* theme. You can identify this by the @import lines at the top of the file, as shown in Example 13-2.

Example 13-2. resources/sass/app.scss

//❶

```
@import 'sencha-touch/default';
@import 'sencha-touch/default/all';
```

//❷

❶   Write your Sencha variables here.

❷   Insert your custom Sass code here.

This code imports the Sass variables and mixins from the *default* resources folders. These can be found in *<touch>/resources/themes/Style Sheets/sencha-touch/*.

Above the import of mixins, you can define Sencha variables. Underneath the mixins, you can start writing your own custom styles and mixins.

After writing your Sass theme, use the following command from the *resources/sass* folder to compile to *app.css*:

```
sencha ant sass
```

Sencha Cmd 4 and higher have the command `sencha app watch`. You can compare this with the Compass command `compass watch`. Sencha Cmd *watches* the app and every time you hit Save, Sencha Cmd builds your app and compiles your Sass stylesheets. When changes are detected, only the minimum amount of work necessary is performed to bring your app and its CSS up to date, saving you from rebuilding your Sass. It is so quick that when you navigate to your browser, the latest version is present. Nice!

Instead of extending from the default theme, you can extend from one of the other themes, as shown in Examples 13-3 through 13-7.

Example 13-3. Extend from the Windows theme

```
@import 'sencha-touch/windows';
@import 'sencha-touch/windows/all';
```

Example 13-4. Extend from the BlackBerry theme

```
@import 'sencha-touch/bb10';
@import 'sencha-touch/bb10/all';
```

Example 13-5. Extend from the MountainView Android theme

```
@import 'sencha-touch/mountainview';
@import 'sencha-touch/mountainview/all';
```

Example 13-6. Extend from the Cupertino iOS theme

```
@import 'sencha-touch/cupertino';
@import 'sencha-touch/cupertino/all';
```

Example 13-7. Extend from the Tizen theme

```
@import 'sencha-touch/tizen';
@import 'sencha-touch/tizen/all';
```

My suggestion is to stick with the default theme unless your design really has to be a spin-off of one of the device-specific themes. Also note that not all mixins and variables are the same for each theme. The only way to figure out which variables and mixins apply for the device-specific themes is by opening the Sass files; for example: *<touch>/resources/themes/Style Sheets/sencha-touch/tizen*.

It is also possible to extend from the Base theme (see Figure 13-9). There are no layout styles, like colors, gradients, margins, and padding set in this theme—just the absolute necessary styles for displaying your app. This theme is the starting point for all of the Sencha out-of-the-box themes (see Example 13-8).

Example 13-8. Extend from the Base theme; you have to style everything yourself

```
@import 'sencha-touch/base';
@import 'sencha-touch/base/all';
```

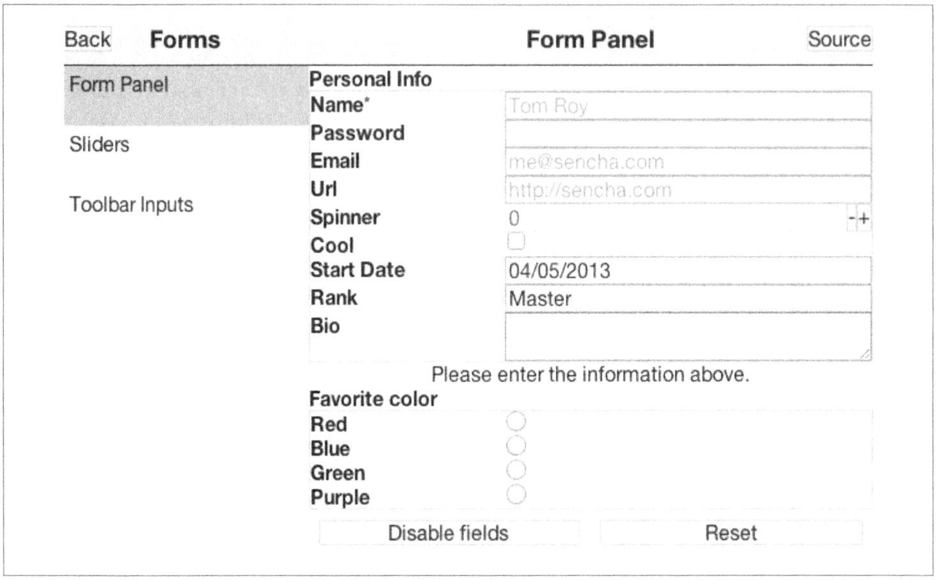

Figure 13-9. The base theme

The advantage of extending from the base theme is that you don't have to override default Sencha styles, because there are none. The base theme lays out only components; you have to style it all yourself. This reduces the file size of your Sassy CSS and therefore results in a much faster CSS compile. Themes will be compiled more quickly because you only need to compile your own custom styling. This makes writing stylesheets much more efficient.

If you want to create your own customized theme, it shouldn't look like any of the out-of-the-box themes. But note that extending from the base theme probably will also take the most time to develop. If just changing some of the base colors is more than enough for you, my suggestion would be to extend from the default theme.

By extending from the Sencha default theme, you can create good-looking themes. There are `Global-CSS` variables—like `base-color`, `neutral-color`, `font-family`—that allow you to change the overall look and feel on the fly. Take a look at the API docs, and check the `Global_CSS` variables. For example, with the variable `base-color`, you can set the main base color for the default theme. Some of the Sencha components also have CSS variables to customize the look of your components. See, for example, Figure 13-10, which shows the variables for lists. Besides CSS variables, there are also a couple of UI component mixins that are quite powerful (see Table 13-2) and global mixins (see Table 13-3).

Figure 13-10. The list component has CSS variables to customize the look of your lists

Table 13-2. Components that have component CSS variables and/or UI mixins

Component	Mixin
Ext.carousel.Carousel	sencha-carousel-indicator-ui($ui-label, $color, $gradient, $active-color, $active-gradient)
Ext.dataview.IndexBar	No mixins available
Ext.dataview.List	No mixins available
Ext.form.FieldSet	No mixins available
Ext.form.Panel	No mixins available
Ext.ActionSheet	No mixins available
Ext.Button	sencha-button-ui($ui-label, $color, $gradient)
Ext.Messagebox	No mixins available
Ext.Panel	No mixins available
Ext.Sheet	No mixins available
Ext.Toolbar	sencha-toolbar-ui($ui-label, $color, $gradient)
Ext.tab.Panel	sencha-tabbar-ui($ui-label, $bgcolor, $gradient, $color)

Table 13-3. Global CSS mixins

Mixin	Description
bevel-box($shadowtype)	Adds a small box shadow (or highlight)
bevel-by-background($bg-color)	Bevels the text based on background color
beveltext($shadowtype)	Adds a small text shadow (or hightlight)
elipsis()	Makes the element text overflow using ellipses to truncate text

Mixin	Description
icon($name, $character, $font-family)	Includes an icon to the stylesheet to be used on buttons or tabs
insertion($width, $height, $top, $left)	Adds basic styles to :before or :after CSS pseudoclasses
mask-by-background($bg-color, $percentage, $style)	Creates a background gradient for masked elements, based on the lightness of their background
toolbar-button($bg-color, $type)	Includes the default styles for toolbar buttons

With mixins, you can create different variants of button, toolbar, or carousel indicators. Out of the box, Sencha Touch ships with some mixins you can use directly on the component by setting the ui config on it. For example, Ext.ToolBar has the UIs light and dark; Ext.Button has the UIs normal, back, forward, round, plain, action, decline, and confirm; and the Ext.carousel.Carousel has the UIs light and dark. With the CSS mixins, you can create many more variants.

To implement a custom Sencha CSS mixin, you have to include the Sencha CSS mixin and pass in all the signature arguments (the first argument is always the custom UI name). Afterward, you can use the mixin in your JS component.

In the *app.scss* file, underneath the @import lines, specify:

```
@include sencha-button-ui('mycustombutton', #99A4AE, 'glossy');
@include sencha-toolbar-ui('alternative', #FF0000, 'glossy');
@include sencha-carousel-indicator-ui('gray', '#EFEFEF', 'glossy', '#FFFFFF',
                                      'glossy');
```

Here's how you can set the ui skin in your Sencha view classes:

```
var cancelBtn = Ext.create('Ext.Button',{
    text: 'Cancel',
    ui: 'mycustombutton'
});
var toolbar = Ext.create('Ext.Toolbar',{
    title: 'My Green Glossy Toolbar',
    ui: 'alternative'
});
var carousel = Ext.create('Ext.carousel.Carousel',{
    ui: 'gray',
});
```

The FindACab App Stylesheet

The stylesheet for the FindACab app extends from the Sencha Touch default theme. It sets some of the Sencha Touch variables, includes a toolbar mixin, and has a custom font and icons (see Figure 13-11). If you are curious, check out the full code of the stylesheet in Appendix B. For now, let's first discuss how to incorporate custom fonts and icons.

Figure 13-11. The FindACab app with a custom theme

There are some great resources on Sass and CSS at the Sass website (*http://sass-lang.com/*). To learn more about Sass, see The Sass Way (*http://thesassway.com/*). Learn Sass at Code School (*http://bit.ly/codeschool-sass*), and check out "Unleash Your Inner Picasso: Advanced Theming by Platform," (*http://bit.ly/picasso-vid*) an online video tutorial by Robert Dougan.

Incorporating Custom Fonts

When you want to incorporate fonts in your theme, you can use @font-face. @font-face is a CSS technique that is often used to incorporate custom web fonts. Where system fonts will be visible only if they're available on your OS, @font-face directly downloads the font from the Internet to display it. Of course, this can create a lot of headaches in terms of licenses and rights. But luckily, there are also a lot of free solutions. You can either download a @font-face kit (a package with multiple font extensions; see FontSquirrel) or use a font service (like TypeKit or Google Fonts).

Read more about `@font-face` on Paul Irish's blog (*http://bit.ly/paul-irish*) and download HTML5 `@font-face` kits from Font Squirrel (*http://www.fontsquirrel.com/*) or at font ex (*http://www.fontex.org/*). You can also use a font service like Adobe Typekit (*https://type kit.com/*) or Google Fonts (*http://www.google.com/fonts*).

Let's talk about downloading a `@font-face` kit. Unfortunately, none of the major browsers have come up with a single web font solution. Instead, they all go their own way. Therefore, you have to embed your web font with multiple extensions into your stylesheet so it works in all browsers. See Table 13-4, which lists font-face compatibility by browser as of October 2013.

Table 13-4. Cross-browser compatibility overview of font-face

Browser	TTF	EOT	WOFF	SVG
Google Chrome	X	_	X	X
Safari	X	_	X	X
Mobile Safari	X	_	X	X
IE10	_	X	X	_
Android Browser	X	_	_	X
BlackBerry Browser	X	_	X	X
Firefox	X	_	X	_

To incorporate `@font-face` fonts, create a *fonts* directory in the *resources/css/stylesheets/* folder and copy the full custom web font folder into this directory.

Would you rather store the custom fonts with your Sass file? That's possible, but then you have to manually copy over the fonts folder to your *resources/css/styles* folder. Hmmm, that might not be so ideal. Therefore, let's automate this. Sencha Cmd has built-in Apache Ant integration.

Open *build.xml* in your root folder and right before the `</project>` closing tag add the following lines of code:

```
<target name="-after-build"/>
    <target name="build"
            depends="init,-before-build,-build,-after-build"
            description="Copy over the font folder and remove temp files"/>

    <copy todir="${basedir}/resources/css/stylesheets/fonts" overwrite="true">
      <fileset dir="${basedir}/resources/sass/stylesheets/fonts">
        <include name="**/*" />
      </fileset>
    </copy>
    <copy todir="${build.dir}/resources/css/stylesheets/fonts" overwrite="true">
      <fileset dir="${basedir}/resources/sass/stylesheets/fonts">
```

```
          <include name="**/*" />
        </fileset>
      </copy>
      <delete dir="${basedir}/${build.dir}"/>
```

When you're building your application, the previous piece of code will automatically copy over the *sass/stylesheets/fonts* folder to the *resources/css/stylesheets/fonts* folder and to the same folder in the build directory.

The next step is implementing the font. You will set the name of the font that will be used throughout your stylesheet code, and you will embed all the font-types used for each different browser:

```
@font-face {
  font-family: 'MyFont';
  src: url('stylesheets/fonts/myfont.eot?22334');
  src: url('stylesheets/fonts/myfont.eot?22334#iefix')
      format('embedded-opentype'),
    url('stylesheets/fonts/myfont.woff?22334') format('woff'),
    url('stylesheets/fonts/myfont.ttf?22334') format('truetype'),
    url('stylesheets/fonts/myfont.svg?22334#myfont') format('svg');
  font-weight: normal;
  font-style: normal;
}
```

You will have to add these lines of code on top of your Sass file.

Base64 Fonts

Maybe you know that images can be saved to Base64 strings (binary to ASCII text). It's a technique that's been used for years for sending email image attachments. If you are not familiar with Base64 strings, they look like this:

```
data:image/png;base64,<LONG BASE64 STRING WITH ENCODED DATA>"
```

An advantage of a string like this is offline storage and caching. The HTML5 Storage API can save only key/value pairs, and thus only character data, so you need to Base64-encode images to store them offline. Also, if an image is Base64 and placed directly in a stylesheet, then it can be cached with the stylesheet—yes, you can save data URLs for images in stylesheets too, but each URL in an image would be a request over the wire. You can also use Base64 encoding for fonts. No longer do you need to worry about hosting a *.ttf*, *.svg*, *.woff*, or *.eot* file somewhere and embedding it.

The trick is to get a Base64 font. Fortunately, you can generate one. Just download a @font-face kit and then upload each extension to an encoder (such as Opinionated Geek's tool (*http://bit.ly/og-base64*)). It will present you with the Base64 string for each font file. These Base64 strings can be implemented in your Sass. See the solution code in Appendix B.

Once you have implemented the font in your Sass file, you will need to assign it to your components. This is easy. Just set a CSS class on a Sencha Touch component to target it from the CSS as follows:

```
{
    xtype: 'button',
    cls: 'mycustombutton'
    text: 'mytext'
}
```

Here's how to incorporate fonts in your Sass stylesheet:

```
.mycustombutton {
    font-family: 'DroidSansRegular';
    line-height: 1.6em;
}
```

Now that you know how to incorporate custom fonts in your Sencha Touch app, let's take a look at incorporating custom icons. Icons in Sencha Touch are icon fonts, so this process is more or less similar to incorporating fonts. You'll just need to make sure that a character maps to a particular font icon. Let's check out the next technique.

Incorporating Custom Icons

Sencha Touch 2.3 uses the Pictos icon font. Before version 2.3, when you wanted to include icons, you had to implement them with a custom Sencha mixin. It had a whole resources folder full of black and white icon images. After using these mixins—for example, `@include pictos-iconmask("wifi");`—you'd use a Base64 string to generate a *wifi* icon into your CSS. To mask the white background away, in your Sencha Touch code, you had to enable the config `iconMask` to `true`.

That was a nice solution, though your CSS file became large and at the end all these icons are PNG pixel images, which means that you would lose quality on retina displays or while scaling or zooming. This is not the case when using vector icon fonts, such as the Sencha Touch out-of-the-box font, Pictos.

With an icon font, icons can be delivered as a font file and are mapped to (Unicode) characters. An icon font can be embedded with CSS like any other custom font.

By using a vector font to render your icons, you can scale them to any size and they will not lose any quality. It also improves load speed and file size; by using a font, you can load all the icons at once and use CSS to change their look for hover and active states. A font made up of a few icons will have a smaller file size than an image sprite with the same number of icons.

By default, Sencha Touch ships with a couple of Pictos icons that are mapped to an `iconCls` class name. To use these, just take the mapped class name, and set the `iconCls` on the tab and button components. See Figure 13-12 for an overview.

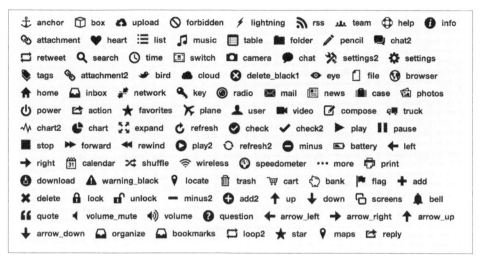

Figure 13-12. Out-of-the-box Pictos icons with their default iconCls mapped names

To incorporate a custom icon set into your design, you can set up your own custom icon font. You can download a ready-made icon font pack or you can create your own. Websites like Fontello.com (Figure 13-13) or Icomoon.io (Figure 13-14) let you choose your own icons and map these to characters and unicodes. Usually, you can specify the default font metrics (e.g., 16px), icon, and font names. Afterward, you download your custom font. The advantage of this technique is that your user won't need to download icons that are not visible and your font size will be smaller. However, for you as a developer or dev team, it might be handy to create an overview icon test page (something like Figure 13-12) so it is clear which characters/Unicodes and icon names are being used.

When you specify your own custom icon font, there's no need to ship your theme to include the Sencha Touch out-of-the-box Pictos icons, because this increases the download size of the theme for your users. It might be a good idea to turn Pictos and default fonts off. Just set the following variables on the top of your Sass file:

```
$include-pictos-font: false;
$include-default-icons: false;
```

Next, incorporate your custom icon font in the stylesheet. This works exactly the same as incorporating any other font: either convert the icon font to a Base64 string and implement this, or link to the font files in the *resources/css/fonts/fontname* folder.

Figure 13-13. Create your own custom font with Fontello.com

Figure 13-14. Create your own custom icon font with IcoMoon.io

Now that your icons are available in your theme, you need to assign them to each `iconCls` class. With an `icon` mixin—`icon($iconCls, $character, $font-family)`— this is easy:

```
@include icon('settings', 'y', 'myfontname');
```

Wow, how does that work? This mixin generates some CSS code that we will apply to a Sencha Touch component (like a button) by passing in an icon CSS class name, `iconCls`. The second argument is the mapped character (or Unicode string). It prepends this character as content in your app, right before the component. The last argument is the `font-family` name of the icon font, so it won't display the readable alphabetical character, but rather the icon.

Some components have no `icon` mixin and `iconCls` class, although it is still possible to incorporate custom icons. It is even possible to change the colors or dimensions for these icons. See the following code, where I have changed the icon for the *list disclosure* button:

```
.x-list .x-list-disclosure:before {
    content: ']';
    font-family: 'myfontname';
    color: #000;
}
```

Just refer to the CSS class of the component you want to target (you can inspect the component with your dev tools, or just add a new CSS class with the `cls` config, on the component). The trick is to use the `:before` or `:after` pseudo-selectors. This will dynamically insert the `content` character before (or after) the component in the DOM. Because these CSS rules also set the `font-family` to the icon font, an icon will be displayed (see Figure 13-15).

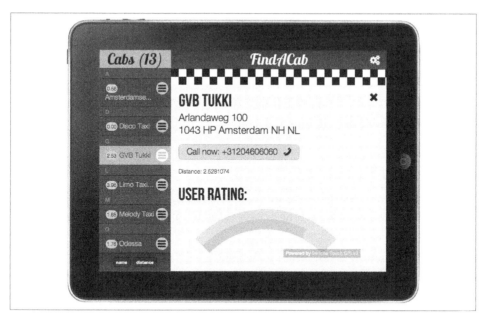

Figure 13-15. The FindACab app with custom icons; see Appendix B for the full code of the stylesheet

This section explained how to incorporate your own custom icons, which creates a custom look with the big advantage that it reduces the file size of the stylesheet (why download all icons in a stylesheet, when you just need some of them?). The next section will discuss in more detail how to optimize your stylesheet.

 Check out the Pictos icon font (*http://pictos.cc/font/*), the Ico Moon icon font (*http://icomoon.io/*), and the Fontello icon font (*http://fontel lo.com/*). There's more information about icon fonts at CSS-Tricks (*http://bit.ly/html-icon-font*), and you can use Branah's tool (*http://bit.ly/branah*) to convert text to unicodes and back.

Optimizing Your Stylesheet for Best Performance

If you want to optimize your Sencha Touch application for performance, optimizing your stylesheet is probably the easiest thing to do, and it's very effective. Custom themes can easily grow in file size. A compiled Sencha Touch CSS of 1.5 MB is not uncommon. However, it can be annoying to put a 1.5 MB stylesheet online, especially when you are visiting (or downloading) your app on a slow cellular network connection, where every kilobyte counts.

Luckily, there are easy tricks that can save many kilobytes; here are the ones we'll discuss in the next few pages:

- Minify your stylesheet
- Import only the required mixins in your stylesheet
- Exclude experimental support for uncommon browsers
- Exclude unusable default fonts and icons

Minifying Your Stylesheet

Set up the theme output style. There are a couple of settings you can choose from, shown in Table 13-5. You'll need the setting `:compressed` to minify the CSS code and reduce the file size.

The compressed setting is not meant to be human-readable. It takes up the minimum amount of possible file size, having no whitespace except what is necessary to separate selectors. It also includes some other optimization tools, such as choosing the smallest representation for colors and removing comments.

Table 13-5. Overview of all style_output settings

Setting	Description
`:compressed`	To fully minify. This reduces the file size. CSS code is not readable.
`:nested`	For easy reading and debugging while CSS is indented; it will also display Sencha comments in your CSS.
`:expanded`	For easy reading and debugging. CSS is not nested. This looks more like it's human made. It will also display Sencha comments in your CSS.
`:compact`	For reading and debugging. Compact style takes up less space than `:nested` or `:expanded`. Each CSS rule takes up one line; it will also display Sencha comments in your CSS.

You can set the `output_style` in the Compass configuration, which is a Ruby file and should be located in the *app/resources/sass/* folder. Actually, if you generated your application with Sencha Cmd, the file will be there and already has a setup for minifying your CSS. If you did not generate your app with Sencha Cmd, just add the following line to your Compass Ruby config (*config.rb*):

```
output_style = :compressed
```

Feel free to experiment with the `output_style` setting to see the file size differences.

Importing Only the Required Mixins in Your Stylesheet

By default, when you generate an application with Sencha Cmd, it will import all available Sencha Touch mixins. See Example 13-9 (and thus CSS rules for every Sencha Touch component that exists in the Sencha framework). That might be a bit more than you need. If your application doesn't use a carousel or slider form fields, it makes no sense to include all these CSS rules in your stylesheet.

Example 13-9. resources/sass/app.scss

```
@import 'sencha-touch/default';
@import 'sencha-touch/default/all';
```

Luckily, you can change this too. Usually, I comment out the `@import` line that imports *all* of the mixins. Then I list all the Sencha Touch mixins myself and I make sure Sencha Cmd is watching/compiling my Sass file (`sencha app watch`). Next, I start to comment out the mixins one by one, based on the classes I think are not being used. This is tricky, though; there are classes that you maybe never directly coded, but they are subclasses from other classes, such as `Class` or `Panel`. That's why you should remove the mixins one by one, while watching your terminal to make sure you don't get any compile errors.

The list of all the available Sencha Touch mixins can be found in *touch/resources/themes/<theme-to-extend-from>/all.scss*. They differ per Sencha theme. When I start listing the mixins in my own Sass file, I need to prefix them with the correct full path from the *touch/resources/themes/* folder, so my compiler won't crash:

```
@import 'sencha-touch/default';
/*@import 'sencha-touch/default/all';*/

@import 'sencha-touch/default/src/_Class.scss';
@import 'sencha-touch/default/src/_Button.scss';
@import 'sencha-touch/default/src/_Panel.scss';
/*@import 'sencha-touch/default/src/_Sheet.scss';*/
@import 'sencha-touch/default/src/_MessageBox.scss';
@import 'sencha-touch/default/src/_Toolbar.scss';
/*@import 'sencha-touch/default/src/_Menu.scss';*/
/*@import 'sencha-touch/default/src/carousel/_Carousel.scss';*/
@import 'sencha-touch/default/src/form/_Panel.scss';
@import 'sencha-touch/default/src/form/_FieldSet.scss';
@import 'sencha-touch/default/src/field/_Field';
/*@import 'sencha-touch/default/src/field/_Checkbox.scss';*/
/*@import 'sencha-touch/default/src/field/_Radio.scss';*/
/*@import 'sencha-touch/default/src/field/_Search.scss';*/
/*@import 'sencha-touch/default/src/field/_Select.scss';*/
/*@import 'sencha-touch/default/src/field/_Slider.scss';*/
/*@import 'sencha-touch/default/src/field/_Spinner.scss';*/
/*@import 'sencha-touch/default/src/field/_TextArea.scss';*/
/*@import 'sencha-touch/default/src/dataview/_IndexBar.scss';*/
@import 'sencha-touch/default/src/dataview/_List.scss';
/*@import 'sencha-touch/default/src/picker/_Picker.scss';*/
/*@import 'sencha-touch/default/src/plugin/_ListPaging.scss';*/
/*@import 'sencha-touch/default/src/plugin/_PullRefresh.scss';*/
/*@import 'sencha-touch/default/src/slider/_Slider.scss';*/
@import 'sencha-touch/default/src/slider/_Toggle.scss';
/*@import 'sencha-touch/default/src/tab/_Panel.scss';*/
```

The previous example is used in the FindACab app. The Sass theme for the FindACab app won't need CSS rules for unused components like textareas and carousels. Therefore, you don't need to import the mixins.

Excluding Experimental Support for Uncommon Browsers

Compass makes it easy to code many of the CSS3 vendor-prefixed properties, without having to type it all out by hand. (No more typos!) For example, if you want to have rounded borders, you could use the Compass mixin border-radius, which will generate all of the vendor-prefixed CSS properties you need:

```
.round {
    @include border-radius(5px);
}
```

This will generate this:

```
.round {
    -moz-border-radius: 5px;
    -webkit-border-radius: 5px;
    -o-border-radius: 5px;
    -ms-border-radius: 5px;
```

```
    -khtml-border-radius: 5px;
    border-radius: 5px;
}
```

Sencha makes use of a lot of these Compass mixins. This can easily increase your CSS file size. Maybe you are building your application only for iOS, or maybe you are displaying a custom theme only for certain platforms. In either case, there is no need to include all these vendor-prefixed properties. IE10 supports HTML5; a lot of CSS properties don't need to be prefixed with `-ms-`; and the browsers Opera and Konquerer are not supported by Sencha Touch (yet).

That's why it might be handy to disable the vendor-prefixed properties. The following code showcases how to disable them for the browsers Konquerer, Opera, and Internet Explorer. Add these variables to the top of your Sass stylesheet (*app/resources/sass/app.scss*), right before the import of the Sencha mixins:

```
$experimental-support-for-opera:false;
$experimental-support-for-khtml:false;
$experimental-support-for-microsoft :false;
@import "compass/css3";
```

Excluding Default Fonts and Icons

Maybe you are not using any icons at all, in which case there is no need to implement the Pictos icon font. Or maybe you are using just a few icons. In those scenarios, it might be better to incorporate your own icon font and disable the out-of-the-box Pictos font. By default, Pictos icons are enabled; disabling them can easily save up to 100KB.

Take a look at the following code. Add these variables to the top of your Sass stylesheet (*app/resources/sass/app.scss*), right before the import of the Sencha mixins:

```
$include-pictos-font: false;
$include-default-icons: false;
```

Summary

Now that you have a whole bag of tricks to reduce the CSS file size, you are ready to go live! Another great way of optimizing your application is to create production builds, a topic we will discuss in the next chapter.

## CHAPTER 14

Builds

While developing the FindACab app, you might have noticed all the JavaScript classes that are loaded in the memory (see Figure 14-1). This is a mix of Sencha Touch framework classes and the custom classes you wrote yourself (i.e., everything that's in the FindACab namespace). Obviously, this is not what you want for production environments, given that every JavaScript file is a separate network request and it can be a huge performance hit, especially on a mobile connection.

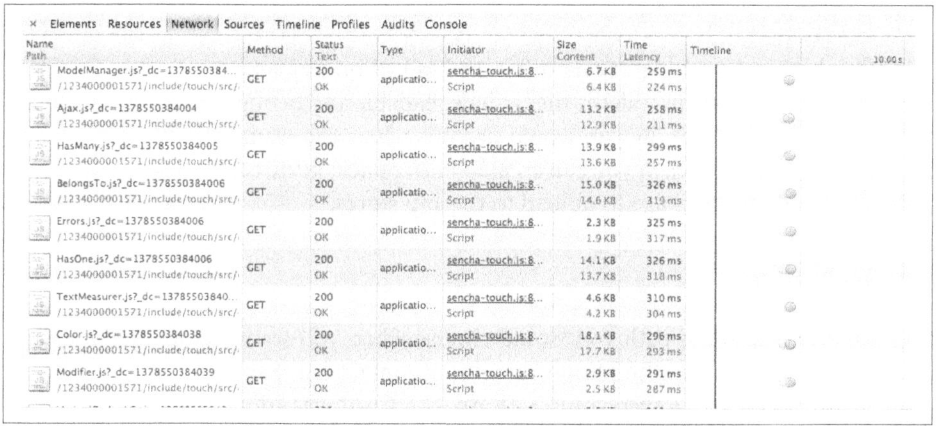

Figure 14-1. All the Sencha Touch JavaScript classes that are loaded in the memory during development

This is why you want to create a *build package*, a small package with only the absolutely necessary code for running your app. The package *concatenates* (joins) all the JavaScript classes that you use in the correct order, whether these are custom classes or Sencha Touch framework classes, and also minifies them to reduce the file size smaller. The creation of the build package is called the *build process*. You'll use the Sencha Cmd tool for this. Remember the process for writing a Sencha Touch application with code? The last step in this process is to create a build with Sencha Cmd (see Figure 14-2). If you have used Sencha Cmd to generate your application, building the app is a piece of cake.

Figure 14-2. The process for writing a Sencha Touch application

 You didn't use Sencha Cmd to generate your folder structure? You might be missing metadata files for Sencha Cmd and therefore your builds can fail. Is this bad? No. Usually in this case, I generate a new folder structure with Sencha Cmd, but with the same namespace as the app that couldn't build. After the folder structure is generated, I copy over the *app* folder (and sometimes also the *app.js* file, if there are no special changes made). Then I start running the build process again. It should work. This tip also works great when you have build errors and you have no idea what's wrong or how to fix it. (It could be an error with your metadata...)

With Sencha Cmd, you can create different kind of build packages. You can create a build for *test environments* (all the files will be readable and debuggable), you can create a *production build* (typically you would use this when you want to host your application on some web server), or you can create a *native* package directly from Sencha Cmd. This can be a native package to upload to the app stores.

Going Native

Going native is also the path you would choose when you want to implement device API capabilities, such as the phone camera or contact list. Sencha Touch ships with device APIs. Version 2.3 even ships with Apache Cordova/Adobe PhoneGap support (see Table 14-1). This means you can build Cordova/PhoneGap packages from the command line with Sencha Cmd, and if you use the device APIs within Sencha, Sencha will use the Cordova/PhoneGap implementations when you create a build for Cordova or PhoneGap.

If you are interested in using those, see the API docs and check out the Ext.device package, or visit the Cordova website (*http://bit.ly/cordova-docs*).

Adobe PhoneGap is built on top of Apache Cordova, and both have access to the API. PhoneGap is commercial and Cordova is open source. PhoneGap and Cordova differ in how their packaging tools are implemented. PhoneGap provides a remote building interface (*http://build.phonegap.com*) that lets you package and emulate an app for a single platform in the cloud. Cordova packaging tools let you build simultaneously for multiple platforms on your own computer when the SDKs are installed. In addition, Cordova is constantly updated by the open source community, and offers lots of plug-ins for download, whereas PhoneGap updates are coordinated by Adobe.

Table 14-1. An overview of all the supported Sencha and Cordova device APIs

Name	Description
`Ext.device.accelerometer.Cordova`	Sencha Touch wrapper for the device's motion sensor device API
`Ext.device.Browser`	Sencha Touch wrapper with the Cordova InAppBrowser
`Ext.device.Camera`	Sencha Touch wrapper with the Cordova device camera device API
`Ext.device.Capture`	Sencha Touch wrapper with the Cordova capture media device APIs
`Ext.device.Compass`	Sencha Touch wrapper with the Cordova compass device API
`Ext.device.Connection`	Sencha Touch wrapper with the Cordova connection device API
`Ext.device.Contacts`	Sencha Touch wrapper with the Cordova contact list device API
`Ext.device.Device`	Sencha Touch wrapper with Cordova device and Cordova events
`Ext.device.FileSystem`	Sencha Touch wrapper with the Cordova filesystem
`Ext.device.Geolocation`	Sencha Touch wrapper with the Cordova geolocation device API
`Ext.device.Globalization`	Sencha Touch wrapper with the Cordova globalization device API
`Ext.device.Media`	Sencha Touch wrapper with the Cordova audio device API
`Ext.device.Notification`	Sencha Touch wrapper with the Cordova notification device API
`Ext.device.Orientation`	Sencha class that listens to the `orientationchange` event
`Ext.device.Push`	Sencha device API that provides a way to send push notifications to a device
`Ext.device.Purchases`	Sencha device that checks whether purchases were made
`Ext.device.Splashscreen`	Sencha Touch wrapper with the Cordova splash screen
`Ext.device.SQLite`	Sencha device API that provides an API for storing data in databases that can be queried using SQL

 There's a nice online Sencha Guide (*http://bit.ly/sencha-apis*) that explains how to implement native device APIs.

Build Resources

Whatever build option you choose, all the build packages will create a *resources* folder with icons, splash screens, and loading images (see Table 14-2). By default, these image resources display the Sencha logo. I know, you don't want this. However, it is very handy to open these images in, for example, Adobe Photoshop and paste your own icon in it. Note that the icons and splash screens are hooked up to the app via the `Ext.applica tion.Application` class in *app.js*. Extra icons or different icon dimensions can be changed in *app.js*.

The generated icons and images are very iOS-device oriented. Apple has special naming conventions for naming an icon or a startup splash screen. See, for example, in Table 14-2 the splash and loading screens. Also notice the dimensions; it takes the height of the device minus 20px of the status bar. For example, the size of an iPad is 768×1,024, so the size of the splash screen should be 768×1,004 in portrait mode.

 There are some design guidelines you need to know with regards to the iOS icons: Apple trims 1 pixel off every icon border for shadows, and you don't have to design the border radius for an icon. You can create your own glow, or have no icon glow at all. In the *app.js* file, when you set `isIconPrecomposed` to `true`, Apple will not add a glossy effect to the icon, so the icon will preserve its exact look.

Table 14-2. Stylesheets that are shipped with Sencha Touch out of the box

Filename	Description
startup/320x460.jpg	Default iPhone splash screen
startup/640x920.png	Retina iPhone splash screen
startup/748x1024.png	iPad splash screen
startup/768x1004.png	iPad splash screen
startup/1496x2048.png	Retina iPad splash screen
startup/1536x2008.png	Retina iPad splash screen
loading/Default-LandScape@2x~ipad.png	2,048×1,496 iPad retina landscape loading screen
loading/Default-LandScape~ipad.png	1,024×748 iPad landscape loading landing screen
loading/Default-LandScapeLeft~ipad.png	1,024×748 iPad landscape loading landing screen
loading/Default-LandScapeRight~ipad.png	1,024×48 iPad landscape loading landing screen (different orientation)
loading/Default-Portrait@2x~ipad.png	1,536×2,008 retina iPad loading screen
loading/Default-Portrait~ipad.png	768×1,004 iPad loading screen
loading/Default-PortraitUpsideDown~ipad.png	768×1,004 iPad loading screen (different orientation)
loading/Default.png	320×480 iPad loading screen
loading/Default@2x.png	640×960 loading screen

Filename	Description
loading/Default~ipad.png	768×1,004 iPad loading screen
icons/icon-spot~ipad.png	Search results on 50×50 iPad RBG icon
icons/Icon.png	Default iPhone 57×57 RGB icon
icons/Icon@2x.png	Retina iPhone 114×114 RGB icon
not available	Retina iPhone 120×120 RGB iOS 7 icon
icons/Icon~ipad.png	iPad 72×72 RGB icon
not available	iPad 76×76 RGB iOS 7
icons/Icon~ipad@2x.png	Retina iPad 144×144 RGB icon
not available	Retina iPad 152×152 RGB iOS 7 icon
icons/iTunesArtwork.png	500×500 RGB icon used by App Store

Adding Non-MVC Folders to Your Build Package

Sometimes you want to add extra (non-MVC) folders with JavaScript classes to your concatenated JavaScript build. Remember how we created a *utils* folder with a JavaScript class that contains `statics`? Sometimes you want to create additional JavaScript classes with logic or statics outside the Sencha MVC folder structure. When these JavaScript files are not within the *app* folder, Sencha Cmd doesn't know they exist when it wants to build your app. Thus, there might be situations in which you want to let Sencha Cmd know about them, which is totally possible. There is an *app* and workspace `class path`. The `workspace.classpath` matters when you have multiple applications and you want to share code (or a copy of the framework) between all apps; in all other situations, the `app.classpath` should be good enough.

For the FindACab app, I have added the *utils* folder to the app classpath in *./sencha/sencha.cfg*:

```
app.classpath=${app.dir}/app.js,${app.dir}/app,${app.dir}/utils
```

Adding Extra Resources to Your Build Package

In other situations, you might want to include extra resources to your build package—for example, a folder with images or a folder with JSON data. There are two ways to include these in your build. I will explain both. First (the easy way, shown in Example 14-1), you can add the folder to the `resources` array in the *app.json* file. By default, Sencha Cmd already created a selection.

Example 14-1. Additional resources that need to be copied during the build process

```
/**
 * Extra resources to be copied along when building
 */
"resources": [
    "resources/images",
    "resources/css",
    "resources/icons",
    "resources/startup"
],
```

 Additional JavaScripts or stylesheets can be entered into the js or css arrays.

The other way of adding resources to your build is what I call the hardcore way, but it's kinda cool so I want to mention it. Sencha Cmd has Apache Ant integration. You can modify the Ant build script *build.xml* totally to your own needs. See Example 14-2; this little Ant script copies a *data* folder from the application root to the *production* build folder. Isn't it awesome?

Example 14-2. Copying a folder to a different location

```
<target name="-after-build"/>
<target name="build"
        depends="init,-before-build,-build,-after-build"
        description="Builds the application"/>

<copy todir="${build.dir}/data" overwrite="true">
  <fileset dir="${basedir}/data">
    <include name="**/*" />
  </fileset>
</copy>
```

Now that you know all the background information about build processes in Sencha Touch, let's create some build packages with the next techniques.

In the next sections, you'll learn how to:

- Create a test build with Sencha Cmd
- Create a production build with Sencha Cmd
- Create a native build with Sencha Cmd and Adobe PhoneGap

Creating a Test Build with Sencha Cmd

With Sencha Cmd on the command line, you can generate a build package optimized for test environments. On the command line, navigate to the *app* folder and run the following:

```
sencha app build testing
```

The test build can be found in the *<myapp>/build/testing/<appname>* folder, which has the following structure (see Figure 14-3):

testing/<appname>/

- *app.js*
- *app.json*
- *index.html*
- *resources*
  - *css/*
    - *app.css*
  - *images*
  - *loading*
  - *startup*

When you create a build for a test environment, Sencha Cmd will concatenate all the used JavaScript class files to one single file, *app.js*. These are all your custom Sencha Touch classes and all framework classes that you use, listed in the correct order. However, this JavaScript file won't be minified and is still readable. In addition, the (framework) comments will be present.

app.css is the CSS stylesheet compiled from the *resources/sass/app.scss* Sass file. In the test package, this file is not minified and still readable.

Another cool thing to know is that Sencha Cmd also verifies (*lints*) your JavaScript during the build process. If it finds a problem, it returns a warning message describing the problem.

When the build succeeds, you can test the package in your browser. For the FindACab app, the URL would look like *http://localhost/findacab/build/testing/FindACab/*.

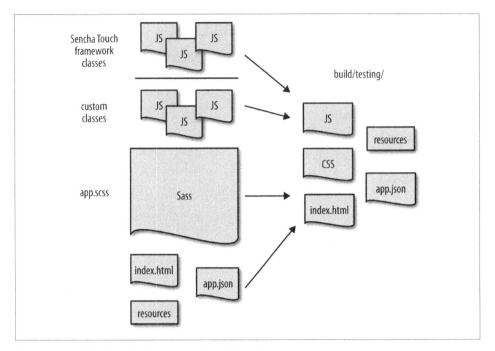

Figure 14-3. The Sencha Touch test build package

Now that you have completed your first test build, you are ready for production. Let's create the first production build!

I'm often asked which tools are good for testing a Sencha Touch application. For UI testing, Siesta is a good tool; for syntax testing, you could use JS Lint; and for unit testing, Jasmine is a popular testing tool. For more information, check out this great blog post (*http:// bit.ly/auto-tests*), which contains all the links to the tools.

Creating a Production Build with Sencha Cmd

Production builds in Sencha Touch are little packages that you want to host on the Web. Usually such a build package can be uploaded to some server so users can browse with their mobile devices to the URL of the app. Once the app is loaded, the app can be bookmarked to the home screen of the user's device. From that moment, visiting your app is no different than opening a native app. The user will see an icon and maybe a splash screen. Data can be available offline, with techniques such as AppCache, Local Storage, or local databases.

With Sencha Cmd on the command line, you can generate a build package optimized for production. On the command line, navigate to the *app* folder and run the following:

```
sencha app build
```

The production build can be found in the *<myapp>/build/production/<appname>* folder, which has the following structure (see Figure 14-4):

production/<appname>

- *app.js*
- *app.json*
- *index.html*
- *cache.appcache*
- *deltas*
- *resources/*
    - *css/*
        - *app.css*
    - *images*
    - *loading*
    - *startup*

When you create a build for production, Sencha Cmd will concatenate all the used JavaScript class files to one single file, *app.js*. These are all your custom Sencha Touch classes and all of the framework classes that you use, listed in the correct order. In production builds, the *app.js* JavaScript file and the *app.css* stylesheet are both minified and comments are removed. This will make the file size nice and small, so it won't take a lot of download time on a mobile network connection.

The bare minimum you will need to upload to your web server and show your app online are the *index.html*, the *app.js*, and the *app.css* files (and when you have images in the *images* folder you'll need that folder, too). However, when you want to have offline capabilities (i.e., the app can be cached offline), you will need a *cache.appcache* file, the deltas folder, and assets like the icons and splash screens for when the app is bookmarked.

The *deltas* folder is an important folder that tracks the version differences every time you edit your application and create a production build. By collecting deltas, you ensure that your user sees a pop up when he opens the app and there is a newer version available. When the user chooses to get the latest version, he will not redownload the full app, only the differences. That's really nice on a mobile network connection!

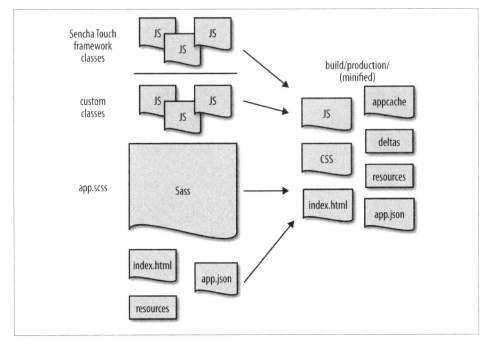

Figure 14-4. The Sencha Touch production build package

When the build succeeds, you can preview the package in your browser. For the FindACab app the URL, would look like *http://localhost/findacab/build/production/ FindACab*. You can see the finalized FindACab app in Figure 14-5.

Let's say you're testing your application. You make a change to fix a bug and then create a build. Refresh the browser—oh no, the bug is not fixed. So again you make a change, create a build... Such processes can be exhausting. Luckily, Sencha Cmd 4 and newer have app watch. Sencha Cmd watches the app and every time you hit Save, it builds your app and compiles your Sass stylesheets. To see the details, you can look at *.sencha/app/watch-impl.xml*, which is imported by the master build script *build.xml*.

Well done! You've completed your first production build. This build is optimized for delivering your application on a web server. Now maybe you want to make some money with it by selling it in an app store. Let's discuss native builds in the next section.

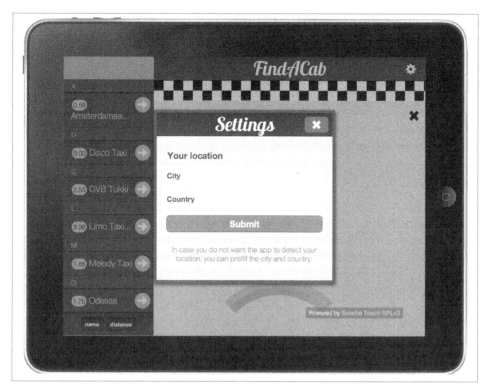

Figure 14-5. The finalized FindACab app

Creating a Native Build with Sencha Cmd and Adobe PhoneGap

You can also create a native package (a hybrid app) with Sencha Cmd to distribute it to various app stores. Currently, there are three products you can use to create a native app from a Sencha Touch code base:

- Sencha Mobile Packager
- Adobe PhoneGap
- Apache Cordova

All products are supported by the Sencha Device API, which allows you to access hardware resources on devices.

Let's go over the differences between these three solutions.

Sencha Mobile Packager

The Sencha Mobile Packager is an old solution and it's included in Sencha Cmd. It uses the *packager.json* file to build iOS or Android build packages locally that can be distributed through the Android Marketplace or Apple App Store. It requires an installation of XCode (for iOS development) or Android Developer Tools (for Android development) to build the package. Because it supports only iOS and Android and getting it to work can be complicated, we won't use this solution for the FindACab app. There are easier solutions supported by Sencha.

Apache Cordova

Apache Cordova is a top-level project within the Apache Software Foundation. Cordova is the free, open source, community-driven version of Adobe PhoneGap. Cordova lets you package apps locally and distribute them through the Android Marketplace, Black-Berry App World, Windows Phone Store, or Apple App Store. Building packages locally via the command line requires an installation of XCode (for iOS development), Android Developer Tools (for Android development), BlackBerry 10 SDK (for BlackBerry 10 development), Tizen SDK (for Tizen development), or Windows 8 Pro with Visual Studio (for Windows Phone development). Sencha Cmd has Apache Cordova integration in the Sencha Cmd build process. Although it's a good solution, we won't use it for the FindACab app, so we don't have to deal with installing all the various SDKs on your machine.

Adobe PhoneGap

Adobe PhoneGap is a commercial solution. You can build locally (which requires the installation of the SDKs) or use the PhoneGap Build cloud service (see Figure 14-6) to remotely package your apps and distribute them through the Android Marketplace, BlackBerry App World, Windows Phone Store, or Apple App Store. It's an easy solution, and you can test applications on your device by scanning a QR code. PhoneGap Build is a commercial service; the free version is limited to one private app. Paid users can access private GitHub repos or upload multiple zip packages.

With PhoneGap Build, you can build native apps to distribute for these platforms:

- iOS
- Android
- Windows
- BlackBerry
- HP
- Symbian

Building packages via PhoneGap Build requires a free Adobe PhoneGap Build account (*https://build.phonegap.com/apps*). To create a PhoneGap account, you will need an Adobe ID (account), and if you want to use the free services you will also need a GitHub account linked to your PhoneGap account.

Figure 14-6. The PhoneGap Build website

 We will use PhoneGap Build in this book. If you would rather use Cordova, you can use the same commands as you see in this chapter, but replace the word phonegap with cordova on the command line. In order to use PhoneGap/Cordova with Sencha Cmd, you will need to have NodeJS, Apache Cordova, or Adobe PhoneGap installed on your machine. See Appendix A for more details.

Initialize a PhoneGap Project

The first step in building a hybrid app is to issue the following command from your project's directory to enable PhoneGap support:

```
sencha phonegap init <APP-ID> <APP-NAME>
```

- The <App ID> follows this pattern: <REVERSED-DOMAIN>.<APPLICATION-NAME>.

- The `<APP-NAME>` should be the same value as the `name` property that you specified in your Sencha Touch *app.json* file.

 If you want to port to an iOS app, you will need to make sure that the App ID is the same one that you registered in your Apple provisioning portal.

Here's the command I used to enable PhoneGap support for the FindACab app:

```
sencha phonegap init com.ladysign-apps.findacab FindACab
```

 Mac OS X users might need to prefix with `sudo` to get administrative rights.

This generated the following structure/files:

- *phonegap* folder structure
- *phonegap.local.properties*
- *config.xml*

The PhoneGap Folder Structure

MyApp/phonegap contains the full PhoneGap file structure. If you used Cordova to initialize a project, the folder will be named *cordova*. This folder structure contains the *platforms* subfolder. When you have a development SDK installed (such as XCode), it allows you to open the SDK project files to build it locally.

The phonegap.local.properties File

The *phonegap.local.properties* file contains the names of the platforms that you want to support when building locally. By default, it takes the local installed SDKs; for example:

```
phonegap.platforms=ios blackberry10
```

The following options are possible:

- `ios` (iOS)
- `android` (Android)

- `blackberry10` (BlackBerry 10)
- `wp` (Windows Phone)

When you run the `phonegap init` command, the property file also gives you settings for the Adobe PhoneGap remote packager. When you have a PhoneGap Build account, you can set up these additional settings to support building remotely from the command line:

```
phonegap.build.remote=true

# Username for PhoneGap Build
phonegap.build.remote.username={username}
# Password for PhoneGap Build
phonegap.build.remote.password={password}
```

When you leave the `phonegap.build.remote` property as `false`, you need to have one of the SDKs (XCode, Android Developer Tools, BlackBerry 10 SDK, or Windows 8 Pro with Visual Studio) installed on your machine.

The config.xml Settings

The *config.xml* file contains references to the icons, splash images, and setups for device API features. The *config.xml* file for the FindACab app could look like Example 14-3.

Example 14-3. config.xml file for PhoneGap

```xml
<?xml version='1.0' encoding='utf-8'?>
<widget id="com.ladysign-apps.findacapp" version="1.0.0"
      xmlns="http://www.w3.org/ns/widgets" xmlns:gap="http://phonegap.com/ns/1.0">
  <name>FindACab</name>
  <description>
      Find nearby Taxi's
  </description>
  <author email="lee.boonstra@sencha.com" href="http://ladysign-apps.com">
      Lee Boonstra
  </author>
  <feature name="http://api.phonegap.com/1.0/device" />
  <preference name="permissions" value="none" />
  <preference name="orientation" value="default" />
  <preference name="target-device" value="tablet" />
  <preference name="fullscreen" value="true" />
  <preference name="webviewbounce" value="true" />
  <preference name="prerendered-icon" value="true" />
  <preference name="stay-in-webview" value="false" />
  <preference name="ios-statusbarstyle" value="black-translucent" />
  <preference name="detect-data-types" value="true" />
  <preference name="exit-on-suspend" value="false" />
  <preference name="show-splash-screen-spinner" value="true" />
  <preference name="auto-hide-splash-screen" value="true" />
  <preference name="disable-cursor" value="false" />
```

```
            <preference name="android-minSdkVersion" value="7" />
            <preference name="android-installLocation" value="auto" />
            <icon src="resources/icons/Icon.png" />
            <icon gap:platform="ios" height="57"
                src="resources/icons/Icon.png" width="57" />
            <icon gap:platform="ios" height="72"
                src="resources/icons/Icon~ipad.png" width="72" />
            <icon gap:platform="ios" height="114"
                src="resources/icons/Icon@2x.png" width="114" />
            <icon gap:platform="ios" height="144"
                src="resources/icons/Icon~ipad@2x.png" width="144" />
            <gap:splash gap:platform="ios" height="480"
                src="resources/loading/Default.png" width="320" />
            <gap:splash gap:platform="ios" height="960"
                src="resources/loading/Default@2x.png" width="640" />
            <gap:splash gap:platform="ios" height="1024"
                src="resources/loading/Default-Portrait~ipad.png" width="768" />
            <gap:splash gap:platform="ios" height="768"
                src="resources/loading/Default-Landscape~ipad.png" width="1024" />
            <access origin="*" />
    </widget>
```

If you want to create apps for iOS 6 or iOS 7, you will need to include a splash screen for retina display with the correct size. The name
should be *Default-568h@2x.png*, and the size in pixels should be
640×1,136. Only when you add this image to the resources and your
config.xml file will the viewport automatically size for iPhone 5 (and
up) screen heights.

Add a *Default-568h@2x.png* splash image to support larger screens as
follows:

```
            <gap:splash gap:platform="ios" height="1136"
                src="resources/loading/Default-568h@2x.png" width="640" />+
```

Building the Native Build Package

After you've initialized your application with PhoneGap or Cordova, it's time to create
a native build.

Run the following from the command line:

```
sencha app build -run native
```

The -run argument makes sure your app will be loaded in an emulator that's installed on your machine. Again, Mac OS X users might
need to prefix with sudo to get administrative rights.

When you're building locally, PhoneGap will build the applications in the *MyApp/phonegap* (or *MyApp/cordova*) folder:

- *platforms/android/bin*: Android *.apk* file
- *platforms/ios/build/*: iOS *.app* file
- *platforms/blackberry10/build/simulator*: BlackBerry 10 *.bar* file
- *platforms/wp8/Bin/Debug*: Windows Phone *.xap* file

When building via the PhoneGap Build service, you will see the various build packages showing up on the PhoneGap Build website. Wow, it's never been so easy!

When you want to delete an application from the PhoneGap Build website, click on the app. Click the Settings button. Scroll down to the bottom of the page and enter the Danger Zone. Click on the Delete button to remove the app.

When you build for iOS, you might run into a build error because you need to *code sign* the iOS app. With PhoneGap Build, you'll need to upload the **.p12 certificate* and the **.mobileprovisioning* mobile provisioning profile. After you've uploaded these two keys, you can unlock the keys and rebuild.

If you're building the app locally (PhoneGap `remote=false` or you use Cordova and the development SDKs), you can open *platforms/ios/Dinmu.xcodeproj* from the *phonegap* or *cordova* folder, and maintain the build settings to code sign the application. Your developer identity should be in the Code Signing Identity list (Figure 14-7). If it's not, you probably need to go through the whole native provisioning process again.

You could also upload a package to PhoneGap Build yourself. In that case, you could create a normal production build for the Web with Sencha Cmd and create a zip package from the *<Workspace>/build/production/<MyApp>* folder, without the *deltas* folder and the *cache.appcache* file.

Figure 14-7. XCode users: note the developer identity in your Code Signing Identity list

Testing a Native Build

If you're using PhoneGap Build, testing the application on Android devices will be very easy. Simply scan the QR code or download, drag, and drop the *.apk* file on the memory card of your phone.

For iOS and Windows Phone, you will need provisioning and code signing, which assures users that the app is from a known source and hasn't been modified since it was last signed. iOS Windows Phone developers will need a (paid) developer account. After creating a signed build, you can scan the QR code or drag the *.app* or *.xap* file over. (iOS developers will need to install the app on their phones with iTunes.)

 Once you have an iOS developer account, you'll need to set up a certificate, an identifier, and a provisioning profile. You will need a Mac machine for this. See Appendix A to review how to make your phone ready for testing on iOS devices.

Previewing your app on your device works really well. Browse to *http://build.phonegap.com* and use a QR reader application to scan the QR code on your app build overview page. This will autoinstall your mobile PhoneGap apps on your device.

Want more information about porting your mobile web app to native? Get help for building iOS apps with PhoneGap in the documentation (*http://docs.build.phonegap.com*); find iOS developer resources at Apple Developer (*https://developer.apple.com/*) and read more about the *config.xml* file in the "Basics" (*http://bit.ly/phonegap-build*) section of the PhoneGap documentation.

Summary

Well done! By now, you can preview your app on your phone or tablet. Congratulations. Now you know all concepts for creating a real-world application with Sencha Touch. I talked about all the basics, like the layout system, events, and the class system. I discussed MVC, and you implemented models, stores, controllers, and views in your application. When you built the FindACab app, you made a remote JSONP connection to the Yelp web service and saved it locally with a client SQL proxy. I discussed several view components like panels, lists, and Google Maps. I showed how to create a custom theme using Sass and how to create both production and native builds.

This is where I will say goodbye. With this Sencha knowledge, you should have the skills to start creating your own awesome Sencha Touch apps! I'm looking forward to seeing those in the app stores!

Help with iOS Certificates and Provisioning

Running test applications on your iOS device can be hard. It's not as simple as dragging and dropping an application via iTunes to your device. No, all iOS builds need to be signed by a developer certificate and a provisioning profile that is tied to your Apple developer account (*http://developer.apple.com*).

You will need a Mac to set up a certificate and provisioning profile. Log into the member center (*https://developer.apple.com/membercenter/*). Click on "Manage your certificates, App IDs, devices, and provisioning profiles." to open the Certificates, Identifiers & Profiles view (see Figure A-1).

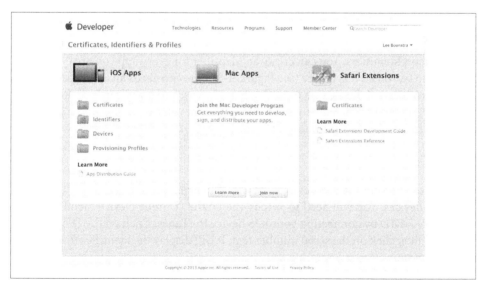

Figure A-1. The Apple developer portal

Certificates

Here are the steps for setting up your certificate profile:

1. Click "Manage your certificates, App IDs, devices, and provisioning profiles."
2. Go to the Certificate Center and create a certificate. For development, you will need an iOS development certificate; when you want to start selling your apps in the App Store, you will need an iOS distribution certificate.
3. While creating certificates, you will need to open the KeyChain Access tool on your Mac. (Use Spotlight search to find the tool if you have never used it before.)
4. Within this tool, click on KeyChain Access Certificate Assistant → Request… and then save the certificate request to your hard disk.
5. In the developer portal, press the Continue button. The next step is to upload this certificate request in your iOS member center.
6. Press the Generate button. It will sign the certificates. After that, you can download the signed certificate and import it in the KeyChain Access Tool by double-clicking on the certificate (*.cer* file).
7. Click Certificates in the left category bar (see Figure A-2). Right-click on one of your Apple developer certificates, and choose Export. Give the certificate the name Developer or Distribution and sign the certificate with your password (*.p12* extension). Save the certificate on your hard disk too. You will use it later.

Identifiers

Next, click on Identifiers. You can create an identifier for every app you are developing and want to test on an iOS device (see Figure A-3). The app needs an app id description (text), app id prefix (choose one from the drop-down), and a wildcard app id (this the bundle ID; remember the name you are using, as you will use it often). The bundle id should be in reverse-domain-name style; for example, *com.domainname.**.

Devices

Now, you can register the iOS devices you would like to test on. It is possible to register up to 100 devices. You will need to specify the UDID (Unique Device identifier). You can get this UDID by connecting your iOS device to iTunes. Click on the Device Summary, and then click on the serial number text. It will display the identifier that you can copy and paste.

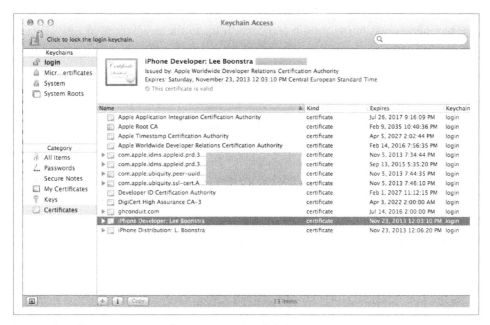

Figure A-2. Export your certificate to your hard disk

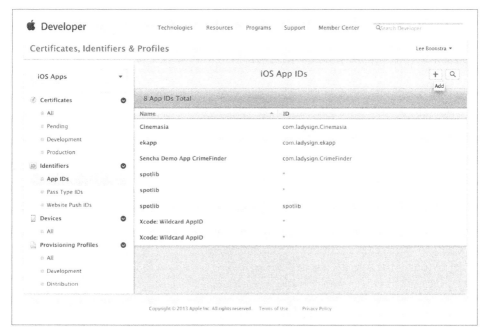

Figure A-3. Create an app identifier in the Apple developer portal

Provisioning Profile

Create a new provisioning profile and hook it up to the newly created App ID (see Figure A-4).

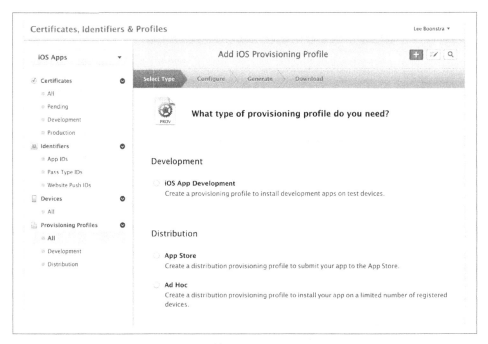

Figure A-4. Create a provisioning profile

Choose a certificate and a device. Then generate your profile. Download the *.mobile-provisioning* profile somewhere safe on your hard disk; you will need it later (see Figure A-5).

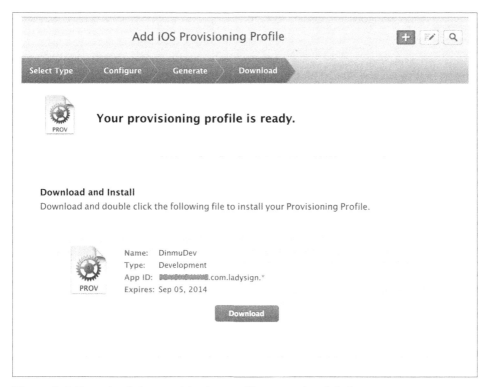

Figure A-5. Download the provisioning profile to your hard disk

iOS Provisioning and PhoneGap

On the PhoneGap Build website, click on the app so it opens edit mode. Next to the iOS build option, you should see a drop-down to enter a key. Click "add new key," and upload the certificate and the mobile provisioning file (see Figure A-6).

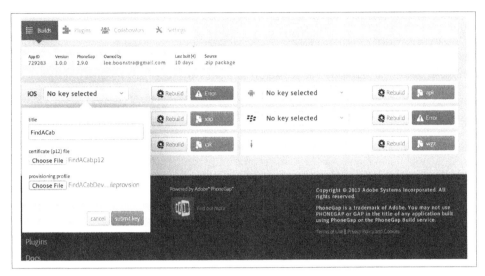

Figure A-6. Upload your certificate and your provisioning profile to the PhoneGap Build site

After uploading, you should be prompted to enter the password you used for the Key-Chain Access tool. (If you're not, click on the yellow lock icon.) When the key is suc-cessfully submitted, you can finally build for iOS.

Custom Stylesheet for the FindACab App

Example B-1 gives the full code of the custom Sass theme for the FindACab app.

Example B-1. resources/sass/app.scss

```scss
@font-face{
 font-family: "Bebas";
 src: url(data:font/ttf;base64,-some-base-64-string) format('woff');
}

$yellow: rgba(250,178,68,1);
$black: #494949;
$base-color: $yellow;
$alternative-color: lighten(#494949, 5%);
$alert-color: #B0886D;
$confirm-color: #FFA500;
$active-color: darken($base-color, 1%);

// GRADIENTS
$base-gradient: 'none';

// LISTS
$list-color: darken($active-color, 20%);
$list-active-color: transparentize($active-color, .2);
$list-active-gradient: 'recessed';
$list-header-bg-color: darken($alternative-color, 10%);
$list-pressed-color: lighten($list-active-color, 10%);
$list-bg-color: #353535;

$global-list-height : 40px;
$list-disclosure-round-size: 2em;
$list-disclosure-size: 1.7em;
$list-round-padding: 20px !default;

$include-pictos-font: false;
$include-default-icons: false;
```

```scss
$experimental-support-for-opera:false;
$experimental-support-for-khtml:false;
$experimental-support-for-microsoft :false;
@import "compass/css3";

@import 'sencha-touch/default';
/*@import 'sencha-touch/default/all'*/;

@import 'sencha-touch/default/src/_Class.scss';
@import 'sencha-touch/default/src/_Button.scss';
@import 'sencha-touch/default/src/_Panel.scss';
/*@import 'sencha-touch/default/src/_Sheet.scss';*/
@import 'sencha-touch/default/src/_MessageBox.scss';
@import 'sencha-touch/default/src/_Toolbar.scss';
/*@import 'sencha-touch/default/src/_Menu.scss';*/
/*@import 'sencha-touch/default/src/carousel/_Carousel.scss';*/
@import 'sencha-touch/default/src/form/_Panel.scss';
@import 'sencha-touch/default/src/form/_FieldSet.scss';
@import 'sencha-touch/default/src/field/_Field';
/*@import 'sencha-touch/default/src/field/_Checkbox.scss';*/
/*@import 'sencha-touch/default/src/field/_Radio.scss';*/
/*@import 'sencha-touch/default/src/field/_Search.scss';*/
/*@import 'sencha-touch/default/src/field/_Select.scss';*/
/*@import 'sencha-touch/default/src/field/_Slider.scss';*/
/*@import 'sencha-touch/default/src/field/_Spinner.scss';*/
/*@import 'sencha-touch/default/src/field/_TextArea.scss';*/
/*@import 'sencha-touch/default/src/dataview/_IndexBar.scss';*/
@import 'sencha-touch/default/src/dataview/_List.scss';
/*@import 'sencha-touch/default/src/picker/_Picker.scss';*/
/*@import 'sencha-touch/default/src/plugin/_ListPaging.scss';*/
/*@import 'sencha-touch/default/src/plugin/_PullRefresh.scss';*/
/*@import 'sencha-touch/default/src/slider/_Slider.scss';*/
@import 'sencha-touch/default/src/slider/_Toggle.scss';
/*@import 'sencha-touch/default/src/tab/_Panel.scss';*/

//mixins
@include sencha-toolbar-ui('light', darken($black,10%), 'recessed');

@include icon('settings', 'y', 'findacabfontello');
@include icon('delete', '*', 'findacabfontello');
@include icon('phone', 't', 'findacabfontello');

.x-list .x-list-disclosure:before {
    content: ']';
    font-family: 'findacabfontello';
    color: #000;
}

.callnow:after {
    content: 't';
    font-family: 'findacabfontello';
```

```
        padding-left: 10px;
}

// Custom code goes here..

.x-toolbar .x-innerhtml {
    font-family: "Lobster";
    font-size: 1.2em;
    line-height: 2em;
}

.x-list .x-list-item {
    color: #ccc;
}

/* template */

body {
    font: {
        family: HelveticaNeue-Light, Helvetica, sans-serif;
    }
}

.taxitpl {
    h1 {
        font-family: "Bebas";
        font-size: 1.8em;
    }

    p,
    address {
        margin: 0 0 20px 0;
        font-size: 1.4em;
    }

    p {
        margin-top: 20px;
        font-size: 0.8em;
    }

}
.taxitpl .x-dock-horizontal {
    background: url(../images/stroke.png) repeat-x;
    padding: 35px 0;
}

.distance {
    display: inline-block;
    padding: 3px;
    white-space: nowrap;
    overflow: hidden;
    background: #ccc;
```

```
        color: #000;
        -webkit-border-radius: 20px;
        -moz-border-radius: 20px;
        border-radius: 20px;
        margin-left: 2px;
        font-size: 0.7em;
}

.callnow {
        display: inline-block;
        font: {
            size: 1.2em;
        }
        line-height: 1.6em;
        padding: 0 20px;
        text-decoration: none;

        &:hover {
            background: darken(#ccc, 20%);
        }

}

.error input {
            border: 3px solid red;
}

.x-form-fieldset-instructions {
        text-align: left;
}
```

Index

Symbols

$sencha-button-ui, 195
@font-face, 263

A

Access-Control-Allow headers, 123, 148
accessors and mutators (get and set methods), 48
accounts, Sencha Network, 6
activeItem, 77
addListener() method, 40
Adobe PhoneGap (see PhoneGap)
AJAX
    comparison to JSONP, 140
    saving or retrieving data from external domain with, 148
    saving or retrieving data from same domain, 132
AJAX proxies, 131, 132–140
    connecting to a model or a store, 133
    implementing, 132
    implementing an AJAX request, 137–140
ajax proxy, 120, 122
AJAX requests
    cross-domain restrictions, 122
    posting data to the server, 243
alert() messagebox, 186
align property, 68

all.js version of Sencha Touch, 28
Android OS
    animation types in Android 2, 77
    SVG, 226
    themes for, 253
Android SDK, 23
Android Tools, 21
animation
    loading animation, 109
    Sencha Touch charts, 226
    showing and hiding overlays, 219, 221
animation object, setting type and direction, 77
Ant
    build scripts in .sencha folder, 93
    modifying build script (build.xml), 280
Apache Cordova (see Cordova)
Apache web servers, 20
API documentation for Sencha Touch, 10
app classpath, 112
app folder, 59, 93
    classes outside of, loading, 110
    generating a model in, 98
app.css file, 253
app.js file, 88, 95
    controllers array, 99
    isIconPrecomposed, 278
    models array, 99
    stores array in, 100

We'd like to hear your suggestions for improving our indexes. Send email to index@oreilly.com.

About the Author

Lee Boonstra works for Sencha, which equips developers with frameworks, tools, and services to help them build awesome mobile web applications using HTML5 and JavaScript. As a technical trainer, Lee teaches Sencha Touch and Ext JS to engineers from all over Europe. She also writes course material for the official Sencha trainings.

Lee likes to speak at conferences and events, and she is the organizer of the Sencha Technology User Group in Amsterdam. This user group regularly organizes meetups, workshops, and presentations in the Sencha office in Amsterdam.

Lee has been developing sites and applications for the Web since 2003, using technologies that include JavaScript (and lots of its frameworks), HTML5, Sass, CSS3, SQL, PHP, and Java. She has worked as a server-side consultant and lead client-side developer for many companies, such as UPC, Heineken, Phillips, and KLM Royal Dutch airlines. In her spare time, she is a video game addict.

If you want to keep in touch, you can find Lee on Twitter (@ladysign) or check out her technology blog (*http://www.ladysign-apps.com*) where she posts handy Sencha Touch tips and tricks every now and then.

Colophon

The animal on the cover of *Hands-On Sencha Touch 2* is a fossa (*Cryptoprocta ferox*). The fossa is a medium-sized (12 to 20 pound) carnivorous mammal that is unique to Madagascar. The classification of the fossa is controversial because it exhibits traits that are similar to the mongoose, the cat, and the civet all at once. However, due to Madagascar's closed ecosystem, the fossa is closely related to all other carnivorous mammals on the island.

As the largest mammal on Madagascar, the fossa enjoys a varied diet, with lemurs being the staple. They hunt during both day and night, and have been known to eat lizards, birds, rodents, and tenrecs (small opposum-like mammals). Fossas are only found in forested areas, and are very comfortable in the treetops, where they catch most of their prey. Unfortunately, this propensity for trees means that the species is extremely affected by habitat destruction; it is currently listed as "vulnerable" by the International Union for Conservation of Nature.

Male and female fossas look almost exactly the same, with mongoose-like heads and cougar-like bodies. They generally have short, reddish-brown fur and semi-retractable claws that are used to grip trees. The long tail also aids in balance and helps the fossa anchor itself to branches. One peculiar physical feature of the fossa is its external genitalia—the male's penis has a long, spiny bone (the *baculum*) that can be almost an inch long. Females also have spiny clitorises that are supported by a bony protrusion called the *os clitoridis*.

Fossas are considered solitary animals and keep to their own territories, which can be up to five square miles. On occasion, it has been observed that male fossas will hunt cooperatively, although this behavior is thought to be a vestige of a time when more than one fossa was needed to take down the (recently extinct) giant lemur.

The total population of fossas living within protected areas is estimated to be 2,500 adults, but this number is probably too high. Among the local people, taboo (known as *fady* in the Malagasy language) generally keeps the fossa safe, but some villagers still hunt it for meat despite this tradition. The collision between humans and nature has resulted in a dwindling fossa population that is increasingly vulnerable to health risks, such as canine distemper, which has begun to show up in wild fossas. It is thought that the disease is transmitted by stray dogs or those used to hunt the fossa for meat or game.

The cover image is from Lydekker's *Royal Natural History*. The cover fonts are URW Typewriter and Guardian Sans. The text font is Adobe Minion Pro; the heading font is Adobe Myriad Condensed; and the code font is Dalton Maag's Ubuntu Mono.

Get even more for your money.

Join the O'Reilly Community, and register the O'Reilly books you own. It's free, and you'll get:

- $4.99 ebook upgrade offer
- 40% upgrade offer on O'Reilly print books
- Membership discounts on books and events
- Free lifetime updates to ebooks and videos
- Multiple ebook formats, DRM FREE
- Participation in the O'Reilly community
- Newsletters
- Account management
- 100% Satisfaction Guarantee

Signing up is easy:

1. Go to: oreilly.com/go/register
2. Create an O'Reilly login.
3. Provide your address.
4. Register your books.

Note: English-language books only

To order books online:
oreilly.com/store

For questions about products or an order:
orders@oreilly.com

To sign up to get topic-specific email announcements and/or news about upcoming books, conferences, special offers, and new technologies:
elists@oreilly.com

For technical questions about book content:
booktech@oreilly.com

To submit new book proposals to our editors:
proposals@oreilly.com

O'Reilly books are available in multiple DRM-free ebook formats. For more information:
oreilly.com/ebooks

Lightning Source UK Ltd.
Milton Keynes UK
UKOW06f1802070814

236521UK00012B/64/P

31192020626295